ERRATA

p. IX. The contents entry for Chart 3 should read, "The Educational System of the Hungarian People's Republic: 1967" instead of 1965.

The page reference in the next entry should read p. X instead of p. XII.

p. 38 The bottom three lines on the page were intended for the printer only and should have been omitted in the final publication.

OE-14140

Education in the Hungarian People's Republic

by

Randolph L. Braham
The City College of the City University of New York

U.S. DEPARTMENT OF HEALTH, EDUCATION, AND WELFARE
OFFICE OF EDUCATION
Robert H. Finch
Secretary
James E. Allen, Jr.
Assistant Secretary and Commissioner of Education
Institute of International Studies
Robert Leestma
Associate Commissioner for International Education

This report was made by Randolph L. Braham, The City College of the City University of New York, pursuant to Contract No. OEC-1-6001002-0802, with the Office of Education, U.S. Department of Health, Education, and Welfare.

Opinions expressed in the report are those of the author and do not necessarily reflect official policy of the U.S. Office of Education.

Superintendent of Documents Catalog No. FS 5.214:14140
U.S. GOVERNMENT PRINTING OFFICE
Washington : 1970

For sale by the Superintendent of Documents, U.S. Government Printing Office
Washington, D.C. 20402 - Price $1.25

Foreword

This report on Hungarian education is one of many Office of Education reports over the years on education in countries outside the United States. A comprehensive study of all major levels and types of education in the Hungarian educational system, it is the first such scholarly study, as far as can be ascertained, to present a report on Hungarian education under Communism to American readers.

The author, Dr. Randolph L. Braham, professor at The City College of the City University of New York, brings to the present study his previous experiences in preparing two other publications for the Office of Education—*Education in the Rumanian People's Republic* (1963) and *Israel: A Modern Education System* (1966). To the task of preparing all three studies he has brought painstaking scholarship, fluency in the native languages, and personal knowledge of the countries.

For this study on Hungarian education the author has again engaged in extensive documentary research. In the United States he consulted collections on Hungarian education located at Teachers College in New York, the Library of Congress in Washington, and the library of the U.S. Department of Health, Education, and Welfare in Washington. In Hungary, he examined major collections located at various libraries and archives, including the Pedagogical Library in Budapest.

The education specialists whom the author consulted in Hungary included some associated with the Hungarian Ministry of Culture, as well as others associated with educational and cultural institutions and organizations. He consulted also with U.S. officials stationed in Budapest. He received advice and suggestions from many education specialists in the United States.

The Office of Education and the author wish to thank all these specialists and officials for their interest and help. Particular thanks are due Mr. Ed Alexander, Cultural Officer, U.S. Embassy in Budapest; Dr. Sándor Kiss, sociologist and national editor of *East Europe*, and Miss Marion Szigethy, librarian, both in New York.

ROBERT LEESTMA
Associate Commissioner for International Education

Contents

Appendixes

Tables

Page

Charts

Map

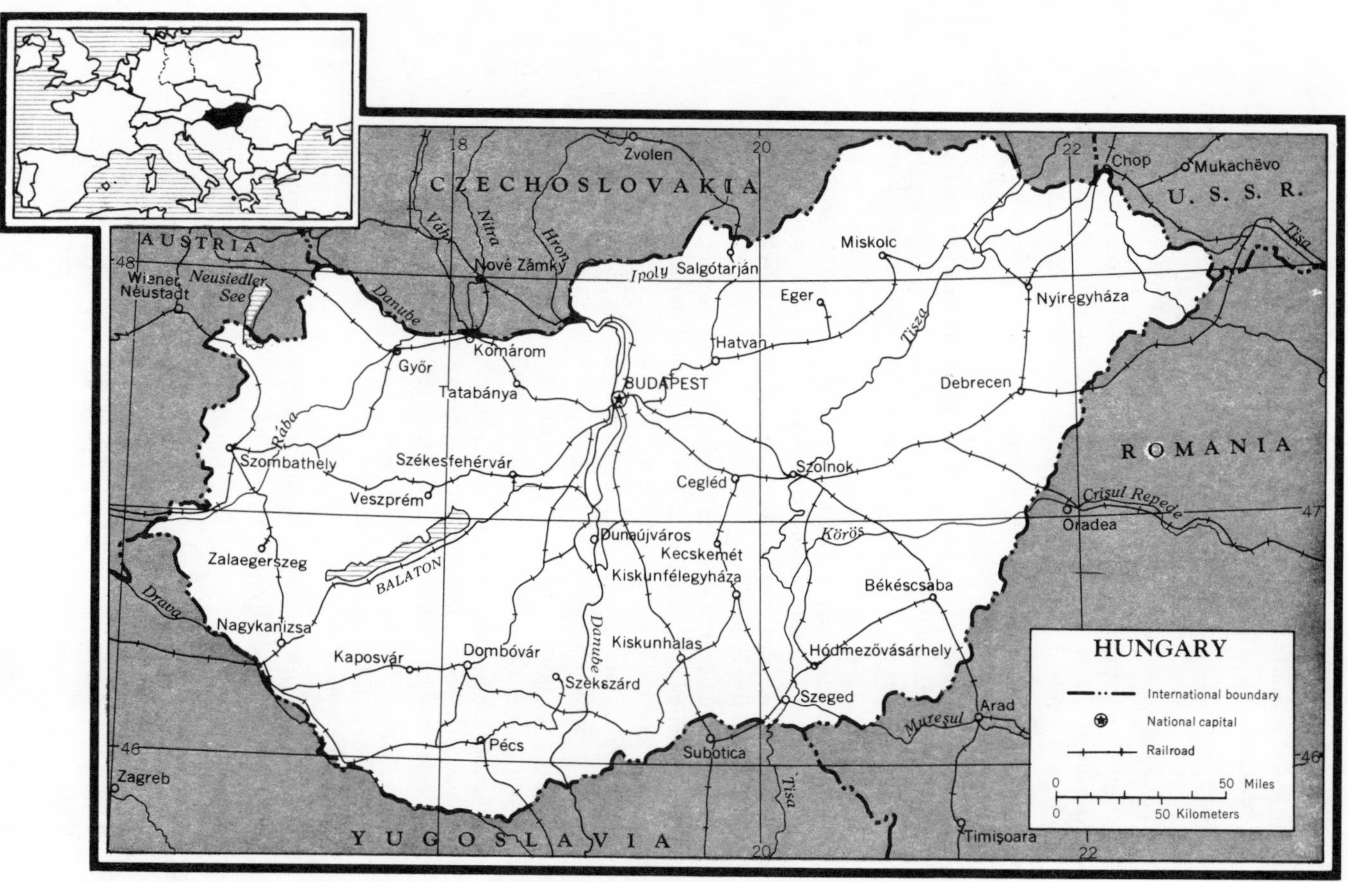

The Hungarian People's Republic: 1968

I. The Country's Background

Geography

Situated in the Carpathian basin of Central Eastern Europe, Hungary (*Magyarország*) is a landlocked country bordered by Czechoslovakia on the north, Rumania on the southeast, Austria on the west, Yugoslavia on the south, and the USSR on the northeast. Occupying an area of 35,911 square miles, Hungary is composed of three major geographic areas: the Great Hungarian Plain (*Alföld*) in the east covering about two-thirds of the country's territory—a densely populated and fertile farming plain; Transdanubia (*Dunántul*) west of the Danube, a hilly region with Lake Balaton—the popular resort area—at its center; and the Northern Uplands (*Észak-Magyarország*), encompassing the Mátra Mountains and most of the country's forests.

The main waterways are the Danube, entering from Austria in the west and crossing through Budapest flowing south to Yugoslavia; and the Tisza, flowing across the Great Plain from northeast to southwest.

Hungary's climate is predominantly continental, with four clearly distinguishable seasons. The average annual temperature is 50 degrees—January and July temperatures averaging 31 and 71 degrees, respectively.

Although considerable progress was made in the country's postwar drive toward industrialization, Hungary is still relatively agricultural. Except for its bauxite deposits (which constitute 9 percent of known world reserves), Hungary is poor in natural resources, depending on imports for its developing industries.

From the political-administrative point of view, Hungary is divided into 19 counties (*megyék*),[1] which, in turn, are divided into districts (*járások*). Its largest and most industrialized city is the capital, Budapest, with a population of about two million. It was legally established in 1873 through consolidation of the three adjoining towns of Pest, Buda, and Obuda. Hungary has four additional cities with populations exceeding 100,000: Debrecen, Miskolc, Pécs, and Szeged.

People

In 1966, Hungary had a total population of 10,160,380, of which 4,909,957 were males and 5,250,423 females. Age distribution was as

[1] Baranya, Bács-Kiskun, Békés, Borsod-Abaúj-Zemplén, Csongrád, Fejér, Győr-Sopron, Hajdú-Bihar, Heves, Komárom, Nógrád, Pest, Somogy, Szabolcs-Szatmár, Szolnok, Tolna, Vas, Veszprém, and Zala.

follows: 23.0 percent under 15; 36.3 percent between 15 and 39; 24.9 percent between 40 and 59; and 15.8 percent above 60. The estimated population on January 1, 1967 was 10,197,000. (Hungary has one of the lowest population growth rates in the world).[2] Hungarians or Magyars account for almost 97 percent of the population; the other 3 percent is composed of small minority groups of Germans (about 240,000), Slovaks (about 27,000), Serbo-Croatians, and Romanians. Approximately two-thirds are Roman Catholic (Hungary marks the farthest extension of majority Roman Catholicism in southeastern Europe), one percent Jewish,[3] and the rest Protestant, predominantly Presbyterian and Lutheran. Hungary's literacy rate of 95 percent is one of the highest in the world, according to official statistics.

History

Hungarians trace their history to the Magyar tribes of the Finno-Ugric group of people living near the Ural-Altai mountains in Central Asia. Under the leadership of Árpád they settled during the era of the Great Migrations in the Danubian Basin, the territory known in Roman times as Pannonia. Although the occupation of the future Hungarian homeland took place around 895-896 and Árpád gave the name to the dynasty that ruled until 1301, it was Prince Géza (970-997) who laid the foundations of the Hungarian State by organizing the tribes. The real founder of the Hungarian Kingdom, however, was Géza's son, István (Stephen) I (1001-1038).

Responsible for the introduction and spread of Christianity in Hungary, Stephen was rewarded by Pope Sylvester II with a special crown and the title of Apostle. He was canonized in 1083. His successors have come to be known as Apostolic Kings of Hungary and the Holy Crown of St. Stephen became the symbol of the Hungarian Nation.

For about two centuries after the reign of Stephen, Hungary was the scene of a series of raids arising both within and without the country, and culminating in the Mongol invasion of 1241. Following the drive of the Ottoman Turks to push northward in the Balkan Peninsula during the 14th century, Hungary emerged as the champion of Christianity and Western civilization in attempting to block the spread of the Turks and of Islamism. This attempt was at first partially successful, especially during the reigns of Sigismund (Zsigmond) I (1387–1437), who was also the elected Holy Roman Emperor and King of Bohemia; John Hunyadi (Hunyadi János), a powerful frontier lord, who acted as Regent; and his son, Mathias Corvinus (Hunyadi Mátyás, 1458–90).

The reign of Mathias Corvinus was one of the most illustrious in Hungary's history. A patron of Renaissance learning, he did much to advance the country's intellectual life by establishing institutions of higher learning and the renowned *Bibliotheca Corvina,* consisting of more than 10,000 manuscripts and books. After his death, internal strife and renewed Turkish military operations laid the ground for the

[2] *Statistical Pocket Book of Hungary 1967.* Budapest: Publishing House for Economics and Law, 1967. p. 11-12.
[3] In 1941, Hungary had a Jewish population of 825,007. By 1967, it was reduced to about 80,000, most of them living in Budapest.

Mohács disaster of August 29, 1526, and the subsequent occupation of two-thirds of Hungary by the Turks for about 150 years. A "rump" Hungary, however, continued to operate in the northwest corner of the country under the rule of the Austrian Hapsburgs, who maintained their claim to the Hungarian crown. The ideal of a free and independent Hungarian Nation was maintained in the eastern ranges of the Carpathians in the semi-independent Hungarian State ruled by the Transylvanian dukes.

The defeat of the Turkish armies at Vienna in 1683 and the subsequent liberation of Buda (1686) and all of Hungary by 1718 under the terms of the Peace of Passarowitz, however, did not see the reestablishment of Hungarian independence. Succession to the Hungarian throne having been conferred upon the male line of Austria,[4] Hungary came under full Hapsburg control in 1699. The rise of Hungarian nationalism and the long insurrection (1703–11) led by Francis (Ferenc) Rákóczi (1676–1735) failed to dislodge the Hapsburgs, though the Hungarians were granted full religious liberty and recognition of their ancient rights and privileges (Treaty of Szatmár, 1711).

The rule of Maria Theresa (1740–80) and Joseph II (1780–90) characterized by the spirit of enlightened absolutism was followed by a period of reforms induced by the revolutionary spirit of enlightenment emanating from France. The spirit of change during the 1840's crystallized around two positions represented by two towering figures of Hungary at the time: (1) *reformism,* advocating the necessity of cultural, economic, and technical reforms as a precondition of national and political transformation and represented by Count Stephen (István) Széchenyi; and (2) *revolution,* seeking "freedom first" for the attainment of national independence, and represented by Lajos Kossuth. The latter won out and on April 13, 1849, the Diet proclaimed Hungary's emancipation from Austria and elected Kossuth as governor. Four months later, however, the Revolution was crushed by the forces of Tsar Nicholas I at the request of the Austrian Emperor Franz Josef.

In 1867, a compromise was reached under the leadership of Ferenc Deák, establishing the Dual Monarchy of the Austro-Hungarian Empire. Under the provisions of the compromise, both units obtained complete autonomy in strictly domestic matters; but the ministries of foreign affairs, war, and finance were centrally administered. Emperor Franz Josef was crowned King of Hungary in the same year.

Despite the many differences between the ruling Austrian and Hungarian elements, Hungary entered a period of general cultural and economic progress, halted only by the outbreak of World War I. Under the Treaty of Trianon (June 4, 1920) Hungary lost 71.4 percent of its prewar territory and about 60 percent of its population.[5]

Following the 1918 abdication of King Charles, Hungary was pro-

---

[4] Inheritance of the throne by females in default of male heirs was made possible by the *Pragmatica Sanctio* (Pragmatic Sanction) which the Hungarian Diet accepted in 1723.

[5] Transylvania and two-thirds of the Banat, or 31.5 percent of the territory went to Romania; Croatia-Slovenia and one-third of the Banat, or 19.6 percent, went to Yugoslavia; Slovakia, Sub-Carpathian Ruthenia, and the city of Bratislava (Pressburg or Pozsony), or 18.9 percent, went to Czechoslovakia; 1.2 percent to Austria (Burgenland); 0.2 percent to Poland (part of Orava and Spis); and less than 0.004 percent to Italy (Fiume). *Hungary.* Edited by Ernst C. Helmreich. New York: Praeger, 1957. p. 13.

claimed a republic, overthrown, however, by the proletarian dictatorship of Béla Kun (March-August, 1919). Kun's regime in turn was crushed by the intervention of the Romanian army, an act paving the way for the monarchical regime of Nicholas (Miklós) Horthy, who served as Regent.

Pursuing a pro-German, revisionist policy, Horthy's Government increasingly alined Hungary with the objectives of the Axis Alliance, which attacked the Soviet Union in June 1941. Under the Treaty of Peace of 1947, Hungary had to cede the territories it had acquired from Czechoslovakia, Romania, and Yugoslavia between 1938 and 1941. Occupied by Soviet troops, Hungary then fell under the control of Soviet policies in the area.

Hungary's gradual transformation into a full-fledged "People's Republic" *(Népköztársaság)* was achieved in a few well-differentiated phases. Following a brief period of democracy characterized by the existence of a genuine coalition government, the preservation of basic liberties, the operation of parties, and the pursuit of economic reform measures (1945–47), the Hungarian Communist Party with the assistance of the Red Army gradually infiltrated the sources of power, thereby laying open the way to transform the country along socialist lines.

The Party's open assumption of power began in 1947, when the drive against the Smallholders' (*Kisgazdapárt*) Party and all other opponents of "progress" was launched, preparing the ground for the elections of August 31, 1947. The Communists accelerated their program for the "building of a socialist society" while maintaining the façade of a parliamentary democracy. The program involved, among other things, the absorption of the Social Democratic Party into the Communist Party; the nationalization of industry, transportation, and education; the collectivization of land; and the inauguration of the system of economic planning. With the adoption of the Constitution of August 20, 1949 (currently still in effect), Hungary was proclaimed a "People's Republic."

Government

From the formal point of view, the Government of the Hungarian People's Republic is parliamentary in character with the executive being "elected" by and "responsible" to the legislative branch. Nominally, the highest organ of State power is the unicameral National Assembly (*Országgyülés*) composed of 340 members and 173 alternates elected to 4-year terms. In reality, however, the assembly merely ratifies the decisions taken by the Government and Party between assembly sessions. Hungary has a collective head of State—the Presidential Council *(Elnöki Tanács)*—consisting of 20 members and a secretary elected from among the members of the National Assembly. The chairman of the Presidential Council acts in the name of the Council as the titular head of the Hungarian People's Republic.

The highest executive-administrative organ of the Government is the Council of Ministers (*Minisztertanács*) or, as it is formally known, the

Hungarian Revolutionary Worker-Peasant Government (*Magyar Forradalmi Munkás-Paraszt Kormány*). This branch of the Government has real power primarily because many of its influential members are also members of the leading organs of the Party, reflecting the Party character of the Hungarian State.

The judiciary is headed by the Supreme Court (*Legfelsőbb Biróság*) which, like the Council of Ministers, is nominally elected by and responsible to the National Assembly. The Court supervises the activities of the lower courts and reviews their decisions. One of the primary functions of the courts, according to article 41 of the 1949 Constitution, is to "punish the enemies of the working people, protect and safeguard the State [and] the social and economic order and the institutions of the people's democracy." In fulfilling these tasks, the courts are assisted by the Chief Public Prosecutor (*Legfőbb Ügyész*) and his subordinates.

The local organs of Government or State power are the people's councils (*tanácsok*) of the counties, districts, towns, and boroughs. Each council elects its own executive-administrative unit, the executive committee (*végrehajtó bizottság*), from among its members. The committee in turn elects a chairman (*elnök*), whose functions are roughly equivalent to those of a mayor in the United States.[6]

All governmental organs are guided by the twin principles of "democratic centralism" and "dual responsibility," which in theory means that all power emanates from the bottom up; in reality, however, all power flows from the top down, freedom of discussion at the bottom merely denoting how best to implement a decision made by the higher organs.

The Communist Party

Although theoretically all power emanates from the people acting through their elected representatives in the National Assembly (the highest organ of State power), in reality ultimate decisionmaking power lies in the top leadership of the Communist Party.

Background

Institutionally, the history of the Hungarian Communist Party is traced to 1890, when the Social Democratic Party of Hungary (*Magyarországi Szociáldemokrata Párt*), the first formal Marxist movement in Hungary, was established. Following the Bolshevik initiative in Russia, the left wing of this Social Democratic Party seceded at the end of World War I. Together with Hungarian prisoners-of-war returning from Russia (many of whom had participated in the historical events of 1917–18) the left wing established the Communists' Party of Hungary (*Kommunisták Magyarországi Pártja*) in 1918. One year later it was temporarily transformed into the Socialist Party of Hungary (*Magyaror-*

[6] The chairmen, deputy chairmen, and secretaries of the executive committees are expected to take the 1-year course in economics and public administration offered by the People's Council Academies (*Tanácsakadémiák*). See Cabinet Resolution No. 1013/1963. (VI.15.), in *Magyar Közlöny* (Hungarian Gazette), Budapest, No. 41, June 15, 1963. p. 272.

szági Szociálista Párt).

With the suppression of the Béla Kun proletarian dictatorship, the Communist movement was outlawed, and hence operated only underground. The right wing of the Socialist Party reorganized itself into the Social Democratic Party *(Szociáldemokrata Párt),* which continued to function until March 1948, when it was absorbed by the Hungarian Communist Party (*Magyar Kommunista Párt*), which had been revived in 1945. The two amalgamated parties came to be known as the Hungarian Workers' Party (*Magyar Dolgozók Pártja*), which, having disintegrated during the revolutionary events of October-November 1956, was reorganized soon after the intervention of the Red Army into the present Hungarian Socialist Workers' Party (*Magyar Szociálista Munkáspárt*).[7]

Structure and Functions

From the formal point of view, the Communist Party's supreme organ is the Party Congress (*Pártkongresszus*) meeting once in 4 years. Its primary function includes the review of past policy, the "formulation" of future policy, and the "election" of a Central Committee (*Központi Bizottság*) to guide the Party between its sessions. Real power, however, lies in the Central Committee, especially the Political Committee *(Politikai Bizottság)* or Politburo, composed of 13 members and six alternates. Its decisions are carried out under the auspices of the Party's main administrative unit, the Secretariat (*Titkárság*), consisting of nine members led by the First Secretary (*Első Titkár*).

Like the governmental organizations, the Party organizations are theoretically highly "democratic" institutions with all power emanating from the bottom up, guided by the twin principles of "democratic centralism" and "dual responsibility"; in reality, however, power flows from the top down, with all decisionmaking power concentrated in the Political Committee.

The functions of the Party organizations are all-pervasive. National policy in all spheres of life is determined by the Party; the primary function of the governmental organs, both central and local, is to implement this policy (chart 1). Supervising the implementation of policy is entrusted not only to the governmental organs normally in charge of this function, but also to the Party organizations established in every sphere of social endeavor. In education, for example, Party cells or basic organizations are established in each school and (depending upon the size of the institution) in each faculty, department, or specialty. They act as the eye and the ear of the Party, assuring implementation of a given Party line.[8]

In education, as in all other spheres of life, national policy is deter-

[7] In this text the Party is referred to as the Communist Party, regardless of the official nomenclature employed at any particular time. The all-pervasive character of the Party is not necessarily revealed by the size of its membership, officially established at 584,849 in November 1966. It "legitimizes" its rule through the Patriotic People's Front *(Hazafias Népfront),* which the March 19, 1967 elections declared had obtained 99.7 percent of the valid votes cast. U.S. Department of State. *World Strength of the Communist Party Organizations* (20th Annual Report, Department of State Publication 8375). Washington: The Department, 1968. p. 59.

[8] See also p. 29-30

Chart 1. The Hungarian Party State: The Interlocking Leadership

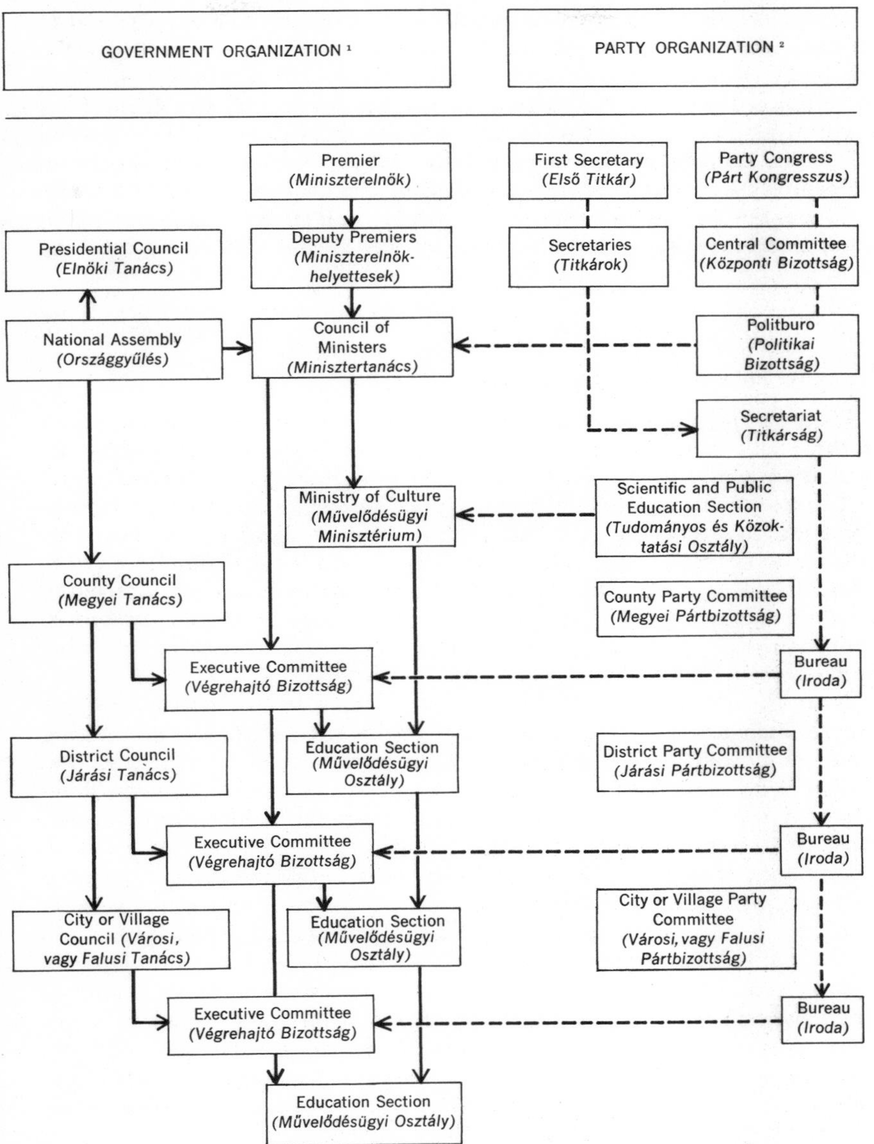

Key: ——— indicates the flow of formal political-governmental authority.
– – – indicates the flow of real political-governmental authority.

[1] The official name of the Government is the Hungarian Worker-Peasant Government (*Magyar Forradalmi Munkás-Paraszt Kormány*).

[2] The official name of the Party is the Hungarian Socialist Workers Party (*Magyar Szocialista Munkáspárt—MSZMP*).

mined by the Party Central Committee or Politburo. The details of this policy are normally worked out by the Scientific and Public Education Section (*Tudományos és Közoktatási Osztály*) of the Central Committee. Following the formal decisions of the central Party organ (s), the policy is then translated into legalistic language and issued in the form of laws, decrees, or resolutions, by the Presidential Council, the Council of Ministers, or the Ministry of Culture (*Művelődésügyi Minisztérium*).[9]

The policies of the Government and Party are highly synchronized primarily because, in the interlocking leadership system of the Party-State, the leading members of the Council of Ministers are also members of the central organs of the Party (chart 1).[10]

[9] See footnote 37 of chapter III.

[10] In the 1960's, for example, Pál Ilku, the Minister of Culture, was also a member of the Central Committee, an alternate member of the Politburo, and a member of the Agitation and Propaganda Section *(Agitációs ès Propaganda Osztály)* of the Party.

II. The Educational Inheritance

Retrospect

The educational legacy which the people's democratic regime inherited from the prewar era proved to be of mixed value. Like the educational systems of most Central and even Western European countries before World War II, Hungary's educational system included some outstanding though highly selective institutions. This system was, however, considerably archaic, inequitable, and restrictive. In fact, from approximately the Middle Ages, it paralleled to a large degree the cultural and educational development of Western Europe. Thus, for centuries education had been vested in the hands of the Christian churches, especially the Roman Catholic church.[1] Until the middle of the 19th century the churches played a dominant role and until 1948 continued to exercise great influence. That year, when the Hungarian schools were nationalized, education became exclusively a State affair.[2]

The Hungarian educational system's development and modernization are intimately connected with the contributions of two men, Baron Joseph (József) Eötvös (1813–71), Minister of Culture in 1848 and 1867; and Count Kuno Klebelsberg, Minister of Culture (1922–31).[3]

A moderate liberal Catholic, Eötvös, the statesman-philosopher, moved in the forefront of many reform movements and in many of his writings he exposed the corrupt practices of county governments.[4] A large number of the educational reform measures adopted during the post-World War I period resulted from the initiative taken by Count Klebelsberg. These measures included the adoption of a scholarship system and of a series of laws designed to raise the cultural standards in rural areas.

Although little of the educational heritage is reflected in the basic content, goals, and principles of the people's democratic system of education, some of the elements characterizing the pre-World War II administration and structure of public education played a considerable role in its evolution.

[1] In 1850, Leo Thun, the Minister of Religion and Education of Austria, ordered that the Hungarian school system be placed under Vatican supervision. Aron Moskovits. *Jewish Education in Hungary, 1848-1948.* Philadelphia: The Dropsie College for Hebrew and Cognate Learning, 1964. p. 29-30.

[2] For a detailed historical account of Hungary's prewar system of education, see Julius Kornis's *Education in Hungary.* New York: Teachers College, Columbia University, 1932. 289 p. See also Joseph Somogyi's *L'Instruction publique en Hongrie* (Public Education in Hungary) (Publications du Bureau International d'Education, No. 87). Geneva: The Bureau, 1944. 122 p. (This publication will be cited henceforth as "Joseph Somogyi.")

[3] See footnote 37 of chapter III.

[4] One of his most important writings on this subject is *A falú jegyzője* (The Village Notary), also available in English translation.

Administration

Ministry Departments

The administrative center of public education before World War II was the Ministry of Religion and Education (*Vallás-és Közoktatásügyi Minisztérium*) acting in accordance with laws passed by Parliament. Reflecting its complex tasks, the Ministry was divided into the following 11 departments: [5]

1. Art and music
2. Commercial schools and institutions for the mentally handicapped
3. Elementary education and teacher training
4. Institutions of higher learning and science
5. Pensions
6. Physical education
7. Public funds for education and public real estate funds
8. Religious affairs
9. Secondary education
10. Technical education
11. Urban schools and teacher-training

The Ministry's major functions were to—

1. Determine the curriculum.
2. Supervise schools (including the denominational ones).
3. Administer city, endowed, cooperative, and private educational institutions.
4. Appoint teachers.
5. Prepare and implement educational laws.

In fulfilling these tasks, the Ministry was assisted by the National Council of Education (*Országos Közoktatási Tanács*), a body of 50 members appointed by the Minister for 5 years and concerned primarily with elementary and secondary education; and by a textbook committee.

Inspection

For educational inspection, prewar Hungary was divided into six districts, each headed by a superintendent appointed by the Regent on the recommendation of the Minister of Culture. The superintendents were concerned mostly with supervision of secondary schools, including the denominational ones. The inspection and supervision system for the elementary and upper elementary (*polgári*) schools was regulated by Laws No. XXXVIII of 1868 and XXIII of 1876, respectively. In accord with these laws, elementary and upper-elementary inspection and supervision were entrusted to the school boards in charge of the particular school levels. In turn, the local school boards operated under the control of the school inspectors, who were charged with general inspection of kindergartens, elementary and upper-elementary schools, trade schools, and teacher-training institutions throughout the counties under their jurisdictions.

[5] Dennis A. Jánossy. *Public Instruction in Hungary*. Budapest: Press of the Royal Hungarian University, 1929. p. 4. (This publication will be cited henceforth as "D. A. Jánossy.")

Structure

Prewar Hungary's educational system covered a network of pre-elementary, elementary, intermediate or secondary, and higher educational institutions (chart 2).

Kindergarten Education

The first kindergarten in Hungary—the "Angel's Garden" (*Angyalkert*)—was founded in Budapest in 1828 by Countess Therese Brunswick (1775–1861), who was deeply influenced by the ideas of Pestalozzi. Her endeavors, however, remained basically fruitless because strong opposition arose against establishing preschool institutions. In 1873 there were still only three private kindergartens in Budapest. The first State-sponsored kindergarten in the country was established at Liptószentmiklós in 1876.

Kindergarten education was regulated by Law No. XV of 1891, which required that kindergartens for children 3 to 6 years of age be established in communities having at least 40 children "without proper supervision." Kindergartens could be maintained by townships, the State, religious denominations, associations, and private groups. Kindergartens run by the first two were free.

Table 1—Number of kindergartens, teachers, and pupils, by type of kindergarten: 1937-38 and 1941-42

Item	Total		Regular kindergartens		Permanent homes		Summer homes	
	1937–38	1941–42	1937–38	1941–42	1937–38	1941–42	1937–38	1941–42
Kindergartens	1,309	2,895	1,140	1,966	45	51	124	878
Teachers	1,767	3,499	1,593	2,570	45	51	129	878
Pupils	124,523	216,714	112,143	161,782	3,776	4,284	8,604	50,648

SOURCE OF DATA: Joseph Somogyi. *L'Instruction publique en Hongrie* (Public Education in Hungary). (Publications du Bureau International d'Education, No. 87). Geneva: The Bureau, 1944. p. 14-15.

Three types of kindergartens existed in prewar Hungary: regular kindergartens, permanent homes, and summer homes.

Ultimate State control over these institutions was exercised by the Ministry of Education exclusively until 1936, and by the Ministry in conjunction with the Ministry of the Interior after 1936.

Of the total 1,309 kindergartens in 1937–38, 404 were State and 629 communal; the others belonged to various associations, denominations, or private individuals (table 1). Sponsorship in 1941–42 was similar to that in 1937–38.[6]

Elementary Education

The first attempt at establishing a unified public education system in Hungary can be traced to Maria Theresa's *Ratio Educationis* of

[6] Joseph Somogyi, op. cit. p. 14-15. See also D. A. Jánossy, op. cit. p.10; Alice Hermann. "Az óvoda és az óvónőképzés" (The Kindergarten and the Education of Kindergarten Teachers). *In: Nevelésügyünk húsz éve, 1945-1964* (Twenty Years of Our Educational System, 1945-1964). Budapest: Tankönyvkiadó, 1965. p. 365-75; Julius Kornis, op. cit. p. 43-47.

Chart 2. The Educational System of Hungary: 1929

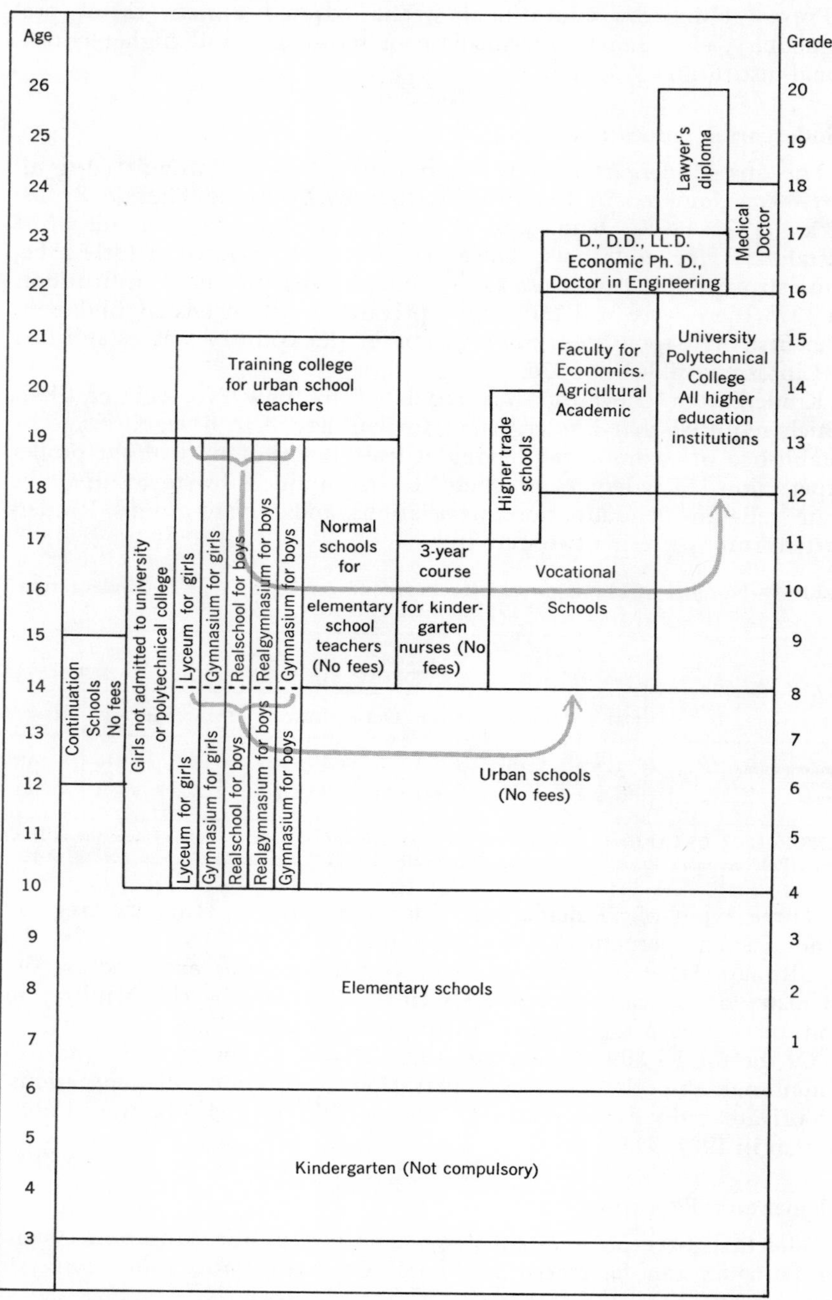

SOURCE OF DATA: Dennis A. Jánossy. *Public Instruction in Hungary.* Budapest: Press of the Royal Hungarian University 1929, p. 9.

1777. This royal edict aimed to regulate Hungarian education on a national basis by providing, among other things, that all schools, whether Catholic or Protestant, must be uniformly supervised by the State in administration, curriculum, methods of teaching, and discipline. Supervisory control power was entrusted to nine royal directors. Although the major provisions of this edict were never really enforced, the *Ratio Educationis* of 1806 issued by Francis I, far more precise and compact than the one of 1777, proved more effective, for it guided the Hungarian institutions of learning from 1806 to the Revolution of 1848–49.

In 1860, an edict by Emperor Francis Joseph transferred control over Hungarian education from Vienna to Buda. Following the Compromise of 1867 (which provided that the Dual Monarchy of Austria-Hungary be established and the Emperor be crowned King of Hungary) Hungarian education developed new momentum under the dynamic leadership of the new Minister of Education, Baron Joseph Eötvös. Through his guidance, Parliament passed Fundamental Education Law No. XXXVIII of 1868, which (as amended by Law No. XXX of 1921) regulated elementary education practically until the end of World War II. The law provided compulsory education for children of 6 through 12 years of age in public elementary schools *(népiskola)* and during 3 further years in so-called continuation or supplementary schools (*ismétlő iskola*).

The 3-year continuation school classes were held within the physical facilities of the elementary schools for 7 hours weekly in the winter and 4 hours weekly in the summer. (Children in the upper elementary schools (*polgári*) were not required to attend the continuation classes.)

In addition to the continuation schools, other special schools were established in sparsely settled rural areas with the financial and physi-

Table 2—Number of hours per week, per subject, in the 8-year elementary schools, by grade: 1941-42[1]

Subject	Grade							
	1	2	3	4	5	6	7	8
Total	29	23	26	27	32	32	32	32
Arithmetic	5	5	5	5	4	4	4	4
Drawing and handwork	0	2	2	2	4	4	4	4
Elements of natural history, economics, and hygiene	0	0	0	0	5	5	5	5
Geography	0	0	0	2	2	2	2	2
History:								
Civics	0	0	0	0	0	0	1	1
Hungarian	0	0	0	0	2	2	2	2
Hungarian:								
Grammar	0	2	2	2	2	2	1	1
Language exercises	2	2	4	3	0	0	0	0
Reading	0	4	4	3	3	3	3	3
Sentence structures	8	1	1	2	2	2	2	2
Writing	8	1	1	1	2	2	2	2
Physical education	3	3	3	3	2	2	2	2
Religion and morals	2	2	2	2	2	2	2	2
Singing	1	1	2	2	2	2	2	2

[1] The curriculum of the urban and rural primary schools varied slightly.

SOURCE OF DATA: Joseph Somogyi. *L'Instruction publique en Hongrie* (Public Education in Hungary). (Publications du Bureau International d'Education, No. 87). Geneva: The Bureau, 1944. p. 19.

Table 3.—Number of regular elementary schools, teachers, and pupils: 1937-38 and 1941-42; and number of continuation elementary schools, teachers, and pupils: 1937-38

Item	Total	Regular		Continuation
	1937–38	1937–38	1941–42	1937–38
Schools	11,336	6,899	12,068	4,437
Teachers	26,647	20,149	35,153	6,498
Pupils	1,130,310	963,087	1,251,426	167,223

SOURCE OF DATA: Joseph Somogyi. *L'Instruction publique en Hongrie* (Public Education in Hungary). (Publications du Bureau International d'Education, No. 87). Geneva: The Bureau, 1944. p. 28-29.

cal cooperation of the peasants. Law No. VII of 1926 required peasants living in isolated locations to maintain an elementary school "for every 2½ square miles of territory if there are at least 20 families with 30 children of compulsory school age living in that territory." [7]

After World War I, the 6-year elementary schools were gradually converted into 8-year ones in some communities. Under Law No. XX of 1940, 8-year public elementary schools were eventually adopted for the whole country.

In 1941–42 the curriculum of the State 8-year elementary schools (table 2) varied slightly between urban and rural schools. The former had somewhat more grammar and arithmetic and somewhat less natural history.

After finishing fourth grade, children could either continue to the upper elementary grades or enter the first year of an 8-year high school, a vocational school, or a so-called upper elementary school (*polgári*), which was the equivalent of the German *Bürgerschule*.[8]

Table 4.—Number of hours per week, per subject, in the 4-year upper elementary (*polgári*) schools for boys, by grade: 1938-39

Subject	Total for all grades	Grade			
		1	2	3	4
Total	125	31	31	31	32
Arithmetic and geometry	15	4	4	4	3
Bookkeeping	1	0	0	0	1
Botany and zoology	6	3	3	0	0
Drawing	11	3	3	3	2
Elements of agriculture and industry	4	1	1	1	1
Elements of economics and civics	2	0	0	0	2
Elements of hygiene	2	0	0	0	2
Geography	10	3	2	3	2
Geology and chemistry	3	0	0	0	3
German	12	3	3	3	3
Guidance	4	1	1	1	1
History	8	0	2	3	3
Hungarian language	16	5	4	4	3
Physical education	10	3	3	2	2
Physics	3	0	0	3	0
Religion	8	2	2	2	2
Shop	6	2	2	1	1
Singing	4	1	1	1	1

SOURCE OF DATA: Joseph Somogyi. *L'Instruction publique en Hongrie* (Public Education in Hungary). (Publications du Bureau International d'Education, No. 87). Geneva: The Bureau, 1944. p. 40.

[7] D. A. Jánossy, op. cit. p. 12.
[8] See p. 15-16.

Although primary education was free and compulsory under Law No. XX of 1940, its compulsory attendance provisions were loosely enforced, particularly in rural areas, because there schools were few and far between. Coeducation was permitted only where local financial conditions were inadequate to provide for separate teaching of boys and girls.

Like kindergartens, elementary schools could be maintained by the State and by associations, communities, individuals, private groups, or religious denominations. In 1937–38, for example, the 6,899 regular elementary schools were distributed as follows:

2,856	Roman Catholic	131	Uniate
1,287	State	112	private
1,079	Calvinist	34	variously affiliated
826	communal	23	Greek Orthodox
395	Lutheran	11	association-sponsored
145	Jewish		

Four years later, in 1941–42, the 12,068 regular elementary schools included 4,925 State and 906 communal. The rest, mostly denominational, were primarily Roman Catholic.[9]

Vocational Education

Before the war, Hungary had a relatively well-developed network of agricultural, industrial, and commercial vocational schools.

A predominantly agricultural country, Hungary had a variety of agricultural vocational schools, offering both basic and technical instruction. For example, special schools offered training in apiculture, dairying, forestry, viniculture, and viticulture. Most of these schools admitted graduates of the 4- or 6-year public elementary schools.

Industrial vocational education for apprentices was organized according to Law No. XVII of 1884 and Law No. XII of 1922 as amended by Law No. VII of 1936.

Admitting graduates of the 6-year elementary schools, the vocational schools for apprentices provided 9 hours of schooling per week, one of them devoted to religion and four to vocational subjects.

In 1937–38 Hungary had 376 industrial schools for apprentices with a total enrollment of 56,643. By 1941–42 the enrollment in these schools had increased to 98,782, although the number of schools actually declined to 375.

The commercial vocational schools for apprentices operated under the same laws governing the industrial vocational institutions and had generally similar conditions. In 1937–38 there were 28 commercial vocational schools for apprentices, with 2,893 pupils; in 1941–42, 33 schools with 4,672 pupils.[10]

Upper Elementary Education

Emulating the German and Austrian school systems, Hungary introduced the upper elementary (*polgári*) or *Bürgerschule* schools. Oper-

[9] Joseph Somogyi, op. cit. p. 28-29. See also Julius Kornis, op. cit. p. 47-66, 277-80.
[10] Ibid. p. 29-35. See also D. A. Jánossy, op. cit. p. 23-27; and Julius Kornis, op. cit. p. 175-212.

ating mostly in cities and larger towns, these schools were first established in Hungary toward the end of the 18th century and were regulated by Law No. XXXVIII of 1868 and Law No. XII of 1927. Immediately before World War II the upper elementary schools were 4-year institutions, separate for boys and for girls. They admitted children who had completed 4 years of elementary school. Graduates of upper elementary schools were qualified for admission to the higher vocational schools, and could transfer to the fifth year of gymnasiums if they passed special supplementary qualifying examinations.

The curriculum for boys consisted of 18 subjects, all told, for the 4 years (some subjects not offered in certain years) ; and the number of hours per week amounted to 31 in each of the first three years and 32 in the last year (table 4). The curriculum for girls varied slightly.

In 1937–38 Hungary had 397 upper elementary schools enrolling 93,561: boys, 45,538; girls, 48,023. By control, the 397 schools were distributed as follows:

160	State	14	Calvinist
101	communal	7	association-sponsored
80	Roman Catholic	6	Jewish
28	private	1	Lutheran

By 1941–42 the number of schools had increased to 482, enrolling 137,427: boys, 64,889; girls, 72,538. The distribution by control remained about the same as in 1937–38.[11]

Secondary Education

The history of Hungarian secondary education can be traced to the *Ratio Educationis* of 1777 and the *Ratio Educationis* of 1806. Following the failure of the Revolution of 1848–49, the Hungarian secondary schools were regulated by the Austrian education law of 1849.

After the establishment of the Austro-Hungarian Dual Monarchy in 1867, secondary education was gradually reorganized and, under Law No. XXX of 1883, evolved into two types: (1) gymnasiums (*gimnázium*), emphasizing classical academic education; and (2) *réal* (scientific) schools (*reáliskola*) offering a more modern education and de-emphasizing Latin. This system prevailed until 1924, when, under Law No. XI, three types of secondary schools were established: (1) gymnasiums; (2) *réal* gymnasiums (*reálgimnázium*), which taught Latin but no Greek and emphasized modern languages; and (3) *réal* schools.

The curriculum of the first 4 years in all three types of schools was basically the same, and the number of hours per week in all three types was identical throughout: 28 in the first two grades and 30 thereafter. The largest part of the curriculum was devoted to the humanities, with the remainder allocated to *réal* (or scientific) subjects and to physical education. The percent distribution among the three subject areas in 1924 was as follows: [12]

[11] Ibid. p. 39-42. See also D. A. Jánossy, op. cit. p. 15-17; and Julius Kornis, op. cit. p. 67-74, 280-81.

[12] József Fekete. "A gimnáziumi tantervek országos vitája" (The National Debate on the Gymnasium Curricula). *Köznevelés* (Public Education), XIX:2:43, January 22, 1963. Budapest.

	Gymnasiums	*Réal* gymnasiums	*Réal* schools
Humanities	73.3	71.6	57.5
Physical education	6.7	6.7	6.7
Réal (science) subjects	20.0	21.7	35.8

The secondary schools were not coeducational. The first ones for girls were established in 1916, and Law No. XXIV of 1926 provided that three types of these schools be established: (1) gymnasiums *(leánygimnázium)*, similar to the academic gymnasiums for boys; (2) lyceums *(leánylíceum)*, similar to the *réal* gymnasiums for boys; and (3), so-called "colleges" *(leánykollégium)* to provide terminal education for girls not intending to continue with higher education.

The uniform prewar secondary school system resulted from Law No. XI of 1934, which established the so-called 8-year gymnasiums. They admitted children who had completed the first four primary grades, usually 10 years old but no older than 13.

For the most part, the gymnasium curriculum was traditional: heavy emphasis on Hungarian language and literature, Latin and Greek, mathematics and geometry, modern European languages (two), and religion and morals. As an offset to the academic side, however, the curriculum provided physical education, singing, and a "sport afternoon" (table 5).

Table 5.—Number of hours per week, per subject, in the 8-year gymnasiums: 1938-39

Subject	Grade									
	1–8	5–8	1	2	3	4	5	6	7	8
Total	273	149	31	31	31	31	33	33	34	34
Chemistry	3	3	0	0	0	0	0	3	0	0
Drawing and art appreciation	10	2	2	2	2	2	0	0	1	1
Economics and social studies	2	2	0	0	0	0	0	2	0	0
English, French, or Italian	15	15	0	0	0	0	4	4	4	3
Geography and ethnography	11	2	3	4	2	0	0	0	2	0
German	20	12	0	0	4	4	3	3	3	3
Greek	15	15	0	0	0	0	4	4	4	3
Guidance	1	0	1	0	0	0	0	0	0	0
History	17	11	0	0	3	3	3	3	2	3
Hungarian language and literature	29	12	5	5	4	3	3	3	3	3
Hygiene	2	1	0	0	0	1	0	0	0	1
Latin	34	16	5	5	4	4	4	4	4	4
Mathematics and geometry	27	12	4	5	3	3	3	3	3	3
Natural history	12	5	2	2	0	3	5	0	0	0
Natural science	10	8	0	0	2	0	0	0	4	4
Penmanship	1	0	1	0	0	0	0	0	0	0
Philosophy	2	2	0	0	0	0	0	0	0	2
Physical education	31	15	4	4	4	4	4	4	4	3
Religion and morals	16	8	2	2	2	2	2	2	2	2
Shorthand	2	0	0	0	0	2	0	0	0	0
Singing	5	0	2	2	1	0	0	0	0	0
"Sport afternoon"	8	8	0	0	0	0	2	2	2	2

SOURCE OF DATA: József Fekete. "A gimnáziumi tantervek országos vitája" (The National Debate on the Gymnasium Curriculums). *Köznevelés* (Public Education), XIX:2:44, January 22, 1963. Budapest.

Control.—Like kindergartens and elementary schools, secondary schools could be maintained by associations, communities, private groups or individuals, religious denominations, and the State. Each secondary school was headed and administered by a director (*igazgató*) acting under the control of inspectors appointed by and responsible to the Ministry of Religion and Education.

In 1937–38, Hungary had 126 secondary schools for boys and 47 for girls. Of the boys' secondary schools, 33 were gymnasiums, 75 *réal* gymnasiums, and 18 *réal* schools. By control, they were distributed as follows:

Boys' schools

51	State
29	Roman Catholic
19	Calvinist
8	Lutheran
6	"Royal Catholic"*
3	private
2	association-sponsored

Girls' schools

16	Roman Catholic
10	State
5	Calvinist
5	communal
5	private
3	Lutheran
2	association-sponsored
1	Jewish

* Government-sponsored Catholic.

The total number of teachers (not including those for religion) in the two sets of schools was 3,488; of students, 69,993—boys, 52,034; girls, 17,959. By 1941–42 the number of secondary schools for boys had increased to 191; for girls, to 59.[13]

Lyceums.—Established by Law No. XIII of 1938, the lyceums (*líceum*) were 4-year institutions offering secondary education of a general practical character and admitting graduates of the 8-year elementary schools or children no older than 18 years who had completed the fourth year of a gymnasium. Operated under the same jurisdictional principles as the gymnasiums, the lyceums were separate for boys and girls.

Graduates of the lyceums, like those of the other secondary schools, had to pass a baccalaureate (*érettségi*) examination before they could be admitted to an institution of higher learning.

Following the territorial acquisitions of 1938–1940,[14] the increased need for teachers led to the reorganization in 1941 of the lyceums, consolidating them with the 5-year teacher-training institutes. Under the 1941 law passed in response to Law No. II of 1939 relating to national defense, the upper grades of the teacher-training institutes were transformed into lyceums offering a teacher's license instead of a baccalaureate diploma.

In 1941–42, 84 lyceums were operating—34 for boys and 50 for girls—distributed by control as shown below:

Boys' lyceums

14	State
5	Calvinist
5	Roman Catholic
3	Greek Catholic
3	Lutheran
2	"Royal Catholic"
1	association-sponsored
1	Jewish

Girls' lyceums

32	Roman Catholic
7	Calvinist
7	State
2	Greek Catholic
1	Jewish
1	Lutheran

[13] Joseph Somogyi, op. cit. p. 51.

[14] In the fall of 1938 and spring of 1939, Hungary acquired the southern and eastern parts of Slovakia; in August 1940, the northern half of Transylvania; and in April 1941, the southern region (Délvidék), including part of the Bácska (Bačka) from Yugoslavia.

Total 1941–42 enrollment was 12,933—boys, 4,750; girls, 8,183. Teachers numbered 1,361.[15]

Teacher Training

Elementary School Teachers

The first teacher-training school in Hungary was established in 1828 by László Pyrker, Archbishop of Eger. The first law relating to such schools was Law No. XXXVIII of 1868, which established 3-year institutions admitting students who had completed 4 years of secondary schools or *réal* schools. After graduation, students of the teacher-training institutes spent 2 years in practice-teaching and then took an oral, a written, and a practical examination leading to a teacher's license. The training was extended to 4 years in 1881 and to 5 years in 1923.

The graduates of the teacher-training institutions could apply for admission to the following: higher teacher-training schools for the preparation of secondary school teachers, higher schools for physical education, higher schools of applied arts, institutes for the preparation of teachers for the handicapped, and institutes for the preparation of agricultural school teachers.

The teacher-training system was reorganized in 1938 by Law No. XIV. Under this law the training of elementary school teachers was entrusted to 2-year academies admitting secondary school graduates who held baccalaureate degrees and passed an admissions examination. The curriculum consisted of the following: economics and hygiene (elements), education (theoretical and practical elements), music, physical education, religion and morals, and singing. After the second year, students took a State examination which consisted of written, oral, and practical parts. If they passed it, they were granted a teacher's license. In addition to the academies, in 1941 the lyceums also started to train teachers for the elementary schools.[16]

In 1937–38, Hungary's teacher-training schools numbered 55: 32 Roman Catholic, 11 State, 10 Protestant, and two Jewish. Excluding those who taught religion, the teaching staff numbered 857; the students, 8,336 (boys, 2,672 and girls, 5,664).[17]

Kindergarten Teachers

Separate institutions, first established in 1837, trained kindergarten teachers. Setting up a 2-year curriculum, Law No. XV of 1891 assured the uniform organization of institutions for training kindergarten teachers. In 1926 the curriculum became a 3-year one, and the institutions admitted graduates of the upper elementary schools or children who had completed 4 years of secondary school.

---

[15] Joseph Somogyi, op. cit. p. 51-56. For further details on the historical background of secondary education, see Gyula Simon. "Középiskolai reformjaink néhány kérdése 1883-tól" (A Few Questions of Our Secondary Educational Reforms Since 1883). *Pedagógiai Szemle* (Review of Education). XIII:2:150-59, 1963. Budapest. See also Julius Kornis, op. cit. p. 75-126, 282-84.

[16] Ibid.

[17] Joseph Somogyi, op. cit. p. 62.

In 1937–38 four kindergarten-training institutions were operating—three Roman Catholic and one State. Their total teaching staffs numbered 58 and their students 450. Four years later, in 1941–42, five such schools were operating—four Roman Catholic and one State. They had 71 teachers and 603 students.[18]

Secondary School Teachers

In 1937–38 and also in 1941–42, the institutions of higher learning were responsible for training secondary school teachers and they still are.

Higher Education

The first institution of higher education in Hungary was the University of Pécs, founded by Louis the Great (Nagy Lajos) in 1367. His successors, Sigismund (Zsigmond) and Mathias Corvinus (Mátyás), established other universities at Buda and Pozsony (Pressburg or Bratislava) respectively.[19] By 1547, however, all three of these were extinct.

Of the universities operating in the prewar period, the earliest one was established in 1635 at Nagyszombat by Péter Pázmány, Archbishop of Esztergom. In 1777 this university was transferred by Maria Theresa to Buda, and by her successor Joseph II to Budapest. In 1848, Law No. XIX placed the university under the jurisdiction of the Ministry of Education. In 1921 it assumed the name of its founder, becoming the Royal Hungarian Péter Pázmány University (*Magyar Királyi Pázmány Péter Tudományegyetem*); at that time it operated with four schools—law, medicine, philosophy, and theology.

The next university was that of Kolozsvár (Cluj), founded under Law No. XIX of 1872. In 1881 it became known as the Royal Hungarian Francis Joseph University *(Magyar Királyi Ferenc József Tudományegyetem)*; it operated with schools of law and political science; medicine; philosophy, linguistics, and history; and mathematics and natural sciences. After Romania's occupation of Transylvania at the end of 1918, Law No. XXV of 1921 brought about the university's transfer to Szeged.[20]

The University of Pozsony (Bratislava) and the University of Debrecen were founded under Law No. XXXVI of 1912. The former came to be known as the Royal Hungarian Elizabeth University (*Magyar Királyi Erzsébet Tudományegyetem*) ; it operated with four schools: law and political science; medicine; philosophy, linguistics, and history; and mathematics, natural sciences, and agricultural sciences. When the city became a part of the newly created Czechoslovakia, the university was transferred by Law No. XXV of 1921 to Pécs, where it operated until

[18] Ibid. p. 64. See also p. 56-79; D. A. Jánossy, op. cit. p. 27-35; and Julius Kornis, op cit. p. 221-38, 281-82.

[19] Sigismund established the *Universitas Budensis* in Buda in 1389 and Mathias founded the *Academia Istropolitana* in Pozsony in 1467. For details see Mátyás Bajkó. "Fejezetek a magyar felsőoktatás történetéből" (Chapters From the History of Hungarian Higher Education). *Felsőoktatási Szemle* (Review of Higher Education), Budapest, XV:4:205-10. April 1966.

[20] With the transfer of Northern Transylvania to Hungary in August 1940, the university returned to its original location, where it operated until Soviet and Romanian troops retook the area in the fall of 1944.

the end of World War II with faculties of law, medicine, philosophy, and theology. The University of Debrecen came to be known as the Royal Hungarian István (Stephen) Tisza University (*Magyar Királyi Tisza István Tudományegyetem)* and operated with the five schools of Calvinist theology; law and political science; medicine; philosophy, languages and history; and mathematics and natural sciences.[21]

In 1940, when the University of Kolozsvár was temporarily reestablished, the institution at Szeged acquired the name of the Royal Hungarian Miklós (Nicholas) Horthy University *(Magyar Királyi Horthy Miklós Tudományegyetem).* It operated with the four schools of law and political science; medicine; philosophy, languages, and history; and mathematics and natural sciences.

During World War II the universities did not operate at full capacity: some of their schools were suspended.

In addition to the universities, Hungarian higher education included a number of polytechnical universities *(műszaki egyetem),* economic institutes, institutes of fine and applied arts and of music, and military academies.

In academic year 1937-38, Hungary had 16 institutions of higher education with 1,724 members of the teaching staffs and 11,747 undergraduate students, of whom 14.5 percent were women. In descending order of enrollment, these undergraduates were divided among the fields of study as follows: [22]

4,671	law
1,576	liberal arts, philosophy, and natural sciences
1,451	medicine
1,052	engineering and architecture
775	economics
621	agriculture
581	teacher-training
322	fine and applied arts
173	pharmacy
525	other

To get into an institution of higher education a student needed to have a baccalaureate diploma and to pass admission examinations. Depending upon his course, he would have to study from 4 years in the schools of law and political science; in philosophy, linguistics, and history; in mathematics and natural sciences; and in theology; to 5 years in the schools of medicine.

Although some institutions were of high caliber, having international reputations in specific areas, the prewar higher educational system was basically restrictive and inequitably selective. For example, Law No. XXV of 1920 and Law No. XIV of 1928 (the so-called *numerus clausus* laws) limited the admission of Hungarian citizens of Jewish faith to a percent equal to the percent of Jews in the total population. The composition of the student body in general was not

[21] For further details on the prewar higher educational system, see Julius Kornis, op. cit. p. 127-74, 285-88.
[22] *Statistical Pocket Book of Hungary 1967.* Budapest: Publishing House of Economics and Law, 1967. p. 182.

correlated with that of the country: the number of students of peasant and working-class background was extremely limited. These inequities were eliminated, however, in the post-World War II period.[23]

[23] In addition to the sources listed in the footnotes of this chapter, consult the following references on the historical background of Hungary's educational system before World War II: (1) Magda Jóború. "*A középiskola szerepe a Horthy-korszak művelődéspolitikájában*" (The Role of the Secondary School in the Cultural Policy of the Horthy Era). Budapest: Tankönyvkiadó, 1963. 159 p. (2) Sándor Köte. *A magyar nevelésügy a polgári demokratikus forradalom és a tanácsköztársaság idején* (Hungarian Education at the Time of the Bourgeois Democratic Revolution and the Soviet Republic). Budapest: Tankönyvkiadó, 1963, 131 p. (3) János Ravasz, László Felkai, Béla Bellér, and Gyula Simon. *A magyar nevelés története a feudalizmus és a kapitalizmus korában* (The History of Hungarian Education in the Era of Feudalism and Capitalism). Budapest: Tankönyvkiadó, 1961. 279 p. (4) *Tanulmányok a magyar nevelés történetéből, 1849-1944* (Studies on the History of Hungarian Education, 1849-1944). Budapest: Pedagógiai Tudományos Intézet, 1957, 323 p.

III. The Postwar Educational System

Evolution

The educational system of the Hungarian People's Republic as it crystallized in the late 1960's evolved as a result of measures adopted in a series of well-differentiated phases. Each phase was characterized by distinct historical changes in the country's drive toward the achievement of what is referred to as "full socialism." These changes in turn were heralded by and reflected in the pronouncements of the Communist Party.

The First Phase: 1945–48

During the immediate postwar period the Party, for tactical reasons, adopted a moderate stand, participating in a genuinely popular coalition government. In accordance with the spirit of the times, it adopted a democratic program which, among other things, called for the elimination of fascist elements and influence from the field of culture and education. It embraced a plan for the democratic re-education of youth, the retraining of teachers [1] and the establishment of a democratic system of education. These aspirations of the Party were shared by most other parties participating in the Hungarian National Independence Front (*Magyar Nemzeti Függetlenségi Front*) and in the Provisional National Government (*Ideiglenes Nemzeti Kormány*), including the Social Democratic Party and the National Peasant Party.

In order to implement the educational goals, the Government in May 1945 established the National Council of Public Education (*Országos Köznevelési Tanács*) by combining the National Council of Public Instruction (*Országos Közoktatási Tanács*) and the Council of Higher Education (*Felsőoktatási Tanács*). The Council's primary function was to advise and assist the Minister of Culture.[2]

A great help in propagating the new educational ideas were certain new educational journals, including the *Köznevelés* (Public Education), the official organ of the Ministry of Culture; and *Embernevelés* (Education of Man), the official organ of the Teachers' Union.[3]

The farthestreaching and most positive change during this first period was the establishment in August 1945 of the "general" school

[1] For details on the retraining of teachers, see p. 140-42.
[2] See footnote 37 in this chapter.
[3] See p. 167-68.

(*általános iskola*), a revamped elementary school. Organized under Decree 6650–1945.M.E. of the National Provisional Government and calling for an ultimate 8-year "general" (elementary) school that would be free and compulsory for children ages 6 to 14 (in place of the former 4- and 8-year elementary schools and 4-year upper elementary schools), the "general" schools were introduced gradually.[4]

When the campaign to organize the "general" schools was begun in late summer 1945, there were 7,068 elementary schools of which 4,605 were denominational, 1,539 State-sponsored, 797 village-maintained, and 127 enterprise-sponsored (or private). There were also 367 upper elementary schools.[5]

The original plan called for the opening of 1,476 "general" schools in 1945–46, but because of lack of space and personnel only 816 were actually opened, of which 286 were State-sponsored, 419 denominational, and 111 village schools.[6]

Based upon the experience of the first year's operation, the Ministry of Culture's Decree No. 70.000/1946VKM amplified the scope and nature of the "general" school and called for the speedy transformation of the existing elementary schools into new elementary or "general" schools. At the beginning of the 1946-47 school year, the total number of old elementary schools was reduced to 2,830, while the number of new "general" schools rose to 4,182.[7] By 1947–48, the last year of the first phase, the number of "general" schools increased to 4,847, while that of the old elementary schools decreased to 2,650.

The "Socialization" Process

The second phase in the country's educational transformation began with the first political changes that led to the establishment of a "people's democratic" regime. It extended from the Fourth Congress of the Party in June 1948 to March 1950, when the Party again adopted a major decision relating to education. That decision stipulated several major tasks for education: "the termination of the cultural monopoly of the propertied classes; the nationalization of the schools; the elimination of chauvinism and national hatred from the schools; the correct teaching of societal evolution and the broadening of national scientific knowledge; and the synchronization of general education with training for life." [8]

School nationalization was carried out under Law No. XXXIII of 1948, which immediately affected over two-thirds of the country's 9,274 schools.[9] It brought into the State school system 639,335 pupils and

[4] See p. 50.

[5] At this time the number of gymnasiums was 174, of which 128 were for boys and 46 for girls. Gyula Simon and József Szarka. *A magyar népi demokrácia nevelésügyének története* (History of the Educational System of the Hungarian People's Republic). Budapest: Tankönyvkiadó, 1965. p. 99. (Referred to hereafter as Simon and Szarka.)

[6] Ibid. p. 100.

[7] Of the 4,182 "general" schools, 2,392 were denominational, 1,213 State-sponsored, 493 village schools, 72 private, and 12 consolidated. Ibid. p. 112.

[8] Ibid. p. 30.

[9] Even before the formal nationalization law was adopted, many "general" and other elementary schools, especially those operated by mining and industrial enterprises, were already transformed into State institutions (February and September 1947).

approximately 18,000 teachers from the denominational "general" and other elementary schools.

The Government entered into special agreements with the various denominations, regulating general relations between the State and the churches, including education.[10] To administer State-church relations, the Government established the State Office for Denominational Affairs (*Állami Egyházügyi Hivatal*).[11] One of its primary functions, in addition to administering general religious affairs, was to give material assistance to the general gymnasiums operated by the various denominations [12] and to effectuate religious instruction in these denominational schools.[13]

Another major transformation during this phase related to the social composition of the secondary school student body. Wishing to raise a new generation of working class-based intelligentsia, the regime proceeded with increasing zeal to break what it called the "monopoly position of the class enemy in the field of education." [14]

In response to this policy objective, the system of admission to secondary schools was radically altered, social origin having emerged as one of the determining criteria. As a result of the measures adopted during this period in Budapest, for example, the proportion of children of working-class background in the first grade of the secondary schools increased from 8 to 9 percent in 1948 to 42.5 percent in 1949.[15] This record was duplicated in most other communities.

The transformation in the social composition of the secondary school student body was made possible, in part, by the Ministry of Culture's Decree No. 51.700/1948VKM, which gave working-class children who graduated from either the 4-year upper elementary school or the 8-year elementary ("general") schools, an opportunity to enter the 5th grade of the then 8-year gymnasiums without having to take supplementary examinations.

From the structural point of view, this period saw the reorganization of the secondary schools into 4-year institutions admitting graduates of the 8-year "general" schools. The new system was gradually implemented beginning with the 1948–49 school year.[16]

Among the organizational-administrative changes of this period by

---

[10] The agreement with the reform and unitarian churches was signed on October 7, 1948; that with the Jewish community on December 7, 1948, with the Evangelical Church on January 15, 1949, and with the Roman Catholic Church on August 20, 1950. For the text of the agreements, see *Köznevelés*, IV:20:185-87. IV:24:209-11. V:1-2:4-5.

[11] Law No. I of 1951.

[12] See p. 77.

[13] In the course of the 1949 curriculum revision, religion was made an elective rather than a required course (Decree No. 5 of 1949). In the wake of the 1956 revolt, the issue of religious instruction was again brought to the fore. It has been regulated in the spirit of Article 54 of the Constitution of August 20, 1949, relating to the separation of church and state and freedom of religious worship. Accordingly, "general" and secondary school pupils desirous of religious instruction are provided this opportunity within the framework of the public schools. The organization of classes for religious instruction is the responsibility of the principals. The teaching of religion cannot be used for "political purposes directed against the State, social, or economic order of the Hungarian People's Republic." "A Magyar Forradalmi Munkás-Paraszt Kormány 21/1957 (III.24.) számú rendelete a vallásoktatásról" (Decree No. 21/1957 (III.24.) of the Hungarian Revolutionary Worker-Peasant Government on the Teaching of Religion). *Magyar Közlöny* (Hungarian Gazette), Budapest, No. 35, March 24, 1957. p. 222-23.

[14] The impending measures in this sphere were reflected in a speech by József Révay, then chief theoretician to the Party, at the MÁVAG machine-building plant of Budapest on September 16, 1948. In it he insisted that "socialism must be built in the sphere of culture as well."

[15] Simon and Szarka, op. cit. p. 34.

[16] At first the nationalization law of 1948 affected only 113 gymnasiums. Ibid. p. 134.

far the most important ones related to the dissolution and replacement of the National Council of Public Education by the National Scientific Institute of Education (*Országos Neveléstudományi Intézet*), which 18 months later was itself dissolved by the 1950 Party decision for harboring bourgeois tendencies in the field of education. Its tasks were assumed by the Minister of Culture and until the Scientific Pedagogical Institute (*Pedagógiai Tudományos Intézet*) was established in 1954–55,[17] no meaningful scientific organization existed in Hungary to effect research in the theory and practice of education.

This period also saw the establishment (1948) of the National Council for the Protection of Children and Youth (*Országos Gyermek- és Ifjúságvédelmi Tanács*) and of the National Office for Collegiums (student homes and dormitories) and Student Welfare (*Országos Diákjóléti és Kollégiumi Hivatal*).

The Socialist Educational System

The third and final phase in the transformation of Hungary's educational system began with the adoption of the March 1950 resolution on education by the Central Committee of the Party.[18] Evaluating the recent historical evolution of the country as one characterized by the replacement of the "democratic dictatorship" by a "dictatorship of the proletariat," the resolution called for the complete reorganization and reorientation of education along Marxist-Leninist lines.

The measures adopted for this purpose included revising the curriculums and syllabuses, restructuring the educational institutions at all post-elementary levels, and changing the admission and examination systems.

An important factor in the implementation of these measures was the founding of the Association of Working Youth (*Dolgozó Ifjúság Szövetsége*) (better known by its abbreviated name DISZ), which was modeled after the Soviet *Komsomol* system.[19]

The emergence of the present socialist educational system during the third phase was not entirely even, major changes having been effected in 1954, 1957, and 1961.

The 1954 changes were motivated by the launching of the so-called "New Course" "liberalization" program following the death of Stalin and the subsequent removal from power of the Hungarian "Moscovites." In education, these changes were based on the January 1954 resolution of the Party's Central Committee, which, among other things, called for the "greater appreciation of the treasures of Hungarian national culture" in all schools.[20] This directive led to the rediscovery of the "progressive," "revolutionary" national heroes of Hungarian art, literature, and poetry, such as Ady, Arany, Balassi, Csokonai, Jókai, Mikszáth, Móricz, Petőfi, and Vörösmarty. It also called for improving the quality

[17] See p. 163.

[18] The resolution can be found in the April 15, 1950, issue of *Köznevelés* (Public Education), Budapest.

[19] See p. 181-84.

[20] "A Központi Vezetőség határozata a közoktatás helyzetéről és feladatairól" (Resolution of the Central Committee Concerning the Status and Tasks of Public Education). *Társadalmi Szemle* (Social Review). Budapest, IX:1:96-103, January 1954.

of teaching, the level of students, the production of textbooks and educational equipment, and (in order to promote research in education) for establishing a Scientific Pedagogical Institute.

The 1957 changes reflected the regime's interpretation of the consequences of the October-November 1956 revolt.[21] In its attempt to protect the people's democratic system against what it called "counter-revolutionary" elements, the Party adopted a series of measures to "further the building of socialism in the field of education." In a resolution adopted in 1958, the Party launched a long-range educational program calculated to assure the education of youth in the spirit of Marxism, expand the network of schools (especially the elementary ones) and tie education more closely to life.[22]

The general overhauling of the educational system in the 1960's was first decided upon at the Seventh Congress of the Party in November 1959. On the basis of Party directives, a School Reform Committee was established which by September 1960 had published its "Guidelines for the Further Development of Our Educational System" (*Irányelvek oktatási rendszerünk továbbfejlesztésére*).

The guidelines and the general scope of the reforms became the subject of a nationwide discussion by laymen and cultural and educational experts alike.[23] The basic principles enunciated in the guidelines, as well as many of the positive suggestions made by leading Hungarian educators, were largely incorporated in Law No. III of 1961, the fundamental education act of the present Hungarian system of education, adopted by Parliament on October 11, 1961.[24]

The law outlines the general principles and goals of Hungary's socialist educational system, the framework of compulsory schooling requirements, and the scope, basic structure, and general content of the various types of schools.

In accordance with the basic objectives of the fundamental education law of 1961, new curriculums were adopted and gradually implemented in both elementary and secondary schools.[25] The teachers and administrators were provided with new regulations relating to the unfolding of the educational process in these institutions and to their specific tasks and responsibilities. Major changes were made in the vocational-technical education system and in the teaching of Marxism-Leninism at institutions of higher learning. To assist the Minister of Culture in an advisory capacity, the Government established late in 1965 a National Council of Education (*Országos Oktatási Tanács*). Its assigned primary

---

[21] The educational process during the revolt was interrupted throughout the country, especially in Budapest, where the fiercest fighting took place. One week after the entry of Soviet tanks on November 4, the schools were ordered to reopen "if the material prerequisites were available." See Resolution No. 7/1956. (XI.12.) of the Government in *Magyar Közlöny*, No. 93, November 12, 1956. p. 570.

[22] "A Magyar Szociálista Munkáspárt művelődési politikájának irányelvei" (Guidelines Concerning the Educational Policy of the Hungarian Socialist Workers' Party), in *Mai kulturális életünk főbb kérdései* (The Major Questions of Our Contemporary Cultural Life). Budapest: Kossuth, 1958. p. 22-27. For full text see *Társadalmi Szemle*. XIII:7-8:116-51. July-August 1958.

[23] Ferenc Tihanyi, *ed. Oktatásügyünk továbbfejlesztéséért. Tanulmányok és dokumentumok* (For the Further Development of Our Educational System. Studies and Documents). Budapest: Tankönyvkiadó *for the* Pedagógiai Tudományos Intézet, 1961. 191 p.

[24] "1961. évi III. törvény a Magyar Népköztársaság oktatási rendszeréről" (Law No. III of 1961 Concerning the Educational System of the Hungarian People's Republic). *Magyar Közlöny*, No. 74, October 17, 1961. p.566-70.

[25] See p. 57-65.

function is to coordinate and assure the ideological, methodological, pedagogical, political, and professional unity of education. Prototypes of the council were also established under the auspices of the executive committees of the district people's councils.[26]

The successes and failures of the educational system in the first 5 years after the adoption of the fundamental law were the subject of a major policy statement by the Minister of Culture in Parliament on November 11-13, 1965.[27] In that statement he was enthusiastic about the almost universal enforcement of the 10-year compulsory school system covering children between 6 and 16 years of age,[28] but gloomy about the future of "general" (i.e., academic) or secondary education.

Admission to the general academic secondary schools, especially their day sessions, was to be curtailed and applicants were to be directed towards vocational-technical training in order to assure that they would enter employment immediately after graduation rather than pursue higher studies. The original 5+1 plan (5 days of theoretical and 1 day of practical training) in the secondary schools was to be used only "where the material prerequisites" were available within the school's framework so as to relieve the pressure on the factories and plants. Where facilities were not available, practical training was to be reduced to 2 hours per week. Intermediate technical training was to be provided only within the framework of shops and plants, with formal schooling in technical areas being confined to the vocational secondary schools teaching clusters of skills and giving instruction culminating in the baccalaureate diploma.

In higher education, the thrust of the criticism was directed towards the inadequate teaching of Marxism-Leninism. Students, the Minister insisted, were not only to become acquainted with the tenets of Marxism-Leninism, they were also to be led to embrace them. Political-ideological training was to be provided within the framework of every subject. The extent to which the recommendations were carried out has not yet been ascertained.[29]

Principles and Goals

The basic principles underlying the educational system were summarized in the Fundamental Law of 1961. According to this law, education is expected to—

1. Assure close ties between the schools and production, and prepare all students for participation in productive life.
2. Raise the general and professional cultural level by taking into consideration the age characteristics of the students.
3. On the basis of a socialist outlook and morality, raise true patriots, upright

[26] For details see p. 5, 33-35.

[27] Pál Ilku. "Népünk általános és szakmai műveltségének emeléséért" (For Raising the General and Professional Cultural Level of Our People). *Köznevelés*, XXI:23:881-89, December 23, 1965.

[28] See p. 50-51.

[29] For a general review of the effect of the educational reform, see the following article in the theoretical journal of the Party's Central Committee: Imre Kurucz. "Az oktatási reform végrehajtása alapelvei tükrében" (The Implementation of the Educational Reform in Light of Its Fundamental Principles). *Társadalmi Szemle*, Budapest. XX:12:42-53, December 1965.

and law-abiding citizens devoted to their fatherland and the people, dedicated to the service of socialism, peace, and brotherhood among nations and to the building and protection of the people's state.

4. Increase the number of students and of persons who study while engaged in productive employment, thereby preparing for the gradual implementation of a general and compulsory secondary education system.[30]

Also according to the 1961 Fundamental Law, the goal of the educational system of the Hungarian People's Republic is to—

1. Provide, by means of a planned educational system, general and professional knowledge; and satisfy the requirements of the economy for skilled labor.
2. Raise the level of general and professional culture.
3. Develop and strengthen in the students a Marxist-Leninist concept of life and socialist morality.
4. Raise conscious, educated, patriotic, upright, and law-abiding citizens who will be faithful to the people, will cooperate in building socialism with useful work, will build and protect the people's state, and will serve with dedication the cause of peace and brotherhood.[31]

The basic principles and goals of Hungary's educational system reflect Article 48 of the Constitution of August 20, 1949, which stipulates that—

1. The Hungarian People's Republic shall insure the right to education to every worker.
2. The Hungarian People's Republic shall implement this right by extending, to all, educational facilities through (1) a free and compulsory "general" (elementary) school system, (2) secondary and higher schools, (3) educational facilities for adult workers, and (4) financial aid to those receiving any kind of education.[32]

Organization and Administration

The educational institutions of Hungary are organized and administered under the direction or auspices of a series of central and local Party and governmental organs and with the cooperation of various cultural, scientific, and social organizations.

The Communist Party

Ultimate decisionmaking power in education, as in all other fields, lies with the central executive organs of the Communist Party.[33] The Party's main organ for dealing with educational matters is the Scientific and Public Education Section (*Tudományos és Közoktatási Osztály*) of the Party Central Committee. Its studies and proposals usually emerge as Party policy, following which they go out as directives and resolutions of the Central Committee. They are then translated into legislative language and issued in the form of decrees or decisions by the Government, the Ministry of Culture, or any other ministry responsible for particular educational tasks.

---

30 Preamble to Law No. III of 1961. op. cit.

31 Article 1 of Law No. III of 1961. op. cit.

32 *Constitution of the Hungarian People's Republic*. Budapest: Athenaeum, 1949. 20 p.

33 See p. 5-8.

In addition to formulating broad policy decisions, the Party also exercises day-to-day supervision over their implementation. At each organizational level and for each type of education there exists a Party base organ to insure that the policies of the Government are implemented. Strict adherence to the Party line is also assured by the fact that politically influential educators hold leading Party positions and a large number of the members of committees or commissions concerned with education or student-faculty life are also members of the Party or the Communist Youth League (*Kommunista Ifjúsági Szövetség*).

Although decisionmaking power rests almost exclusively with the Party, the central and local governmental and school administrative organs have considerable latitude for implementing educational policy.

The Ministry of Culture

Evolution.—A number of organizational and structural changes have taken place since 1951 in the Ministry having charge of educational affairs. The following tabulation gives a profile of the Ministry's name changes and of related events since pre-World War II days:

Year	*Name*	*Related Events*
Before 1951 (Pre-World War II days).	Ministry of Religion and Public Education (*Vallás- és Közoktatásügyi Minisztérium*)	----------
1951 ----------	Ministry of Public Education (*Közoktatásügyi Minisztérium*)	State Office for Denominational Affairs established to handle state-church relations.[34]
1953 ----------	Ministry of Education (*Oktatásügyi Minisztérium*)	Consolidated under Law VI with the Ministry of Higher Education (*Felsőoktatási Minisztérium*)[35]
1956 ----------	Ministry of Culture (*Művelődésügyi Minisztérium*)[36 37]	Consolidated with the Ministry of Public Culture (*Népművelési Minisztérium*)

Structure and Functions.—The competence and responsibilities of the Ministry are outlined in a 1957 Government resolution.[38] According to this resolution, the Ministry of Culture—

1. Guides, supervises, and directs kindergartens, general schools, gymnasiums, and teacher-training institutes; coordinates and supervises vocational secondary schools and universities; and regulates academic matters of the institutions of higher learning, including admissions, scholarships, the teaching of Marxism-

[34] See p. 25.

[35] The Ministry of Higher Education had been established in 1952 under Law 21/1952.

[36] *Magyar Közlöny*, No. 106, December 29, 1956. p. 613.

[37] Literally, the *Művelődésügyi Minisztérium* means Ministry of Cultural Affairs. In the present publication, regardless of the official nomenclature for the Ministry in any particular year, the term Ministry of Culture is used at all times.

[38] "A Magyar Forradalmi Munkás-Paraszt Kormány 1.045/1957. (IV.25.) számú határozata a Művelődésügyi Minisztérium ügyköréről" (Resolution No. 1,045/1957. (IV.25.) of the Hungarian Revolutionary Worker-Peasant Government Concerning the Competence of the Ministry of Culture). *Magyar Közlöny*, No. 47, April 25, 1957. p. 276

Leninism, and the grading of institutions that operate under the jurisdiction of other ministries or governmental organs.

2. Aids and guides the work of professional artists and supervises artistic institutions and enterprises, including those in publishing, cinematography, and the theatre, as well as national museums and archives and some of the large libraries of the country. Further, it guides the work of organizations engaged in the propagation of mass culture, including the Institute for Popular Culture *(Népművelési Intézet)* and the Association for the Propagation of the Social and Natural Sciences (*Társadalom- és Természettudományi Ismeretterjesztő Társulat*). Also exercises direct control over cultural institutions and enterprises administered by the people's councils, and issues general rules and guidelines concerning landmarks and historical monuments.
3. Exercises control over the education sections of executive committees of the local people's councils.
4. Exercises State control over the national education associations.

The Ministry of Culture also exercises direct control and supervision over the State Office for Denominational Affairs [39] and over the Hungarian Office for Physical Education and Sport *(Magyar Testnevelési és Sport Hivatal)*.[40]

The Ministry is divided into a number of specialized sections or divisions dealing with various aspects of its activities. Among these parts of the Ministry are the following:

1. Section of kindergarten (*Óvodai Osztály*)
2. Division of Public Education (*Közoktatási Főosztály*)
3. Division of Secondary Education (*Középfokú Oktatási Főosztály*)
4. Division of Vocational Education (*Szakoktatási Főosztály*)
5. Division of Teacher and Kindergarten-Teacher Training (*Tanító- és Óvónőképző Szakosztály*)

In formulating and implementing its policies, the Ministry cooperates with a number of advisory and governmental agencies, other interested ministries, and mass organizations.

The National Council of Education

Modeled after the original National Council of Public Education,[41] the National Council of Education (*Országos Oktatási Tanács*) was established in late 1965 to serve the Ministry of Culture in an advisory capacity, especially with regard to educational matters affecting other ministries. Headed by the Minister of Culture, it consists of representatives of the various ministries, with the Minister of Labor (*Munkaügyi Miniszter*) serving as deputy chairman. Among its primary functions is to synchronize substantive and organizational questions affecting schools and institutes that operate under the jurisdiction of ministries other than the Ministry of Culture.[42]

---

[39] See p. 25.
[40] See p. 193.
[41] See p. 23.
[42] Decree No. 27/1965. (XII. 1). See also "Megalakult az Országos Oktatási Tanács" (The Establishment of the National Council of Education). *Köznevelés*, XXI:24:934, December 17, 1965.

Since its inception in 1965, the Council has been concerned with—

1. Preparation of general guidelines for the curriculums and syllabuses of vocational secondary schools.
2. Evaluation of the status of vocational secondary schools and their development plans.
3. Formulation of major principles concerning the content and structure of vocational secondary schools for adults with emphasis on admission of those coming from vocational schools for apprentices.
4. Effective utilization of available classrooms in elementary and secondary schools and in vocational schools for apprentices.
5. Revision of the network of secondary schools and the establishment of long-range plans concerning the proportion of various types of secondary schools in the 1970's.[43]

The Institute for Cultural Relations

Operating for a few years under the direct jurisdiction of the Minister of Culture, the Institute for Cultural Relations (*Kulturális Kapcsolatok Intézete*) functions under the immediate supervision of the Council of Ministers (*Minisztertanács*).[44]

The primary task of the Institute is to:

1. Propagate and popularize Hungarian culture abroad.
2. Propagate and popularize other people's cultures in Hungary.
3. Prepare and help implement cultural agreements.
4. Deal with questions relating to the development of cultural relations decided upon by the Council of Ministers.

In 1963, the Institute was also placed in charge of the Hungarian National Commission for UNESCO and its Secretariat.

The Hungarian National Commission for UNESCO

Hungary originally joined UNESCO in 1948, but, like the other "people's democratic" countries, took no active part in its work until after the death of Stalin and the subsequent "liberalization" trend. By far the most important Hungarian governmental agency in charge of UNESCO affairs is the Hungarian National Commission for UNESCO (*Magyar UNESCO Bizottság*). Reorganized in 1954, 1956, and again in 1958, the Commission consists of the Plenary Session, the Executive Council, and the Secretariat. Headed by a President, it is composed of 60 full members representing various important national institutions involved in UNESCO activities as well as experts in culture, education, and science.

Under the rules of the Commission, the Plenary Session is convened

---

[43] *Report on Educational Progress in the 1966/67 Academic Year Presented at the XXXth Session of the International Conference on Public Education, Geneva, July 1967.* Budapest, 1967, p. 22-23.

[44] "A Magyar Forradalmi Munkás-Paraszt Kormány 1016/1962. (VI. 30.) számú határozata a Kulturális Kapcsolatok Intézetéről" (Resolution No. 1016/1962. (VI. 30.) of the Hungarian Revolutionary Worker-Peasant Government Concerning the Institute of Cultural Relations). *Magyar Közlöny*, No. 48, June 30, 1962. p. 414.

at least once a year and the Executive Council every month, or as required. The Council includes, in addition to the President and Secretary-General of the Commission, representatives of the Ministry of Culture, the Institute for Cultural Relations, the Hungarian Academy of Sciences (*Magyar Tudományos Akadémia*), and the Association of Technical and Scientific Societies (*Műszaki és Természettudományi Egyesületek Szövetsége*).

The UNESCO program in Hungary is carried out under the auspices of eight subcommittees, one for each of the following areas: adult education and youth activities, communication, culture, the "East-West Major Project," hydrology, natural sciences, public education, and social sciences and anthropology.[45]

Other Ministries and Agencies

Certain intermediate and higher vocational-technical and professional institutions are under the jurisdiction of the ministries in charge of the particular field. Thus, medical universities operate under the auspices of the Ministry of Health (*Egészségügyi Minisztérium*), forestry and agronomy universities and colleges under the Ministry of Agriculture and Food (*Mezőgazdasági és Élelmezésügyi Minisztérium*), and technikums and vocational-technical schools under the corresponding economic ministries.

Most vocational schools for apprentices operate under the jurisdiction of the Ministry of Labor (*Munkaügyi Minisztérium*), although some function under the direction of the various ministries of industry and domestic and foreign trade.

With regard to academic matters proper, however (including examinations and grading, some aspects of the curriculum, inspection, methodology, and basic educational principles), the Ministry of Culture shares authority over all of these institutions.[46]

General plans concerning the economy's requirements for skilled workers in the various skill areas and concerning quotas for admission to the various institutions of higher learning are determined by the National Planning Office (*Országos Tervhivatal*). To determine these quotas the Office collaborates with the central and local governmental and educational authorities.

The People's Councils

Identified as the highest organ of State power at the local level, the people's councils (*tanácsok*) exercise considerable power in education. The councils, composed of so-called working people's deputies, carry out their policies through their executive committees (*végrehajtó bizottságok*), whose chairmen are roughly equivalent to American mayors. Each executive committee is divided into special administrative sections (*szakigazgatási szervek*) dealing with various areas of public interest

[45] Sándor Maller. "Hungary and UNESCO," *The New Hungarian Quarterly*, Budapest, VII:23: 148-52, Autumn 1966. See also Máté Kovács. "Hungary and the East-West Project," Ibid. p. 152-55; Sándor Maller. "Magyarország és az UNESCO" (Hungary and the UNESCO). *Köznevelés*, XX:2:67-68, January 24, 1964.

[46] Article 29 of Law No. III of 1961, cited above.

such as culture, education, health, roads, sanitation, and so on. The executive committees operate within the framework of general rules and guidelines emanating from the various ministries.

As a result of the liberalization-decentralization measures adopted in 1967, the special administrative sections are now directly responsible to the executive committees of their particular people's councils rather than to the corresponding ministries.[47]

With a few exceptions, local people's councils exercise direct control over all institutions of learning at the secondary and lower levels. They exercise this control through their educational sections (*művelődésügyi osztályok*), roughly corresponding to American boards of education. The chiefs of these sections are appointed by and responsible to the executive committees of their people's councils. The committees, in turn, are responsible in educational matters to the Ministry of Culture.

Although, from the operational point of view, the educational sections work under the immediate control and guidance of the executive committees, they are also subject to those general rules, regulations, and directives issued by the Ministry of Culture that are national in scope. The Ministry also supervises the instructional-educational process in the schools through periodic inspections organized on either the national or the regional level.

The people's councils are organized on a hierarchical basis, each executive committee being responsible to the council that elected it and to the executive committee immediately above it. According to the 1955 regulation which specified the educational responsibility of the educational sections of the various people's councils, the 19 county people's councils (*megyei tanács*) through their educational sections guide and supervise the work of the educational sections of the district people's councils (*járási tanács*).

The educational sections of the county people's councils also direct and supervise general gymnasiums, teacher-training institutes, intermediate *technikums,* and institutes for the handicapped, as well as student homes and dormitories attached to such institutions. The educational sections of the district councils control and guide the basic educational institutions.[48]

The communal or village people's councils (*községi tanács*) operate without separate educational sections within their executive committees. In the field of education, they are primarily concerned with the organization and supervision of kindergartens, the establishment of school districts, and the registration and attendance of children of compulsory school age.

---

[47] "A Magyar Forradalmi Munkás-Paraszt Kormány 1023/1967. (VIII.8.) számú határozata a tanácsok végrehajtó bizottságai szakigazgatási szerveinek iráyitásáról" (Resolution No. 1023/1967. (VIII.8.) of the Hungarian Revolutionary Worker-Peasant Government Concerning the Guidance of the Special Adminstrative Sections of the Executive Committees of the People's Councils). *Magyar Közlöny*, No. 54, August 8, 1967. p. 401-03.

[48] Between 1957 and 1961-62, the educational sections of the district people's councils were abolished and their tasks assigned to the educational sections of the county people's councils. For further details on the responsibilities of the people's councils in the field of education, see, Aurél Hencz. *A művelődési intézmények és a művelődésigazgatás fejlődése, 1945-1961* (The Evolution of Educational Institutions and Administration, 1945-1961). Budapest, Közgazdasági és Jogi Könyvkiadó, 1962. p. 124-33; (2) Jenő Lugossy. "Közoktatáspolitikánk néhány időszerű kérdéséről" (Concerning a Few Timely Questions About Our Educational Policy). *Köznevelés*, XXIII: 17:641-45, September 8, 1967.

Concurrently with the establishment of the National Council of Education,[49] county councils of education (*megyei oktatási tanácsok*) were also established to serve as advisory bodies to the executive committees of the county people's councils on matters affecting all primary and secondary educational establishments, the coordination of classrooms, the distribution of teachers, and the educational-instructional process in general.

The Mass Organizations

To implement their educational policies, the Party and governmental organizations have the assistance and cooperation of a number of mass organizations, including the Communist youth organizations,[50] the trade unions, and the Parental Work Collectives (*Szülői Munkaközösségek*).

The trade unions are basically Party-subordinated organizations concerned not only with advancement of the material and professional interests of school employees but also with implementation of Party decisions. To help accomplish the latter purpose they work closely with Party units operating in the educational institutions.[51]

The Parental Work Collectives were first organized in 1948 at the initiative of the Democratic Association of Hungarian Women *(Magyar Nők Demokratikus Szövetsége)*.[52] Their objective, as defined by the Ministry of Culture in 1959, is to help promote the development of the socialist school and to assure the education of youth in a socialist spirit through synchronizing the educational process in the school and the home.

The Parental Work Collectives aim to:

1. Assist teachers in strengthening student discipline and struggling against absences and lateness.
2. Assist teachers and Communist youth organizations in supervising homework so as to improve educational performance.
3. Mobilize parents to assure conditions for effective study at home, proper supervision of homework, and acquisition of the required materials for school work.
4. Propagate the objectives of the Communist youth organizations among parents, and assist in establishing and equipping youth clubs.
5. Assist in providing summer employment for school children.
6. Participate in improving the material conditions of the schools through social campaigns.
7. Assist in organizing parents' meetings to sponsor cultural and social events.[53]

[49] See p. 31-32.
[50] See p. 180-89.
[51] See also p. 29-30.
[52] Decree No. 43.300/1948 (V. 15). VKM of May 15, 1948, of the Minister of Culture. For details on the role of parental organizations in the field of education, see Sándor Komlósi. "Az iskola és a család kapcsolata" (The Relationship Between the School and the Family). *In: Nevelésügyünk húsz éve, 1945-1964* (Twenty Years of Our Educational System, 1945-1964). Budapest: Tankönyvkiadó, 1965. p. 271-318.
[53] Aurél Hencz. *A művelődési intézmények és a művelődésigazgatás fejlődése, 1945-1961*, op. cit. p. 117-18. See also present publication's chapter V, p. 55-57.

Financing Education

Methods

Since 1948 financing education has become the concern of the State, exclusively. Education is financed from the general State budget, from budgets of ministries sponsoring educational units, and from budgets of the people's councils.

Budgets: Central and Local

In the budgetary process the principal or director of each educational institution submits estimates to the authority having immediate jurisdiction over it. The main budgetary items for education are the following: construction, equipment for laboratories, libraries, and shops; repair and maintenance, salaries of the teaching and auxiliary staff, scholarships, and student welfare.

Following necessary adjustments, the individual budgetary proposals are consolidated into the budgets of the people's councils and into the State budget prepared by the Ministry of Finance *(Pénzügyminisztérium)*.

The total 1967 budget for all educational establishments amounted to 8 billion, 886 million forints[54] as against 8 billion, 94 million forints

Rate	*1959*	*1960*	*1961*	*1962*	*1963*	*1964*	*1965*	*1966*	*1967*
Official	11.74	11.74	11.74	11.74	11.74	11.74	11.74	11.74	11.74
Tourist/financial	23.48	23.48	23.48	23.48	23.48	23.48	23.48	23.48	23.48
Unofficial	43.00	51.00	44.90	44.75	59.00	53.25	54.60	50.00	58.00

SOURCE OF DATA: *Pick's Currency Yearbook 1968*. New York: Pick Publishing Corporation, 1968. p. 254, 56.

in 1966—an increase of 792 million forints (9.8 percent). The 1967 educational budget was 8.5 percent of the entire State budget and of the State's gross income.[55]

Fees, Tuition, and Scholarships

Hungary's free educational system comprises elementary schools, schools for the handicapped, secondary schools,[56] vocational schools for training skilled workers, and elementary schools for adults. Everyone enrolled in any of these institutions, however, must provide his own supplies and textbooks.

Schools other than those named above charge a tuition which varies according to the student's grades and general educational achievement, the parents' or guardian's income, and (in some cases) the parents' contributions to the socialist State. Tuition and registration fees, however, are offset by a liberal scholarship and student welfare program.

State assistance is basically of two types: social benefits and scholarships. Social assistance (table 6) involves placement of students in

[54] Exchange rates for the Hungarian forint (defined as 75.758 milligrams of fine gold per U.S. dollar) from 1959 to 1967 were the following:

[55] *Report on Educational Progress in the 1966/67 Academic Year*, op. cit. p. 23. Sources did not reveal any breakdown of these figures by ministries, people's councils, and educational levels.

[56] Secondary education became free in 1962 under Decree No. 9/1962. (III. 25.) of the Government. See footnote 50 of chapter V.

Table 6.—Number of nursery, kindergarten, and elementary school pupils and number of secondary and higher education students receiving social assistance, by type of assistance: 1966-67

Type of assistance	Nurseries and kindergartens	Elementary schools	Secondary schools	Higher education collegiums
Grants	—	—	1,803	31,409
Living quarters	1,416	22,857	35,906	24,523
Meals	186,662	219,936	87,682	40,528
Study rooms	—	203,784	35,018	—
Vacations	—	71,164	20,569	—

SOURCE OF DATA: *Report on Educational Progress in the 1966/67 Academic Year Presented at the XXXth Session of the International Conference on Public Education, Geneva, July 1967.* (Budapest, 1967) p. 34.

dormitories or residences, regular and emergency financial aid, and meals at low prices. For purposes of assistance, students are divided into three categories according to the income of the parents or guardians. Scholarships are awarded on the basis of educational performance, and may be granted by State organs as well as by social organizations and enterprises. Scholarships awarded by the latter two also give serious consideration to the recipient's social background, with priority for children of manual workers.

Scholarships are normally awarded on the basis of a contract under which the recipient undertakes to work after graduation for a specified time at a location set forth in the contract.[57]

Types of Education and Training

The educational system of the Hungarian People's Republic provides education and training starting at the 3-year kindergarten level and continuing through the compulsory 8-year elementary level, the 4-year secondary level, and (depending upon career objectives) the 2-to-6 year higher education level. At various spots in the system are the continuation schools, the vocational schools, the adult education schools, and the evening and correspondence sections of the universities and higher institutes (chart 3).

Kindergarten

Pre-elementary education is provided in the kindergartens *(óvodák)*, which are organized on a voluntary attendance basis. Enrolling children of 3- to 5-years of age, kindergartens are administered by central or local educational or government authorities, industrial or agricultural enterprises, or social organizations including trade unions. They normally fulfill a dual task, providing educational background for the children while at the same time freeing the mothers for productive work.[58]

[57] For details on the tuition and scholarship system at the secondary and higher education level, see p. 69-70 and 125-27, respectively.
[58] See chapter IV.

Chart 3. The Educational System of the Hungarian People's Republic: 1967

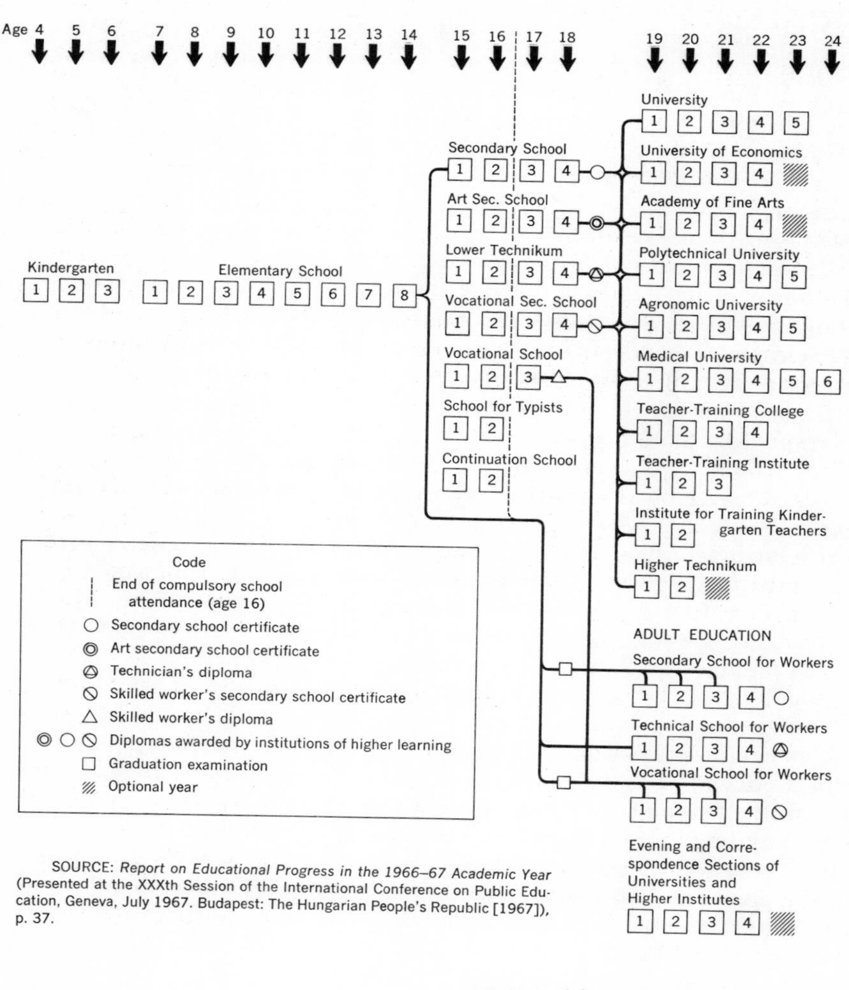

SOURCE: *Report on Educational Progress in the 1966–67 Academic Year* (Presented at the XXXth Session of the International Conference on Public Education, Geneva, July 1967. Budapest: The Hungarian People's Republic [1967]), p. 37.

Jacket 356 - 544 Illus. No. 5a
Width 26½ picas Depth 29½ picas Focus 56 %
[ ]Sq. Ht. [X]Line [ ]Comb. [ ]Sil'te [ ]Broad

Elementary Education

The so-called "general" school *(általános iskola)* provides 8 years of elementary education. The product of one of the farthest reaching and most positive educational reforms of the postwar era, the *általános iskola* is free and compulsory for children age 6 through 14. The compulsory attendance requirement, however, extends through the age of 16. Children graduating from the *általános iskola* at age 14 have three choices: (1) continue schooling at a secondary institution, (2) take part-time employment in production, or (3) pursue their education at a continuation school.

Established by local government authorities, the continuation schools *(továbbképző iskolák)* operate under the same jurisdictional principles as the 8-year elementary schools. They are 2-year institutions offering a basically industrial or agricultural course for children who graduate from the general schools before reaching age 16 and are not planning to work or to continue their education in a secondary school.

Secondary Education

Academic secondary schools or gymnasiums *(gimnáziumok)*, art secondary schools *(művészeti gimnáziumok)*, secondary *technikums*, and vocational secondary schools provide secondary-level education. All are 4-year institutions offering both theoretical and practical training.

The gymnasiums operate under the overall jurisdiction of the Ministry of Culture, and their graduates who have earned a baccalaureate diploma *(érettségi)* may apply for admission to any institution of higher education, primarily the regular, polytechnical, and medical universities.

The vocational secondary schools offer training in a group of related skills; their graduates who have passed both the baccalaureate and the practical-skill examinations may pursue their studies in a higher education institution corresponding to their particular specialty.

The *technikums*, established in the 1950's, are of three types: agricultural, economic, or industrial. Any of their students who graduate with the technical secondary school certificate are entitled to apply for admission to a higher technical institution that offers courses in their particular specialty. Such graduates are also entitled to hold jobs in production commensurate with their training.

The *technikums* and the art secondary schools are gradually to be transformed, beginning in 1969, into vocational secondary schools. Both the secondary *technikums* and the vocational secondary schools function under the jurisdiction of their corresponding agricultural, economic, or industrial ministries. From the strictly operational point of view, however, like the other secondary schools (and like the elementary schools), they operate under the immediate control and guidance of the educational sections of the executive committees of the people's councils in the counties where they are located.[59]

[59] For details on elementary ("general"), continuation, and secondary schools, see chapter V. For a brief survey of Hungary's postwar lower educational system, see Gyula Simon. "Húsz év a magyar iskolaügyben" (Twenty Years of Hungarian Education). *Pedagógiai Szemle* (Review of Education), Budapest. XV:4:342-54, 1965.

Higher Education

The primary objective of the higher education institutions is to educate professionally competent and politically reliable individuals. Hungary's institutions of higher education fall into six types:

1. Agronomic universities and colleges .... (*Agrártudományi egyetemek és főiskolák*)[60]
2. Medical universities .... (*Orvosi egyetemek*)
3. Polytechnical universities .... (*Műszaki egyetemek*)
4. Special colleges, including colleges of applied and fine arts, military schools, and physical education. ....
5. Teacher-training colleges and institutes[61] .... (*Tanitóképző főiskolák és intézetek*)
6. Universities .... (*Tudományegyetemek*)

Jurisdiction over the regular and polytechnical universities and the art and teacher-training institutes and colleges is exercised by the Ministry of Culture. The medical universities operate under the direction of the Ministry of Health *(Egészségügyi Minisztérium)*, while the technical and other institutions of higher learning are under the corresponding ministries or other governmental agencies.

Admission quotas to all these institutions are determined by central governmental organizations, especially the National Planning Office *(Országos Tervhivatal)*, in accordance with the general social and economic requirements of the nation.[62]

Special Education

In addition to the formal standard levels of education, Hungary has a relatively well-developed network of special educational institutions, including schools for adults, schools for the handicapped, art institutions, military schools, and Party schools.[63]

Enrollment

Concerned with the development of education at all levels, the Hungarian Government has made great efforts, especially since the 1948 nationalization of schools, to extend the network of educational institutions of all types. The increase in the number of institutions between 1950-51 and 1966-67 is especially marked for kindergartens, secondary schools, and higher education institutions (table 7). Reflecting the country's general population situation, the elementary schools, however, actually declined in number (tables 8 and 9). And reflecting its general interest in education is the number of graduates from each educational level (table 10).

---

[60] Although "fõiskola" literally means "high school" *(Hochschule)*, to differentiate it from secondary institutions it is rendered throughout this text as "college."

[61] For details on teacher-training institutes and colleges, see chapter VIII.

[62] See chapter VII.

[63] See chapter IX.

Table 7.—Number of kindergartens, elementary schools, and secondary schools; and number of higher education institutions and faculties (schools): 1950–51—1966–67

School year	Kindergartens	Elementary schools	Secondary schools	Higher education[1]	
				Institutions	Faculties (Schools)
1950–51	1,773	6,185	405	19	43
1951–52	1,910	6,156	421	27	49
1952–53	2,072	6,102	427	31	52
1953–54	2,245	6,108	441	33	56
1954–55	2,435	6,168	442	36	54
1955–56	2,503	6,220	455	32	54
1956–57	2,509	6,273	456	31	53
1957–58	2,599	6,291	449	30	51
1958–59	2,656	6,314	435	30	49
1959–60	2,780	6,322	411	43	60
1960–61	2,865	6,307	419	43	60
1961–62	2,951	6,261	425	60	78
1962–63	3,057	6,220	441	87	106
1963–64	3,136	6,162	530	89	108
1964–65	3,185	6,105	593	91	110
1965–66	3,227	6,036	591	92	111
1966–67	3,267	5,954	589	92	111

[1] Includes higher *technikums* and technical schools.

SOURCE OF DATA: *Statisztikai évkönyv 1966* (Statistical Yearbook 1966). Budapest: Központi Statisztikai Hivatal, 1967. p. 341.

Table 8.—Number of kindergarten and elementary school pupils and number of secondary, higher education, and vocational school students: 1950–51—1966–67

School year	Kindergartens	Elementary schools	Secondary schools	Higher educational institutions[1]	Vocational schools
1950–51	106,362	1,229,957	107,925	32,501	56,800
1951–52	121,215	1,205,173	122,292	40,431	60,237
1952–53	130,056	1,196,043	139,484	49,442	57,525
1953–54	131,873	1,203,346	164,410	53,330	45,472
1954–55	118,372	1,207,455	162,461	47,454	52,153
1955–56	145,948	1,226,200	155,264	45,431	61,692
1956–57	167,849	1,255,001	172,786	42,608	75,405
1957–58	162,174	1,259,114	159,388	35,867	88,747
1958–59	170,559	1,268,650	177,738	34,037	101,561
1959–60	179,848	1,314,432	204,401	37,996	116,566
1960–61	183,766	1,392,260	241,036	44,585	125,343
1961–62	171,582	1,444,543	283,747	53,302	134,782
1962–63	177,752	1,472,743	333,747	67,324	143,957
1963–64	184,345	1,468,683	385,419	82,280	151,154
1964–65	187,398	1,445,124	417,446	91,923	163,892
1965–66	189,372	1,413,512	407,485	93,957	172,383
1966–67	191,991	1,380,286	375,734	89,544	183,599

[1] Includes higher *technikums* and technical schools.

SOURCE OF DATA: *Statisztikai évknyv 1966* (Statistical Yearbook 1966). Budapest: Központi Statisztikai Hivatal, 1967. p. 342.

Table 9.—Number of teachers in the kindergartens, elementary schools, secondary schools, and institutions of higher education: 1950–51—1966–67
[—Indicates that source did not show any figures]

School year	Kindergartens	Elementary schools	Secondary schools[1]	Institutions of higher education[2]
1950–51	2,423	35,248	6,174	—
1951–52	3,201	38,089	5,929	—
1952–53	3,785	39,869	6,110	—
1953–54	4,431	43,108	6,970	5,677
1954–55	5,486	45,955	7,535	5,036
1955–56	6,120	50,259	7,810	4,913
1956–57	6,151	52,214	7,935	4,753
1957–58	7,170	53,667	8,053	4,966
1958–59	7,499	55,056	8,402	4,908
1959–60	8,093	56,449	8,360	[3]5,035
1960–61	8,538	57,290	8,778	5,635
1961–62	8,914	58,333	9,232	5,865
1962–63	9,311	59,921	9,619	6,702
1963–64	9,776	61,518	10,631	7,278
1964–65	10,102	62,108	11,561	7,938
1965–66	10,319	62,167	12,049	8,444
1966–67	10,566	62,241	12,317	8,889

[1] Includes day-session teachers only.

[2] Includes lecturers and instructors of physical education, but not visiting professors.

[3] Does not include the faculty of teacher training institutes and colleges for kindergarten and elementary teachers.

SOURCE OF DATA: *Statisztikai évkönyv 1966* (Statistical Yearbook 1966). Budapest: Központi Statisztikai Hivatal, 1967. p. 341.

Table 10.—Number of graduates of the 8-year elementary schools, secondary schools, and institutions of higher education: 1950–66
[—Indicates that source did not show any figures]

Year	8-year elementary schools	Secondary Schools			Institutions of higher education					
		Total	Academic	Industrial *technikums*	Total	Polytechnical	Agricultural	Economics	Medicine	Law
1	2	3	4	5	6	7	8	9	10	11
1950	69,900	16,380	—	—	4,345	1,511	312	404	662	457
1951	79,396	17,219	—	—	5,174	1,252	334	431	1,036	1,112
1952	80,147	17,656	8,268	2,055	4,843	1,329	83	428	816	429
1953	97,453	23,687	12,672	3,452	7,078	1,874	210	712	846	134
1954	101,958	26,479	11,331	5,455	5,644	848	85	818	556	214
1955	97,848	30,264	12,874	6,961	6,442	865	460	771	544	291
1956	101,853	28,535	12,889	7,206	9,746	2,948	597	965	612	361
1957	104,336	31,431	16,133	7,698	7,036	2,205	781	458	539	723
1958	115,892	31,498	17,412	6,741	5,655	1,967	537	364	640	482
1959	106,680	31,072	18,906	5,660	6,178	2,097	715	325	670	614
1960	107,349	33,662	21,004	6,800	5,628	1,644	891	329	830	603
1961	127,178	37,999	24,799	7,300	6,317	1,610	535	324	833	493
1962	140,422	46,722	30,017	8,804	7,251	1,723	574	384	922	577
1963	148,384	52,729	30,749	11,438	9,583	1,888	1,292	484	921	528
1964	154,495	60,946	32,009	13,606	11,065	2,220	1,580	620	959	483
1965	157,797	68,898	37,917	13,941	13,938	3,116	2,152	961	1,015	726
1966	152,349	77,530	41,934	15,248	18,107	5,003	2,783	1,284	982	677

SOURCE OF DATA: *Statisztikai évkönyv 1966* (Statistical Yearbook 1966). Budapest: Központi Statisztikai Hivatal, 1967. p. 342.

IV. Pre-Elementary Education

Evolution

Although the first kindergarten was established in Hungary as early as 1828,[1] pre-elementary education remained relatively undeveloped in quality until after World War II. The total number of kindergartens in 1938 was 1,140; together with the so-called permanent and summer homes[2] there were 1,309 pre-elementary institutions with a total enrollment of 124,523 (table 1) representing 23.6 percent of kindergarten-age children.

The kindergartens were mostly overcrowded and understaffed, with an average of 70.4 children per group.[3]

The scope and functions of pre-elementary education before World War II were specified by Law No. XV of 1891. In accordance with this law, the kindergartens were considered primarily as institutions for the protection and care of children. They emphasized discipline and religious-moral training. During the Horthy era (1919-44), kindergarten education, like all other levels of education in Hungary, acquired certain patriotic-chauvinistic overtones.

Following Hungary's liberation from German occupation in Spring 1945, priority in pre-elementary education was given to the physical rehabilitation of war-damaged buildings and the everyday care, including feeding and clothing, of the children. These tasks were undertaken under the leadership of a number of parent and teacher organizations spearheaded by the Democratic Association of Hungarian Women (*Magyar Nők Demokratikus Szövetsége*).

For the better achievement of this dual aim—physical care and education—the kindergartens were transformed shortly after the cessation of hostilities into day homes *(napközi otthonok)* and continued to operate in this fashion until October 1, 1946. As in the prewar period, the pre-elementary institutions were under the jurisdiction of the Ministry of Public Welfare *(Népjóléti Minisztérium)* until 1949, when they were placed under the Ministry of Culture. On June 16, 1948, the kindergartens, like all other educational institutions, were nationalized,

[1] See p. 11.

[2] Ibid.

[3] Alice Hermann. "Az óvoda és az óvónőképzés" (The Kindergarten and the Education of Kindergarten Teachers). *In*: *Nevelésügyünk húsz éve, 1945-1964* (Twenty Years of Our Educational System, 1945-1964). Budapest: Tankönyvkiadó, 1965. p. 365-418 (referred to hereafter as Alice Hermann). This article is also available in a somewhat abbreviated form in *Tanulmányok a magyar népi demokrácia neveléstörténetéből* (Studies From the History of Education of the Hungarian People's Republic)—Vol. I. Budapest: Pedagógiai Tudományos Intézet, 1961. p. 169-238.

thus assuring that a uniform system of pre-elementary education would be established.

The nationalization of education brought about substantive qualitative changes in the content of kindergarten training, including curriculum revision and teacher retraining.

The new curriculum provided for valuation of psychological factors pertaining to the needs and characteristics of kindergarten children. Teacher retraining was effected through 3-month courses which, in addition to professional subjects, also included political-ideological reorientation.[4] The refresher courses, like teacher-training and other courses in general, came to rely increasingly on Soviet educational materials in Hungarian translation.

The educational-political objectives of the regime were furthered by the launching, in January 1948, of *Gyermeknevelés* (Child Education), the professional journal for kindergarten education. This journal appeared until January 1953, when it was replaced by *Óvodai Nevelés* (Kindergarten Education). The changeover heralded the general revision of pre-elementary education.

The Changes of 1953

The system of pre-elementary education was reorganized in 1953 according to the provisions of Law No. III. The Law defined the primary goal of kindergarten education as follows: "The function of kindergarten education is the education and care of children of kindergarten age in accordance with the goals of socialist education, and their preparation for primary education. Kindergarten education must establish the basis for the healthy, hardy, patriotic, self-confident, courageous, disciplined and multilaterally educated man." [5]

The pre-elementary educational institutions are of two basic types: nurseries and kindergartens.

Nurseries

The nurseries (*bölcsődék*) are educational-welfare institutions operating under the auspices of the Ministry of Health *(Egészségügyi Minisztérium)* and admitting infants from the age of 1 month to 3 years. These cooperate closely with the parents for the proper physical care and correct upbringing of infants under their supervision.

Maintained and operated by people's councils, enterprises, factories, or cooperatives, the nurseries are of various types: permanent nurseries functioning on a year-round, full-day basis; seasonal nurseries, operating only part of the year; 6-day nurseries which care for children from Monday morning to noon on Saturday; and special nurseries for handicapped children.

For admission, the nurseries give preference to children who have working parents or only one parent. Children of nonworking mothers

[4] For greater details see p. 140-44.
[5] Alice Hermann, op. cit. p. 393.

are normally accepted only if the mother suffers from some disability.

Fees depend on the income of the parents and the number of children in the family.[6]

Towards the end of 1964 Hungary had 611 nurseries caring for approximately 34,000 infants and employing an average of one trained nurse for every nine children.[7]

Kindergartens

Kindergartens may be established and maintained only by local people's councils, State agencies and institutions, State plants, enterprises and farms, producer cooperatives, and social organizations, in accordance with the rules and regulations of the education sections of the people's councils.

In contrast to the nurseries, the kindergartens are under the ultimate educational supervision of the Ministry of Culture (*Művelődésügyi Minisztérium*). Depending on local requirements and conditions, the following types of kindergartens may be operated:

1. *Half-day kindergartens (félnapos óvodák)*, representing about 14 percent of all kindergartens, in which children bring along their morning snack and go home at lunchtime.
2. *Full-day kindergartens (egész napos óvodák)*, the most popular type, accounting for 53 percent of all kindergartens (children in these institutions are fed for nominal fees).
3. *Seasonal day-home kindergartens (időszaki napközi otthonos óvodák)*, representing approximately 22 percent of the total, which usually operate during the winter as half-day kindergartens.
4. *Summer day-home kindergartens* (*nyári napközi otthonok*) operating as full-day kindergartens during the summer agricultural season.
5. *Six-day kindergartens (hatnapos óvodák)* providing full room and board during working days.
6. *Children's homes* (*gyermekotthonok*) caring for children on a full-time, year-round basis.[8]

The kindergartens admit children between 3 and 6 years of age. Wherever feasible, the children are divided into groups of approximately the same age, each group averaging 25 to 30 children. At the end of 1964, approximately 35 percent of the kindergartens, however, did not have age subdivisions.

An August 5, 1969 resolution by the Minister of Culture gave the following directives: (1) Establish kindergartens for national minorities in localities inhabited by non-Magyars. (2) Transform existing Hungarian-language kindergartens into kindergartens for the national minorities if at least two-thirds of the parents of the enrolled children request such kindergartens. (3) Within the framework of the existing Hungarian-language kindergartens, establish special minority groups if at least 15

[6] See tabulation under "Kindergartens."

[7] Zoltán Halász, *ed. Cultural Life in Hungary*. Budapest: Pannonia Press, 1966, p. 39; Ferenc Abent. "A Magyar Népköztársaság közoktatásügye" (The Educational System of the Hungarian People's Republic). *In: A közoktatásügy Európa szocialista országaiban* (Public Education in the Socialist Countries of Europe). Budapest: Tankönyvkiadó *for the* Országos Pedagógiai Intézet, 1965. p. 273-74.

[8] Ferenc Ábent, op. cit. p. 274.

parents (previously 25) express a preference to have their children taught in their mother tongue.

Applications for admission to kindergartens are screened and decided upon by admission committees consisting of representatives of State and social organizations.

Admission criteria for the kindergartens are similar to those for the nurseries. Normally covering about 40 percent of the food costs, fees are scaled according to family income and size. The 1965 scale of daily fees was as follows: [9]

Parents' monthly earnings (in forints) [10]	*Daily fee (in forints) per child in kindergarten when family has—*		
	1 child	*2 children*	*3 children*
Under 1,000	2.0	1.50	1.40
1,001 to 1,600	3.0	2.50	2.00
1,601 to 2,200	4.0	3.20	2.80
2,201 to 3,000	5.0	4.0	3.50
3,001 to 3,800	7.0	6.0	5.0
3.801 to 4,600	9.0	7.0	6.0
4,601 to 5,600	10.0	8.0	7.0
5,601 to 7,000	12.0	10.0	8.0
Above 7,000	15.0	13.0	11.0

The average monthly income of a Hungarian couple in 1967 was 3,800 forints (about $161).[11]

Kindergarten education is viewed as an organic part of the Communist education system; this is reflected in the three main kindergarten activities, i.e., play, work, and learning. In addition to instilling Communist principles, the other two main objectives of kindergarten education are to provide care for the children while the parents are at work and to prepare children for elementary school. The latter goal is emphasized in the case of children over 5 years old, who are increasingly involved in formalized compulsory activities geared to develop their capabilities for school work.

In their daily work with the children, kindergarten teachers are expected to abide by the procedures and rules and regulations issued by the Ministry of Culture. Soon after the adoption of Law No. III of 1953 relating to kindergartens, the Ministry issued its so-called "Methodological Letter" *(Módszertani Levél)* to guide kindergarten teachers in their approach to kindergarten education. The letter remained in effect until the fall of 1957, when a comprehensive handbook was issued with detailed instructions relating to every facet of pre-elementary education. Special chapters deal with (a) the organization and content of education differentiated in terms of age groups, (b) the crystallization of the fundamental principles underlying the three basic modes of kindergarten education (play, work, and instruction), and (c) the determination of the content of the five major kindergarten subjects: (1) physical education,[12] (2) native tongue and knowledge of surroundings, (3) ele-

[9] Zoltán Halász, *ed. Cultural Life in Hungary*, op. cit. p. 40.

[10] For value of the forint, see footnote 54 of chapter III.

[11] Gloria Emerson. "In Hungary, a New Approach to Children." *The New York Times*, June 26, 1967.

[12] The importance of physical education in the kindergartens is highlighted by the publication of a special teachers' handbook: *Testnevelés az óvodában* (Physical Education in the Kindergarten). Budapest: Tankönyvkiadó, 1964. 204 p.

ments of quantity, form, and space, (4) drawing and handwork, and (5) music and singing. Additional chapters deal with the organization of holiday and summer festivities and the relationship between the kindergarten and the nursery, the school, and the family.[13]

The formalism and inflexibility associated with the required strict adherence to the methodological specifications of the handbook seem to have eased a bit in the mid-1960's. Then, under the initiative of some liberal educators possibly under Western influence in child rearing, demands became ever more vocal for striking a balance between the requirements of the social and the individual education of the child. In line with the new trend, there is a tendency (discernible especially in the progressive kindergartens in large cities) to allow greater freedom for the children. In these kindergartens they are no longer compelled to sing or play with certain toys or participate in group projects, but are encouraged to do things for themselves.[14] Striking a harmonious balance between social and individual upbringing, together with general uplifting of the level of education, continues to be the main problem confronting contemporary pre-elementary education in Hungary.

Enrollment

A gradual increase in enrollment between 1960 and 1966 was matched by a corresponding increase in the number of kindergartens and kindergarten teachers (tables 11 and 12). The percent of children of kindergarten age (3 to 6) attending preprimary institutions gradually increased from 33.7 in 1960 to 49.7, placing Hungary among the leading countries in this respect. The pupil-teacher ratio also improved during the corresponding period by gradually declining from 21.5:1 to 18.2:1.

Table 11.—Number of kindergartens, kindergarten places, teachers, and pupils: 1960-66[1]

Year	Kinder-gartens	Kinder-garten places	Teachers	Pupils	Places per 100 kinder-garten-age children	Percent of 100 kinder-garten-age children in kinder-gartens	Pupils per 100 places	Pupils per teacher	Summer homes	
									Number	Child resi-dents
1	2	3	4	5	6	7	8	9	10	11
1960	2,865	162,282	8,538	183,766	29.8	33.7	113.2	21.5	1,181	44,400
1961	2,951	168,190	8,914	171,582	33.9	34.6	102.0	19.2	952	30,141
1962	3,057	175,326	9,311	177,752	37.9	38.4	101.4	19.1	927	29,681
1963	3,136	178,561	9,776	184,345	40.5	41.8	103.2	18.9	859	27,242
1964	3,185	182,312	10,102	187,398	43.1	44.3	102.8	18.6	784	24,254
1965	3,227	185,768	10,319	189,372	46.2	47.1	101.9	18.4	654	20,489
1966	3,267	189,439	10,566	191,991	49.1	49.7	101.3	18.2	542	17,108

[1] Data are year-end figures.

SOURCE OF DATA: *Statisztikai évkönyv 1966* (Statistical Yearbook 1966.) Budapest: Központi Statisztikai Hivatal, 1967. p. 343.

[13] *Nevelőmunka az óvodában. Útmutatás óvónők számára* (Education Work in the Kindergarten. Guide for Kindergarten Teachers). 5th ed. Budapest: Tankönyvkiadó, 1964.

[14] Gloria Emerson. "In Hungary, a New Approach to Children," op. cit. See also Alice Hermann. "Az óvodai nevelés eszközei közoktatásunk átszervezésének tükrében" (The Techniques of Kindergarten Education in Light of the Reorganization of Our Public Education). *In: Tanulmányok a neveléstudomány köréből, 1961* (Studies From the Sphere of the Science of Education, 1961). Budapest: Akadémiai Kiadó, 1962. p. 275-317.

Table 12.—Number of kindergartens, kindergarten places, teachers, and pupils by municipality and county: December 31, 1966

Municipalities and counties	Kinder-gartens	Kinder-garten places	Teachers	Pupils	Pupils per 100 places	Pupils per teacher
Total	3,267	189,439	10,566	191,991	101.3	18.2
Municipalities						
Budapest	455	32,052	2,537	34,629	108.0	13.6
Debrecen	34	2,585	158	2,963	114.6	18.8
Miskolc	34	2,499	161	2,830	113.2	17.6
Pécs	42	2,835	174	3,046	107.4	17.5
Szeged	44	3,087	170	3,005	97.3	17.7
Counties						
Baranya	90	4,715	254	4,606	97.7	18.1
Bács–Kiskun	174	10,706	504	10,479	97.9	20.8
Békés	180	9,679	511	9,294	96.0	18.2
Borsod–Abauj–Zemplén	148	8,107	394	8,264	101.9	21.0
Csongrád	109	6,330	313	5,942	93.9	19.0
Fejér	121	7,538	444	8,243	109.4	18.6
Győr–Sopron	156	9,594	480	9,383	97.8	19.5
Hajdu–Bihar	141	7,879	398	7,970	101.2	20.0
Heves	104	5,410	290	5,480	101.3	18.9
Komárom	106	7,091	330	7,191	101.4	21.8
Nógrád	115	5,137	261	5,100	99.3	19.5
Pest	278	15,481	782	15,908	102.8	20.3
Somogy	138	6,502	295	5,902	90.8	20.0
Szabolcs–Szatmár	191	9,487	499	9,968	105.1	20.0
Szolnok	163	9,082	492	9,038	99.5	18.4
Tolna	154	7,806	326	7,167	91.8	22.0
Vas	95	4,755	254	4,983	104.8	19.6
Veszprém	123	7,422	360	7,045	54.9	19.6
Zala	72	3,660	179	3,555	97.1	19.9

SOURCE OF DATA: *Statisztikai évkönyv 1966* (Statistical Yearbook 1966). Budapest: Központi Statisztikai Hivatal, 1967. p. 414.

V. Elementary and Secondary Education

Evolution

Of the many sweeping and far-reaching changes in Hungary's postwar educational system, perhaps the most remarkable and positive were those relating to the elementary and secondary school system. These changes involved, basically, the modernization and (at least as originally envisioned) the democratization of an antiquated, clerical-conservative oriented school system.

The prewar, 4-year elementary school *(népiskola)* offered a basic education which was terminal for many pupils. As in many other European countries (some with relatively advanced educational systems), the 10-year-old pupils graduating from public school in Hungary were confronted with the problem of making a choice which did not necessarily reflect their aptitudes or capabilities but which did affect their entire future careers.

Only about 25 percent of the children completing 4th grade—mostly from well-to-do families—entered the gymnasium, the stepping stone to higher education. About 75 percent of the children, mostly from worker and peasant backgrounds, entered the 5th grade, and many of these dropped out before completing 8th grade.[1] About 18 percent, mostly children of the petty bourgeoisie, entered the upper elementary school *(polgári)*[2] and about 7 percent, mostly children of the well-to-do and the intelligentsia, entered the gymnasiums, which were primarily preparatory schools for the institutions of higher learning.[3]

The church influence, especially the Roman Catholic, was considerable; this is reflected in the 1937-38 school year figures for denominational and public schools: 4,619 of the former and only 1,287 of the latter. Almost 50 percent of all elementary schools were the one-teacher kind.[4]

The secondary schools emphasized the humanities and theoretical-philological studies at the expense of the sciences, training students for universities or the civil service. Secondary vocational and technical education was neglected.

The present elementary-secondary school system is based on a series

---

[1] In 1930, for example, only 48.5 percent of the population graduated from 6th grade of the elementary school. Gyula Simon *and* József Szarka. *A magyar népi demokrácia nevelésügyének története* (History of the Educational System of the Hungarian People's Republic). Budapest: Tankönyvkiadó, 1965. p. 170 (Referred to hereafter as Simon and Szarka.)

[2] On the character and scope of the *polgári* school see p. 13-14.

[3] Simon and Szarka, op. cit. p. 8.

[4] Ibid.

of changes that were brought about in well-differentiated phases.[5]

It was during the first phase of the immediate postwar period that Hungary's most far-reaching and positive educational reform was instituted through the establishment of the "general" school *(általános iskola)* system. Under Decree No. 6650-1945.M.E. of the National Provisional Government, the new 8-year "general" (elementary) school was to be gradually established as a free and compulsory institution for children ages 6 through 14 in place of the 4- and 8-year elementary schools, the 4-year elementary schools, and the 4-year lower gymnasiums built on the 4-year elementary schools.

Although certain changes were made in the secondary schools' composition, curriculum, and general orientation,[6] they continued to operate until 1951 in accordance with Law No. XI of 1934. That law was abrogated by Decree No. 14 of 1951, which laid the foundations of the present academic secondary schools.

The present system of vocational secondary schools, including agricultural, economic, and industrial secondary *technikums,* can also be traced to the measures introduced in the 1951-55 period.

The Free and Compulsory School System

Free, compulsory education for children begins on September 1 following the sixth birthday and lasts, at least theoretically, until they reach age 16.[7] When they reach school age, children must be registered in the 8-year elementary ("general") school. If they graduate from that school at age 14 and choose not to pursue their studies either in secondary or vocational school and are not employed for at least 4 hours a day, they must be registered in so-called further-training or continuation schools *(továbbképző iskolák)* until the end of the school year in which they reach age 16.[8] Physically and mentally handicapped but trainable children are subject to the same regulations, but are to be registered in special institutions.[9]

Between March 1 and 15, the parents of children approaching school age must notify the elementary school authorities of the district in which they live, thus enabling these authorities to plan for the next school year. Actual registration takes place in June, normally during the first two working days after the end of the school year.

Hungary's record in implementing the free and compulsory elementary education system is one of the best in the world. By 1965, 98.6 percent of the 6-year-old children were registered in the first grade; of

[5] For the various historical phases underlying the Hungarian educational reforms see p. 23-28 of chapter III.

[6] Hungary has various types of secondary schools (see p. 75-84). When not specifically identified (as, for example, vocational secondary school), the term secondary school(s) as used in this text refers to the gymnasium(s) or, roughly, the academic secondary school(s).

[7] "1961. évi III. törvény a Magyar Népköztársaság oktatasi rendszeréről" (Law No. III of 1961 Concerning the Educational System of the Hungarian People's Republic). *Magyar Közlöny.* (Hungarian Gazette), Budapest, No. 74, October 17, 1961, p. 566-70. See especially Articles 3-5. See also "A Népköztársaság Elnöki Tanácsának 1962. évi 13. számú törvényerejű redelete a tankötelezettségről" (Decree No. 13 of 1962 of the Presidential Council of the People's Republic Concerning Compulsory Education). *Magyar Közlöny*, No. 43, June 16, 1962. p. 389-90. This was implemented by Decree No. 7/1963. (XII. 11.) MM of the Minister of Culture. Ibid. No. 87, December 11, 1963. p. 666-72. Although "törvényerejű rendelet" means literally "decree-law," it is rendered throughout this text simply as "decree."

[8] See p. 71-72.

[9] See p. 172-73.

these, 90 percent completed 8th grade by the time they were 16 years of age, i.e., at the end of the 10th year of compulsory education.[10] At age 14, however, only 77 percent of the students normally graduate from elementary school.[11]

Organization: Structure and Functions

The School Districts

Established, maintained, and supervised by the education sections of the local people's councils,[12] the elementary schools are organized into school districts *(iskolai körzetek)* so as to assure the equitable and proportional distribution of pupils. The districts are established in accordance with local conditions and in terms of the number of schools operating within the particular geographic area. If the principal of the accepting school gives permission, pupils may also, under certain conditions, attend schools outside their district. The network of elementary schools is established in such a way as to assure that central or district upper elementary schools with grades 5 to 8 will be established in sparsely populated areas.

The School Year

The school year begins on September 1 and ends, technically, on August 31. The school attendance year is divided into two semesters, the first starting on the second working day in September and ending on January 25; the second, starting on the first working day after January 25 and ending on June 8—except for students in the last year of high school, whose school attendance year ends on May 8. In cases where the specified number of days of instruction has not been provided by June 8, the school attendance period may be extended up to June 20.

In addition to their classroom responsibilities, third-year secondary school students, immediately after the end of the school year, must spend 2 weeks in production, where they are to be employed for no more than 8 hours a day. Elementary school pupils in grades 7 and 8, whose curriculum includes agriculture—normally in schools located in rural areas—must take part in agricultural work for 4 half-days during the course of the school year.

For excursions and various social activities, the principal may designate 4 days during the school year as days on which no instruction is provided.

In addition to the summer vacation, elementary and secondary school pupils have two shorter vacations during the school year: a winter vacation from December 22 to January 7, and a spring vacation from April

---

[10] Pál Ilku. "Népünk általános és szakmai müveltségének emeléséért" (For Raising the General and Professional Cultural Level of Our People). *Köznevelés* (Public Education), Budapest. XXI:23:882, December 3, 1965.

[11] Jenő Lugossy. "Közokatáspolitikánk néhány időszerü kérdéséről" (Concerning a Few Timely Questions About Our Educational Policy). *Köznevelés*, XXIII:17:643, September 8, 1967.

[12] Concerning the educational functions of the people's councils, see p. 5, 33-35.

5 to April 13. There is no school on the following holidays: November 7, the day of the Bolshevik Revolution; March 15, the national holiday commemorating the 1848-49 Revolution; April 4, the day of the country's liberation from Nazi occupation; Easter Monday; and May 1.[13]

The Class: Size and Instruction Periods

Normally held in the morning, classes start at 8 a.m. Where there is a shortage of classrooms, afternoon sessions may also be organized and may continue as late as 7 p.m., depending on local conditions. Each class period lasts 45 minutes. Exceptions may be made during the winter from November 1 to March 1, when afternoon class periods may be reduced to 40 minutes each.

Class size in both elementary and secondary schools is usually set at 40 pupils; when necessary because of the number of pupils to be accommodated or because of a classroom shortage, class size may be increased to 50 pupils. Parallel classes having a total enrollment of fewer than 41 are consolidated by the principal at the beginning of the school year. Sparsely populated areas with small elementary schools organize groups that are composed of pupils at several grade levels. Recommended groupings of grades for this purpose are grades 1-3, 2-4, 5-6, and 7-8; or grades 1-4, 5-8, depending upon local conditions.[14]

Both elementary and secondary schools are coeducational. To establish a separate boys' or girls' school requires special permission from the Ministry of Culture (*Művelődésügyi Minisztérium*).[15]

Attendance

In both recitation and practical classes attendance is compulsory and is strictly enforced. Unauthorized absences must be reported and justified. Absences due to illness or to weather or transportation difficulties lasting no more than 3 days may be excused by a written statement from parent or guardian; absences of more than 3 days require a medical or official certificate.

Buildings and Equipment

Although the education sections of the people's councils are basically responsible for providing the budgetary means to construct and maintain schools and acquire equipment, it is the principal's task to see that schools and equipment are judiciously and effectively used.

[13] In addition to these holidays, the schools are required to organize festivities at the beginning and closing of the school year and to honor the Bolshevik Revolution and the country's liberation. Commemorative ceremonies and discussions are also organized in connection with the following dates: October 2, international peace day; November 20, day of the establishment of the Hungarian Communist Party; March 8, international women's day; March 15, anniversary of the 1848-49 Revolution; March 21, day of the establishment of the Hungarian Soviet Republic of 1919; April 22, Lenin's birthday; May 1, the day of "proletarian internationalism"; the first Sunday of May, Mother's Day; and in the last week of May, international children's day.

[14] For the curriculum of these various grade groupings, see *Tanterv és utasitás az általános iskolák számára* (Curriculum and Instruction for the General Schools). Budapest: Tankönyvkiadó *for the* Művelődésügyi Minisztérium (Ministry of Culture), n.d. p. 6-12.

[15] See footnote 37 of chapter III.

One of the primary duties of the school principal is to assure that the classrooms and other educational facilities are so organized as to provide the best possible means for the advancement of education. Toward this end he is expected to keep a careful watch over the status of the building (s) and equipment and, in cooperation with the building superintendent, to prepare a list of proposals for the local authorities concerning needed repairs or acquisitions.

The principal is also expected to provide and organize workshops (and garden plots wherever possible) in order to make practice and experimental work an integral part of the curriculum.

Theoretically at least, every elementary and secondary school is expected to have its own library, with one section of books devoted to the teachers' professional interests and another to the children's reading interests. Concerning the cataloging system to be employed and the books to be acquired, the school libraries are expected to follow the instructions and guidance of the National Pedagogical Library (*Országos Pedagógiai Könyvtár*).[16]

Elementary and secondary school buildings can be identified from the outside by an oval-shaped, white-enameled plaque bearing the emblem of the Hungarian People's Republic at the center and the school's name (*"Általános Iskola"*—"General" School; *"Gimnázium"*—Gymnasium; or *"Általános Iskola és Gimnázium"*—"General" School and Gymnasium) surrounding the emblem.

Administration: Structure and Functions

The elementary and secondary school administrative system is extremely complex, involving not only the administrative and educational employees of the particular school but also the parents, as well as representatives of the Party, various trade unions, and other mass organizations.

The Principal

The key role in the administration of an elementary or a secondary school is played by the principal (*igazgató*). Like the manager of a socialist enterprise, the principal is solely responsible for implementing all instructions from the higher educational, governmental, and competent Party authorities.

In his capacity as chief educational director of a school, the principal is expected to:

1. Organize the school's educational processes, including preparation of programs and syllabuses, supervision of classes and extracurricular activities, guidance of the ideological and professional further training of teachers, and rewarding or punishing employees.
2. Establish and develop the "pupil-collectives" and assume educational responsibility for the work of the various youth movements.[17]

[16] See p. 165-66.
[17] See p. 180-92.

3. Synchronize the school's educational processes and the student *collegia* or dormitories (*diákotthon*).
4. Supervise the teachers' class performance by occasional visits.
5 Issue warnings or institute formal procedures against teachers or other employees in case of violations of official instructions or contractual obligations or manifestations of attitudes, whether within or outside the school, which are incompatible with their profession.[18]

Principals are required to put in 48 hours a week and, theoretically at least, are not authorized to leave the school building during the day except on official business.

In determining policy and implementing their duties, the principals have the cooperation of the assistant principals, the school councils, teacher committees, the class advisers, and the work collectives.

The Assistant Principal

In the absence or incapacity of the principal, the assistant principal (*igazgatóhelyettes*) assumes full responsibility for the effective operation of the school. His primary responsibilities are educational-methodological, including guidance of work collectives, visits to classes, and consultations with teachers. His work load and conditions are similar to those of the principal.

The School Council

Schools operating with at least 12 teachers are required to set up a school council (*iskolatanács*), an advisory body to assist the principal in management of the school. Led by the principal, it includes as members the assistant principal, the Party and trade union representatives in the school, the leaders of the youth movements, and a few elected teachers. Depending upon the issues to be discussed, the school council may also invite others to its deliberations.

The council establishes its own work rules and agenda, and can make decisions only with the agreement of the principal.

The Teacher Collective

The teachers and instructors of a school, together with the directors of the student homes and the teachers at the enterprises or institutions operating in conjunction with the particular school, constitute the "teacher collective" (*Nevelői közösség*). Members of the collective are expected to cooperate towards the advancement of the teaching-learning process. The collective makes decisions concerning the school's work program, the unified educational procedures to be used, internal rules, and matters affecting students, including attendance and behavior, examinations, academic failure, and the awarding or penalizing of individual pupils. In all other matters it has only advisory functions. The collective meets in regular and in extraordinary meetings. The regular meetings

[18] *Rendtartás az általános iskolák és a gimnáziumok számára* (Regulations for the General Schools and the Gymnasiums). Budapest: Tankönyvkiadó, 1964. p. 9-11.

are normally held at the beginning and end of the semester. The collective's deliberations and decisions are recorded in the form of minutes.

The Class Adviser

Appointed by the principal, the class adviser (*osztályvezető* or *osztályfőnök*) is expected to encourage the children's collective life and to help operate youth movements. A regular teacher who assumes the class-adviser role as part of his load, he is expected to gain an understanding of the personalities of the children in his group, observing them in class and extracurricular activities and through visits to their homes. In striving to channel the children's development as independent and individual workers through communal living, he is guided at all times by the youth movement statutes.

The class adviser chairs meetings held at the end of each semester to decide on the promotion of students and, together with the chairman of the "parents' work collectives" *(szülői munkaközösség),* guides the work of the latter. He has office hours and periodically informs the parents regarding the attitude and progress of their children.

Work Collectives

Work collectives (*munkaközösségek*) may be organized in schools with at least three teachers or three class advisers or three teachers of the same subject. Work collectives may also be organized on an interschool basis. Based on voluntary participation, work collectives aim to promote the educational process, submit proposals for syllabus changes, arrange exchanges of class visits, help inexperienced teachers, send delegates to educational conferences, and submit proposals for awards or promotions for their members.

The Nonacademic Staff

The principal, assistant principal (s) , and the building superintendent-administrator (*gondnok*) guide the nonacademic employees in their work. Appointed by the education section of the people's council, the building superintendent-administrator is primarily concerned with the school's economic activities: preparing the budget, acquiring and making efficient use of supplies, maintaining and operating the building (cleaning, heating, and lighting it; providing general upkeep; and taking measures to prevent fires) .

Relations With Organizations and Institutions

The elementary and secondary schools maintain working relations with a number of governmental, Party, and social organizations as well as with enterprises and occasionally with foreign organizations.

Higher Authorities

In their dealings with higher authorities, the schools must act according to a well-established procedure. Individual employees of a school may appeal to a higher organ only through the office of the principal.

Schools and/or individual classes may be visited by members of the Central Committee of the Party and of the Government, the parliamentary deputies of the particular district, members of the Scientific and Public Education Section (*Tudományos és Közoktatási Osztály*) of the Party Central Committee,[19] representatives of the educational section of the people's council, associates of the National Pedagogical Institute (*Országos Pedagógiai Intézet*) ,[20] the chairman and deputy chairman of the people's council, the secretaries of the Party committees of the respective communities, individuals authorized by the Ministry of Education, and the school physician when authorized by the principal. These visits may be made only with the knowledge and in the presence of the principal or his assistant.

In the school's day-by-day administration, direct contact is normally maintained with the education section of the people's council in the community.

Party and Social Organizations

The schools are required to maintain regular contact with the Party and social organizations. One of the duties of the principal is to inform the territorial Party organizations and councils concerning the work and problems of his school and to ask their assistance when required. With the exception of the Party, trade-union, and youth-movement representatives in the school and the chairman of the parents' work collective, who are appointed by the organizations, the representatives of the school are appointed by the principal.

Enterprises

The schools are required to maintain close contact with the enterprises, shops, collectives, and institutions that cooperate in implementing the practical aspects of education. Cooperation is normally based on instructions issued by the ministries exercising immediate jurisdiction over the various enterprises. In turn, the latter are expected to cooperate in furthering vocational training, while the schools are expected to contribute to the advancement of the general cultural level of the workers in the enterprises.

Foreign Organizations and Individuals

Requests by foreign organizations or individuals for school documents (whether certificates, transcripts, or any other legal papers) can be handled only through the Ministry of Culture. Visits to Hungarian educa-

[19] See p. 29-30.
[20] See p. 163.

tional institutions by foreigners, like all educational-cultural matters involving foreigners, are handled by the Institute of Cultural Relations (*Kulturális Kapcsolatok Intézete*).[21]

Curriculums and Syllabuses

In the highly centralized educational system of Hungary, the curriculums and syllabuses for all grades in the 8-year elementary ("general") schools and in the secondary schools are prepared and published under the auspices of the Ministry of Culture. Based on the studies, experiments, and recommendations of the National Pedagogical Institute, the centrally issued curriculums and syllabuses are binding for all teachers in all grades.

During a lesson in learning the musical scales

During the post-World War II period, the Hungarian educational authorities revised the curriculums and syllabuses several times, aiming to reflect in them the particular social and political requirements of the regime under the circumstances of the moment.[22]

The elementary and secondary school curriculums and syllabuses in effect during the late 1960's were adopted in 1962 and 1965, respectively. They aim to exemplify the general principles and goals prescribed for the schools.[23]

[21] See p. 32.
[22] See p. 23-28.
[23] See p. 28-29.

Curriculums

A major characteristic of these curriculums and syllabuses in comparison with the earlier ones (especially the prewar) is their scientific-technical orientation. The most noteworthy change in the secondary school curriculum involves the change in 1966-67 from the traditional humanities-*réal* (science) division to a more diversified curriculum for all students, with the large schools also offering subject-specialization classes in various subjects that include chemistry-biology, drawing (art), foreign languages, mathematics, mathematics-physics, music, and physics-chemistry (table 14).[24]

During the 1965-66 school year the subject-specialization curriculum was offered in 864 classes (20.6 percent of the total number of classes) in general gymnasiums. By 1966-67, 1,023 classes were using this curriculum. These 1,023 classes were divided among subject specialties as follows:[25]

Number	*Specialty*	*Number*	*Specialty*
406	Russian	36	Chemistry-physics
139	English	28	Music
108.5	German	21	Mathematics
106.5	French	10	Physical education
69	Math-physics	6.5	Spanish
49	Biology-chemistry	2	Drawing (art)
41	Italian	0.5	Polish

All courses in all grades (tables 13 and 14) are expected to be taught in a "scientific", i.e., dialectical-materialist, manner in order to advance the training of the "new socialist man."

Social Sciences.—In secondary school, elements of the social sciences are taught within the framework of several other subjects, including literature and general science; in elementary school, however, they are concentrated in geography and history courses. In the lower grades, basic elements of history and geography are taught as part of the course on "Knowledge of the Surroundings." In the upper grades, history is taught in the spirit of Marxism-Leninism and it aims to inculcate basic historical and political knowledge concerning societal evolution, with emphasis on the historical development of Hungary; and to develop a dialectical and historical-materialist outlook.[26] Geography in the upper elementary grades emphasizes an understanding of the nature of the subject and knowledge of the various continents and major socialist and capitalist countries.

In secondary school the major objectives of social science teaching are similar to those in elementary school. The history courses stress ancient history in the first year, feudalism in the second, capitalism in the third, and imperialism and the contemporary era in the last year. Geography in secondary school stresses the natural and economic features of the areas studied. The ideological-political training of the students

---

[24] For a succinct evaluation of the secondary school curriculum, see József Bencédy. "A gimnázium új tanterve" (The New Curriculum of the Gymnasium). *Köznevelés* (Public Education), Budapest XXI:13-14:527-29, July 9, 1965.

[25] *Report on Educational Progress in the 1966/67 Academic Year Presented at the XXXth Session of the International Conference on Public Education.* Geneva, July 1967. p. 27.

[26] *Tanterv és utasitás az általános iskolák számára*, op. cit. p. 311, 339.

Table 13.—Number of hours per week, per subject, in the 8-year elementary schools, by grade: 1965-65

Subject	Grade							
	1	2	3	4	5	6	7	8
Total	20	24	26	27	29	30	31	31
Arithemtic-geometry	5	6	6	6	5	5	4	4
Chemistry	0	0	0	0	0	0	2	2
Drawing	0	1	1	2	2	2	2	2
Geography	0	0	0	0	2	2	2	2
Guidance [1]	0	0	0	0	1	1	1	1
History	0	0	0	0	2	2	2	2
Hungarian:								
Composition	0	0	2	2	0	0	0	0
Grammar	0	3	3	3	0	0	0	0
Language and literature	0	0	0	0	6	5	5	5
Reading	10	5	4	4	0	0	0	0
Writing		2	2	2	0	0	0	0
Knowledge of the surroundings	1	2	2	2	0	0	0	0
Music	1	2	2	2	2	2	2	2
Physical education [2]	2	2	2	2	2	2	2	2
Physics	0	0	0	0	0	2	2	2
Practical exercises	1	1	2	2	2	2	2	2
Russian	0	0	0	0	3	3	3	3
The living world [3]	0	0	0	0	2	2	2	2

[1] Includes conferences with the class adviser.

[2] In the first grade, "Play."

[3] Includes elements of biology and zoology.

SOURCE OF DATA: *Tanterv és utasitás az általános iskolák számára* (Curriculum and Instrcution for the General Schools). Budapest: Tankönyvkiadó *for the* Művelődésügyi Minisztérium (Ministry of Culture). No date. p. 5.

is furthered by a special course, "Foundations of Our World Outlook", which emphasizes the systematic study of Marxism-Leninism and the political-economic aspects of the socialist system.

Natural and Physical Sciences.—The proportion of science, including mathematics, in the overall curriculum is rather high in the upper grades of the elementary school, and especially high in the science specialization classes of the secondary school. Elementary grades 6 to 8 teach a physics course emphasizing basic physical concepts and their qualitative and quantitative interrelationships, basic physical laws and their application in everyday life, and technology. Chemistry, taught in grades 7 and 8, emphasizes the nature of the various chemical groups and their applications in chemical production, their physical-chemical characteristics and their uses, and the fundamental laws underlying chemical processes. The upper elementary grades teach a course on "The Living World" that covers elements of anthropology, botany, and zoology.

In all elementary grades mathematics is taught rather intensively. In secondary school, it is taught with special concentration in the mathematics and mathematics-physics specialization classes.

In the first year of secondary school, the stress is on equations; in the second, on plane geometry, trigonometry, logarithms, and powers; in the third, on trigonometry, solid geometry, and differential calculus; and in the fourth, on integral calculus and solid geometry.

Physics and chemistry are taught to all secondary school students, regardless of their specialization, in order to familiarize them with the

Table 14.—Number of hours per week per subject, in secondary schools having both general and subject-specialization classes, by grade: 1965-66

[Grades 1-4 are equivalent to grades 9-12 in the United States]

Subject	General [1]				General [2]				Foreign languages				Mathematics				Math-physics				Physics-chemistry				Chemistry-biology				Drawing				Music			
	Grade				Grade				Grade				Grade				Grade				Grade				Grade				Grade				Grade			
	1	2	3	4	1	2	3	4	1	2	3	4	1	2	3	4	1	2	3	4	1	2	3	4	1	2	3	4	1	2	3	4	1	2	3	4
1	2	3	4	5	6	7	8	9	10	11	12	13	14	15	16	17	18	19	20	21	22	23	24	25	26	27	28	29	30	31	32	33	34	35	36	37
Total	33	33	34	34	33	33	33	33	34	34	34	34	34	34	35	35	33	34	35	35	32	34	35	35	34	34	35	35	32	33	34	34	33	33	34	34
Biology [3]	2	2	2	2	2	2	2/0	2	2	2	2/0	2	2	2	2/0	2	2	2	2/0	2	2	2	2/0	2	4	4	4/2	4	2	2	2/0	2	2	2	2/0	2
Chemistry	2	2	2	0	2	3	3	0	2	2	2	0	2	2	2	0	2	2	2	0	4	4	4	2	4	4	4	2	2	2	2	0	2	2	2	0
Drawing and evaluation of masterpieces	2	0	0	1	2	0	0	1	2	0	0	1	2	0	0	1	2	0	0	1	2	0	0	1	2	0	0	1	4	3	3	4	2	0	0	1
Foundations of world outlook	0	0	0	3	0	0	0	3	0	0	0	3	0	0	0	3	0	0	0	3	0	0	0	3	0	0	0	3	0	0	0	3	0	0	0	3
Geography	2	2	2	0	2	2	2	0	2	2	2	0	2	2	2	0	2	2	2	0	2	2	2	0	2	2	2	0	2	2	2	0	2	2	2	0
Guidance	1	1	1	1	1	1	1	1	1	1	1	1	1	1	1	1	1	1	1	1	1	1	1	1	1	1	1	1	1	1	1	1	1	1	1	1
History	2	3	3	3	2	3	3	3	2	3	3	3	2	3	3	3	2	3	3	3	2	3	3	3	2	3	3	3	2	3	3	3	2	3	3	3
Hungarian language [4]	2	1	1	1	2	1	1	1	2	1	1	1	2	1	1	1	2	1	1	1	2	1	1	1	2	1	1	1	2	1	1	1	2	1	1	1
Hungarian literature [4]	2	3	3	3	3	3	3	3	2	3	3	3	2	3	3	3	2	3	3	3	2	3	3	3	2	3	3	3	2	3	3	3	2	3	3	3
Mathematics	4	4	4	4	5	4	5	5	4	4	4	4	6	6	6	6	7	6	6	6	4	4	4	4	4	4	4	4	4	4	4	4	4	4	4	4
Mathematics exercises	0	0	0	0	0	0	0	0	0	0	0	0	4	4	4	4	0	0	0	0	0	0	0	0	0	0	0	0	0	0	0	0	0	0	0	0
Music	2	1	0	0	2	1	0	0	2	1	0	0	2	1	0	0	2	1	0	0	2	1	0	0	2	1	0	0	2	1	0	0	4	3	2	2
Music–choir [5]	0	0	0	0	0	0	0	0	0	0	0	0	0	0	0	0	0	0	0	0	0	0	0	0	0	0	0	0	0	0	0	0	1	1	1	1

Subject																		
Physical education	2	2	2	2	2	2	2	2	2	2	2	2	2	2	2	2	2	2
Physics	0	2	4	4	0	3	4	5	0	2	4	4	0	2	4	4	0	4
Practical exercises	5	5	5	5	2	2	2	2	2	2	2	2	0	0	0	0	2	2
Psychology [3]	0	0	0/2	0	0	0	0/2	0	0	0	0/2	0	0	0	0/2	0	0	0
Russian [6]	3	3	3	3	3	3	3	3	6	6	5	5	3	3	3	3	3	3
Second foreign language	2	2	2	2	3	3	2	2	3	3	3	3	2	2	2	2	2	2

Subject																		
Physical education	2	2	2	2	2	2	2	2	2	2	2	2	2	2	2	2	2	2
Physics	6	6	0	4	6	6	0	2	4	4	0	2	4	4	0	2	4	4
Practical exercises	2	2	2	2	2	2	2	2	2	2	2	2	2	2	2	2	2	2
Psychology [3]	0/2	0	0	0	0/2	0	0	0	0/2	0	0	0	0/	0	0	0	0/	0
Russian [6]	3	3	3	3	3	3	3	3	3	3	3	3	3	3	3	3	3	3
Second foreign language	2	2	2	2	2	2	2	2	2	2	2	2	2	2	2	2	2	2

[1] General secondary school class with one day per week (5 hours per day) practical work.

[2] General secondary school class with 2 hours of practical work per week.

[3] In the third year of secondary school, biology is taught in the first semester and psychology in the second.

[4] Hungarian language and literature are taught by the same teacher but treated and graded as two separate subjects.

[5] Students receive no grades in this subject.

[6] In case the student does not choose Russian as his major foreign language, but, rather, English, French, Italian, or Spanish, he must then take Russian as his second foreign language.

SOURCE OF DATA: *Tanterv és utasitás a gimnáziumok számára: Óratervek* (Curriculum and Instruction for the Gymasiums: Course Plans). Budapest: Tankönyvkiadó *for the* Müvelődésügyi Minisztérium (Ministry of Culture), [1965]. p. 7-15.

major physical phenomena and laws, especially those constituting the basis of modern technology; the several science specialization classes, of course, study the subjects in greater depth.

Biology is taught in every grade of secondary school with the exception of the second half of the third year, when a beginning psychology course is given instead. In the first year, the biology course emphasizes botany; in the second, zoology; in the first half of the third, anatomy and general biology; and in the fourth, genetics and evolution.

Language and Literature.—In both elementary and secondary schools, Hungarian language and literature are taught throughout the curriculum, constituting over 40 percent of the curriculum in the lower grades. In the upper secondary grades literature courses also include material on world literary masterpieces and the history of literature.

Russian is required starting with grade 5; in secondary school it is taught throughout for at least 3 hours per week (the Russian specialization class has more intensive study of the subject, involving from 5 to 6 hours per week).

Foreign languages other than Russian are also taught in secondary school. Students whose subject specialization is in foreign languages may choose English, French, German, Italian, Latin, or Spanish. Students whose major is a language other than Russian must, however, choose Russian as their minor. Emphasis in foreign language instruction is on acquiring a thorough foundation in grammar and a basic 1,200-word vocabulary: 350 words in the first year, 300 in the second, 300 in the third, and 250 in the fourth. (These 4 years or grades are equivalent to grades 9-12 in the United States.) In addition, students are expected to be able to use this vocabulary in everyday conversation, read and understand more advanced text with the aid of dictionaries, and pursue their studies independently after they graduate from secondary school.

Although the teaching of foreign languages is still based primarily on the traditional methods of rote learning, attention is increasingly focused on using modern audiovisual techniques.[27]

Practical Training: Polytechnization.—Elementary school pupils must devote 1 hour per week in grades 1 and 2, and 2 hours per week in the other grades, to practical agricultural or industrial work. Secondary school students must take pretraining for a skill in any field—one 5-hour day per week in some schools and only 2 hours per week in others. This pretraining takes place in classes that may have two or even three separate sections, depending upon enrollment.

The classes are held in shops, cooperatives, institutions, or agricultural and industrial enterprises with which the school has concluded a contractual agreement by June 30 preceding each school year. Theoretically, each practical work session begins with a general discussion of the principles and techniques involved in the use of tools and the specifics of the particular trade or skill. In addition to the weekly practical work, which is part of the regular curriculum, third-year secondary

[27] *Tanterv és utasitás a gimnáziumok számára. Angol, francia, latin, német, olasz és spanyol nyelv* (Curriculum and Instruction for the Gymnasiums. English, French, Latin, German, Italian, and Spanish). Budapest: Tankönyvkiadó *for the* Művelődésügyi Minisztérium, 1965, 118 p. For further details see also UNESCO. *International Bureau of Education. Modern Languages at General Secondary Schools.* (Publication No. 268). Geneva: 1964. p. 76-78.

Polytechnical training in a secondary school

school students must also spend 2 weeks during their summer vacation in production. Although they are paid for this work, it is considered part of their school performance and is inscribed in their official school record.

Hungarian educators[28] emphasize that in the development of the polytechnical program they were influenced and guided by the Marxist classics[29] and Soviet educational experience. Basically, polytechnical education is work-experience education that aims to combine manual work and academic study and to serve as a means for molding the individual's social, political, and intellectual development—reminiscent of John Dewey's concept of "learning by doing."

Although elements of polytechnical education were introduced in the various postwar curriculums, they were primarily experimental and unsystematic. The first concrete step towards introducing formal polytechnical education was taken in October 1955, when a symposium was organized jointly by the Scientific Pedagogical Institute (*Pedagógiai Tudományos Intézet*)[30] and the Ministry of Culture. As a result of this symposium, the elementary school curriculum was expanded, starting with the 1956-57 academic year, to include in the upper grades "Practical Exercises"—2 hours per week of practical work. To validate the first year's experience (much of which was negative primarily because materials were in short supply), the National Work Collective for Polytech-

[28] István Bori *and* Ferenc Tihanyi. "A hazai politechnikai oktatás" (Our Domestic Polytechnical Education). *In: Nevelésügyünk húsz éve, 1945-1964* (Twenty Years of Our Educational System, 1945-1964). Budapest: Tankönyvkiadó, 1965. p. 151-77; István Bori and Ferenc Tihanyi. "A politechnikai oktatásról" (Concerning Polytechnical Education). *In: Oktatásügyünk továbbfejlesztéséért. Tanulmányok és dokumentumok* (For the Further Development of Our Educational System. Studies and Documents). Edited by Ferenc Tihanyi. Budapest: Tankönyvkiadó. 1961. p. 111-30.

[29] According to Marx, "polytechnism," as it is often called, is "an education which, in the case of every child over a certain age, combines labor with instruction and physical culture, not only as a means for increasing social production, but as the only way of producing fully developed beings. Maurice J. Shore. *Soviet Education: Its Psychology and Philosophy*. New York: Philosophical Library, 1947. p. 52.

[30] See p. 163.

nical Research (*Országos Politechnikai Kutató Munkaközösség*) was organized.

From the Collective's studies and findings, a Government resolution formulated the basic assumptions and directives underlying polytechnical education in elementary and secondary schools.[31] This resolution called for the introduction of polytechnical training in all elementary and secondary schools, thus aiming to further "education for practical life." The purpose of such training was defined as one to acquaint children with the natural laws and phenomena underlying production and with their practical application in production. The children were to be made acquainted, in theory and practice, with the most important raw materials and they were to develop an aptitude for working with tools and machines.

The resolution called for polytechnical education to be introduced in 1958-59 into 500 elementary ("general") and 40 secondary schools.

Although the succeeding years saw the extension of this training to many more schools, the problems besetting this form of education have continued into the late 1960's. One such problem is the reluctance of many secondary school students preparing for the universities to engage in physical (especially agricultural) work, and the lack of modern shops equipped for this activity. Another problem is the adverse effect upon production of the presence of large groups of students in the industrial enterprises, because they interfere with the orderly conduct of regular production. This was especially true in schools that operated under the so-called "5+1" system—5 days of classroom and 1 day of shop work.[32] Resistance to applying polytechnical methods was also shown by many of the teachers. This was reflected in a statement revealed by the official Communist Party daily *Népszabadság* (People's Freedom) in an article of May 21, 1959:

> There still exist among a fraction of pedagogues and primarily among teachers of the humanities a tendency to see in polytechnical education some degradation of human culture. They express their fears openly, saying that polytechnical education brings the school down to the level of the apprentices' school . . . This is an attitude protecting the ideal of the old schools. Practice will, of course, sooner or later convince them . . . that their view is erroneous.[33]

Seven years after the new polytechnical system was installed, however, the problems continue to persist, as revealed by the policy statement of the Minister of Culture at a parliamentary session on November 11-13, 1965. In that statement the Minister stressed that many polytechnical education schools had no adequately equipped shops of their own and that many of their shop instructors were poorly trained for the job. Although well equipped, the industrial enterprises had no space to provide technical training for all the students living in the communities where the enterprises were located. As a partial solution to the problem, the Minister recommended that the "5+1" system be retained only in

[31] "A Magyar Forradalmi Munkás-Paraszt Kormány 1.014/1958. (III. 29.) számú határozata a műszaki-gyakorlati nevelés fokozottabb fejlesztéséről az általánosan képző iskolákban" (Resolution No. 1,014/1958. (III. 29.) of the Hungarian Revolutionary Worker-Peasant Government Concerning the More Intensive Development of Polytechnical-Practical Training in the General Type Schools). *Magyar Közlöny*, No. 29, March 29, 1958. p. 253-54.

[32] See p. 28.

[33] *East Europe*, New York. 8:7:42, July 1959.

schools that were suitably equipped and staffed; and that technical training be reduced to 2 hours per week in the other schools.[34]

Special Subjects.—Some secondary schools organize special courses to advance students' special interests and capabilities. These courses normally last from September 15 to May 31, with two 45-minute classes weekly. Students are accepted in these courses by the school principal on the basis of applications which they submit in response to a public notice outlining the subjects and admission conditions.[35]

Excursions.—With the principal's permission, excursions and trips may be arranged. If one has been planned, it is mandatory for every child in the particular class to participate unless he is excused by the class adviser. Excursions lasting longer than half a day are usually planned to take place on school holidays.

Syllabuses

The Ministry of Culture has published detailed syllabuses for every course taught in every grade of the elementary and secondary schools. It is the principals' responsibility to see that these syllabuses are followed in actual classroom practice.[36] In addition, teachers are also provided with teacher handbooks supplementing the syllabuses for the various courses.[37]

Textbooks

Like the curriculums, syllabuses, and teachers' handbooks, the textbooks for all grades and levels of education are published in State enterprises and are prescribed for all schools. The publication of a textbook involves a long and complicated process including contracting, processing, and distribution.

Contracting and Processing

Textbook writers are selected through competitions announced publicly by the Ministry of Culture. Textbook entries in a competition are first examined critically by a specialized working committee composed of specialists representing the Ministry of Culture, the National Pedagogical Institute, and the *Tankönyvkiadó* (Textbook Publishing House). The working committee then normally submits its selections, for advice, to two educators who specialize in the particular field of the proposed textbooks. After receiving the advice of these educators, the working committee sends the chosen manuscripts to a 3-member approval committee, on whose final recommendation a contract is con-

[34] Pál Ilku, op. cit. p. 881-89.

[35] *Rendtartás az általános iskolák és a gimnáziumok számára,* op. cit. p. 72-73.

[36] The detailed syllabuses for every elementary course appear in *Tanterv és utasitás az általános iskolák számára,* op. cit. 670 p. The 1965 secondary school syllabuses were prepared by the Main Section of Public Education *(Közoktatási Főosztály)* and the National Pedagogical Institute and published in a series of pamphlets by Tankönyvkiadó for the Ministry of Culture under the following general title: *Tanterv és utasitás a gimnáziumok számára* (Curriculum and Instruction for the Gymnasiums). See items under "Curriculums, Syllabuses, Rules, and Instructions" in the present publication's bibliography.

[37] See the list of items under "Teachers Handbooks" in the present publication's bibliography.

cluded between the Textbook Publishing House and the author(s). (The approval committee has for chairman the director of the National Pedagogical Institute. The two other committee members are the director of the Textbook Publishing House and a representative from the appropriate section of the Ministry of Culture.)
the date agreed to in the contract; the publishing house then submits these manuscripts to an official textbook reviewer and to the Teachers Union (*Pedagógus Szakszervezet*) [38] for a so-called "social critique." [39]

These review observations and critiques are summarized by the responsible editor of the publishing house, and the authors are expected to revise the manuscript accordingly. When revisions are completed and accepted, the working committee approves the manuscript's publication.

The publication rights last for 6 years, during which period the publisher at his discretion may issue further printings without obtaining the author's permission and without paying him any additional fees. The fees for all aspects of publishing (including original writing, translations, and editing) are established by special decree.[40] Every literary work is paid for according to its length and classification (or, more precisely, according to the number of 16-page forms it will consist of when printed). The forms are measured according to how many letters of the alphabet they contain; the official measurement is 40 thousand letters of the alphabet per form.

The author's fee for a form in a higher-education textbook ranges from 1,000 to 1,400 forints;[41] in an elementary or a secondary school textbook, from 800 to 1,200; and in a textbook prepared in the language of one of the minority nationalities, from 900 to 1,300. Translating fees per form vary from 500 to 780 forints for translations from Hungarian, and from 250 to 500 for translations into Hungarian. Editorial fees range from 20 to 225 forints per form.

Distribution

It is customary to bring out a textbook in a small first edition for experimental use by a few selected schools. Texts proving successful are then published in an issue totaling 10 percent more copies than there are pupils in the particular grade, to allow enough extra copies for teachers, inspectors, and student teachers. For example, in 1957, 228,000 copies of the primer were printed for 206,800 first-graders.[42] The textbooks, mostly paperbound, are relatively inexpensive. They are not given to the students free, as in some people's democracies. The official list of textbooks is published yearly by the Ministry of Culture.

---

38 See p. 167-68.

39 László Gáspár. "*A pedagógia műhelyei: 5—Tankönyvkiadó*" (The Shops of Pedagogy: 5—The Textbook Publishing House). *Köznevelés*, Budapest. XXI:5:197-98, March 12, 1965.

40 "A művelődésügyi miniszter 2/1959. (I. 18.)M.M. számú rendelete a tankönyvek kiadásáról" (Decree No. 2/1959. (I. 18.)MM. of the Minister of Culture Concerning the Publication of Textbooks). *Magyar Közlöny*, No. 8, January 18, 1959. p. 45-48.

41 Concerning the value of the forint, see footnote 54 of chapter III.

42 UNESCO. *INTERNATIONAL BUREAU of EDUCATION. Primary School Textbooks*. (Publication No. 204). Geneva: The Bureau, 1959. p. 130-32.

Quality

The textbooks as a rule are of good quality, well-designed, and attractively illustrated. Some of the workbooks for practical exercises are produced by photo-offset.

The selection of type, layout, and illustrations is the responsibility of the graphic section of the publishing house.

From the point of view of content, all textbooks must be closely correlated with the corresponding syllabuses and follow a basically dialectical-materialist orientation.

Examinations and Grading

The system of examinations and grading, like that of rewards and punishments, is regulated by the Ministry of Culture,[43] and teachers must follow the Ministry's regulations.

Examinations

Although all elementary and secondary school students must take semester- and year-end examinations, some must also take certain special-purpose examinations: baccalaureate, differential (supplementary qualifying), grade, makeup, and trade-qualification. The student's semester- and year-end performance as a whole is determined by the collective judgment of committees.[44]

Students who have received a failing mark in some subject or in the grade examination are entitled to take a repeat examination *(javitóvizsga)* at a late-August date specified by the school principal. This examination is usually oral. Candidates who fail the repeat examination or who do not report for it must repeat the grade.[45]

Grade examinations *(osztályozó vizsgák)* covering the material studied during the entire year, must be taken by students who missed more than 250 class hours of instruction during the second semester, who were on official leave of absence, or who, older than the regular age, are studying independently. This last group may take cumulative examinations covering 2 years' work at a time, with the exception of grades 7 and 8 of the elementary schools and of the third and fourth years of the secondary schools. Consisting of written, oral, and practical parts, examinations are normally given either at the end or the beginning of the school year.

Differential or supplementary qualifying examinations *(különbözeti vizsgák)* must be taken by secondary school students who are transferring from secondary schools of a different type or from vocational schools,

[43] *Rendtartás az általános iskolák és a gimnáziumok számára,* op. cit. p. 32-48

[44] See next subsection, Grading.

[45] The Hungarian educational authorities have taken various measures to help educationally disadvantaged or under-achieving children, particularly those in one-teacher elementary schools. Special guidance and educational tutoring are also provided for children coming from broken homes or living under conditions not conducive to learning. For details see "A tanulmányi feltételekben hátrányos helyzetben levõ tanulók segitéséröl. A Müvelödésügyi Minisztérium Közoktatási Föosztályának utmutatója" (Concerning the Assistance of Educationally Disadvantaged Pupils. Guide of the Main Public Education Section of the Ministry of Culture). *Köznevelés,* XX:13:481-84. July 13, 1964.

students who are resuming their education after an interruption, and students who started their secondary education outside the country. The examinations, usually given in the middle of June or in late August, consist of written and oral parts. The examination committee is headed by the principal or his assistant.

The trade-qualification examination (*szakmai minösitő vizsga*) may be taken by any secondary school graduate, whether or not he also applies for the baccalaureate examination. A successful candidate is given a diploma as a skilled worker in a particular trade, which is a separate document from the secondary school-completion certificate and from the baccalaureate diploma. The principal of every school is required to notify the education section of the local people's council by April 15 of each year of the number of candidates for this examination in the various trade skills, and of the proposed time and place.

When the student has successfully completed secondary school he takes the baccalaureate examination[46] (*érettségi vizsga*). He does so in the school where he has received his secondary school-completion certificate. By April 15, the principal(s) must inform the education section of the people's council how many applicants there are for the baccalaureate examination in the various fields.

The baccalaureate examination has been the subject of a number of governmental or ministerial decrees and regulations regarding its form and content. The details of the examination procedure valid in the late 1960's were published in 1963.[47] According to these rules, the examination has a written and an oral part and consists of four subjects: three required ones, namely, history, Hungarian language and literature, and mathematics; an elective, which may be either foreign languages, biology, physics, or chemistry, depending on the candidate's subject specialization in secondary school. The student may take the examination at any time within 5 years after he graduates from secondary school.

The examination subject matter is prepared by the Ministry, which sends it to the various schools with instructions and sample questions; on the basis of this, secondary school teachers participating in the examination procedure make up the actual examination questions.

Criticized in the past as favoring children of the privileged classes, the examination and diploma continue to be the subject of controversy. The examination is favored, however, as a means for evaluating the educational and cultural level which the student has achieved by the end of general secondary education, for determining his suitability for further studies, and for stimulating him to study. It is criticized for its effect on the students, for its form, and for its content.

Since it is the only examination for most students and since it has great importance for university-level education and career choice, the baccalaureate examination is said to have a negative psychological impact on the student.[48] This effect is said to be aggravated if the student has

[46] Although the term baccalaureate has a somewhat different connotation in the United States, it is here rendered to denote the comprehensive examination offered at the end of secondary schooling in most European countries.

[47] Order No. 186/1963. (MK24.)MM of the Minister of Culture. For details on the functions of the baccalaureate examination, see Mrs. Dénes Varga. "Gondolatok az érettségi funkciójáról" (Thoughts on Functions of the Baccalaureate Examination). *Pedagógiai Szemle* (Review of Education), Budapest. XVI:3:213-18, 1966.

[48] József Szarka. "A jövő a korszerűbb értékelési módszereké" (The Future Belongs to the More Modern

passed the examination and then discovers that he nevertheless cannot be admitted to a university for lack of space. Another source of criticism is the high prestige value associated with passing the baccalaureate examination, and its use in an attempt to secure material advantages.

Grading

Students are graded by so-called grading conferences composed of teachers and instructors, who in their decisions consider the students' behavior, industriousness, and achievements. The half-year grading conference is headed by the class adviser, and the year-end one by the principal. Marks for behavior range from 5 to 2, 5 being exemplary, 4 good, 3 variable, and 2 bad. The same grades apply for industriousness, except that 2 means "negligent." Academic achievement is marked on a scale from 5 to 1, with 5 being outstanding or excellent, 4 good, 3 average, 2 passing, and 1 failure. Grades in behavior and industriousness are not included in the calculation of grade averages, but are taken into consideration for admission to dormitories, the granting of awards, and the assignment of elementary school pupils to secondary schools.

Awards and Penalties

To stimulate the students' drive for learning, industriousness, and good behavior, the educational authorities have instituted a system of awards. An award may take the form of public recognition in class as an example worthy of being followed, recognition by the principal, praise in the records, a certificate of praise—or it may be the school's highest award. This last form of award is made to a student who has completed 4 years of secondary school with a 5.0 average, and the tangible evidence is a medal inscribed "Outstanding Student" *(Kitünő tanuló)*. It is issued by the educational section of the people's council and presented to its winner during graduation ceremonies.

Unruly students or those not working to capacity, on the other hand, are subject to a series of penalties determined by the teacher, class adviser, principal, or the youth movement, depending on the nature of the infraction. Penalties may be a warning, private or in front of the class, a reprimand by the principal, a transfer, or (for a student who is beyond the compulsory school age) expulsion. The latter measure must have the concurrence of the education section of the people's council. In very serious cases, the school may recommend to the Ministry of Culture that the student be barred from all schools in the country (again, only for a student beyond compulsory school age).[49]

Tuition, Scholarships, and Assistance

Until 1962, secondary education was based on a tuition system combined with a scholarship system for students of worker and peasant

---

Evaluation Methods). *Köznevelés*, XXIII:22:847-48, November 24, 1967. József Fekete. "Az új gimnáziumi érettségi vizsgaszabályzat" (The New Regulation Concerning the Baccalaureate Examination). Ibid. XX:2:41-45 January 24, 1964. "Az általános tanulmányi eredmény megállapitása az érettségin" (The Determination of the Results of General Education During the Baccalaureate Examination. Ibid. XXI:8:284-85, April 23, 1965.

[49] *Rendtartás az általános iskolák és a gimnáziumok számára*, op. cit., p. 33-37.

background and for those with good academic records. Beginning with the 1962-63 school year, all registration and tuition fees in the secondary schools were abolished.[50]

In addition to free education, some students may also be given the additional privilege of boarding at school, staying at so-called day-homes, using study rooms, or eating at school cafeterias.

Boarding school privileges are accorded primarily to deserving secondary school students living in communites that do not have a school of a particular type. Day-homes and study rooms are intended mainly for children both of whose parents work and whose household does not include some other adult able to supervise them, or children who would be entitled to dormitory arrangements but have been accommodated in private homes other than their own for lack of space. Both day-homes and study rooms are set up for groups of at least 20 and no more than 40 children. Day-homes operate on a year-round basis, while the study rooms are open for 3 hours daily during the 10-month school year. Although the dormitories, day-homes, and study rooms are not free, the fees are low and liberal financial assistance is available to pay these fees.

The following tabulation reveals certain 1963-64 school-year statistics, presented in descending order of the number of children assisted: [51]

Number of children	*School level*	*Kind of assistance*
164,223	8-year elementary ("general")	Meals in day-homes
[1] 33,064	Secondary	Dormitory or private home boarding
30,187	do.	Study rooms and school cafeterias [2]
15,426	Upper grades of 8-year elementary	Study rooms
2,276	Secondary	"Social scholarships" [3]
1,160	8-year elementary ("general")	Dormitories [4]

[1] 15.7 percent of the total number of secondary students.
[2] Source did not give separate figures for the two kinds of assistance.
[3] Awarded by such organizations as trade unions.
[4] A total of 16 dormitories.

Types of Schools

Elementary education is offered in two types of schools: (1) the 8-year free and compulsory "general" school and (2) the 2-year continuation or further-training school. Secondary education is offered in the academic gymnasium *(általános gimnázium)* and in three types of vocational school (agricultural, economic, and industrial). All schools are coeducational, although separate classes for boys and girls may be organized with the concurrence of the education sections of the people's councils.

[50] "A Magyar Forradalmi Munkás-Paraszt Kormány 9/1962. (III.25.) számú rendelete a középfokú oktatási intézményekben a beiratási dij és a tandij megszüntetéséről" (Decree No. 9/1962. (III.25.) of the Hungarian Revolutionary Worker-Peasant Government Concerning the Abolition of Registration and Tuition Fees in Secondary Schools). *Magyar Közlöny*, No. 20, March 25, 1962. p. 203.
[51] Simon and Szarka, op. cit. p. 125 and 142.

The 8-Year Elementary ("General") School

Originally launched in 1945, the 8-year free and compulsory elementary ("general") school is the most positive achievement of Hungary's postwar educational reforms. Although the school's basic structure has remained essentially the same since then, its scope and objectives have been redefined.[52] Its principal aim was declared to be one that would lay the foundation for developing the Communist man. Toward this end, the 8-year elementary school is expected to—

1. Provide every pupil with a modern unified basic education. Use the educational process to develop in the children the moral traits characteristic of the Communist man.
2. Provide an education that will lead the children to love their socialist homeland and the people of other countries, respect work and the working man, and take part in the realization of societal aims.
3. Enable the pupils to become conscious workers and protectors of their fatherland and of its future society.[53]

Although the number of schools declined gradually between 1960-61 and 1966-67, owing both to consolidation of small institutions and decline in enrollment (the latter a manifestation of Hungary's declining birth rate), the pupil-teacher ratio as well as class size steadily improved (tables 15, 16, 17).

The total 1966-67 elementary enrollment was 1,380,286 pupils (table 18). The overwhelming majority of the pupils were in elementary ("general") schools having separate classes for each of the eight grades; only 15,876 children were in so-called partial 8-year schools in which a few grades are taught in consolidated classes owing to small enrollment. The remaining 94,321 children attended elementary schools having only one, two, or three classrooms. Of the 29,988 pupils in one-classroom schools, however, only 1,785 were in the upper grades (table 20).

Polytechnical education was accorded great importance (table 19). Although the total number of pupils enrolled for practical education in the upper grades of the elementary schools during 1960-61 was only 223,634 (36 percent of all pupils in those grades), this number had increased by 1966-67 to 654,243 (87.3 percent). As between agricultural and industrial work, the distribution was roughly half-and-half.

The Continuation School

Under Hungary's compulsory education laws, children graduating from elementary schools before age 16 who do not choose to continue their education in either an academic or a vocational secondary school and who are not gainfully employed at least 4 hours[54] a day must

[52] Articles 6 and 8 of Law No. III of 1961 Concerning the Educational System of the Hungarian People's Republic, op. cit. "A Népköztársaság Elnöki Tanácsának 1962. évi 14. számú törvényerejű rendelete az alsófokú oktatási intézményekről (Decree No. 14 of 1962 of the Presidential Council of the People's Republic Concerning the Lower Educational Institutions). *Magyar Közlöny*, No. 43, June 16, 1962. p. 390-92. See also Decree No. 3/1966. (XI.4.) MM of the Minister of Culture implementing Decree No. 14/1962. Ibid, No. 67, November 4, 1966. p. 612-18.

[53] *Tanterv és utasitás az általános iskolák számára*, op. cit. p. 4.

[54] Originally the laws called for a gainful employment of 36 hours per week. See Decree No. 36/1959 in footnote 56.

Table 15.—Number of 8-year elementary schools, classrooms, teachers, pupils, and class sections: 1960–61—1966–67[1]

School year	Schools	Class-rooms	Teachers[2] Total	Qualified as— Teacher	Qualified as— Professor	Pupils	Class sections	Pupils per— Teacher	Pupils per— Section	Pupils per— Classroom	Sections per classroom
1960–61	6,307	30,155	57,290	33,289	22,412	1,392,260	42,763	24.3	32.6	46.2	1.42
1961–62	6,261	30,791	58,333	32,926	22,544	1,444,543	43,478	24.8	33.2	46.9	1.41
1962–63	6,220	31,147	59,921	32,590	23,108	1,472,743	44,109	24.6	33.4	47.3	1.42
1963–64	6,162	31,520	61,518	31,940	23,734	1,468,883	44,518	23.9	33.0	46.6	1.41
1964–65	6,105	31,570	62,108	31,232	24,850	1,445,124	44,473	23.3	32.5	45.8	1.41
1965–66	6,036	31,711	62,167	30,785	25,714	1,413,512	43,949	22.7	32.2	44.6	1.39
1966–67	5,954	31,680	62,241	31,107	26,538	1,380,286	43,323	22.2	31.9	43.6	1.37

[1] Data released at beginning of school year.

[2] Includes all teachers employed in the 8-year elementary school system who have graduated from teacher-training institutes and colleges; also all principals, assistant principals, and directors of day-homes teaching 12 hours or less.

SOURCE OF DATA: *Statisztikai évkönyv 1966* (Statistical Yearbook 1966). Budapest: Központi Statisztikai Hivatal, 1967. p. 343.

Table 16.—Number of pupils in the 8-year elementary schools, by grade: 1960–61—1966–67[1]

School year	Total	Grade 1	2	3	4	5	6	7	8
1960–61	1,392,260	229,151	192,604	175,620	178,288	176,003	164,093	148,539	127,962
1961–62	1,444,543	223,417	212,059	187,607	173,773	180,184	169,951	156,081	141,471
1962–63	1,472,743	204,378	208,574	207,131	185,681	176,359	176,226	164,367	150,027
1963–64	1,468,683	185,086	190,495	203,912	204,525	188,057	171,592	168,754	156,262
1964–65	1,445,124	163,265	173,744	187,368	201,100	207,853	183,067	164,095	159,632
1965–66	1,413,512	161,537	157,971	171,007	184,837	206,686	201,639	175,079	154,756
1966–67	1,380,286	156,063	150,674	155,306	168,713	190,600	199,892	194,007	165,031

[1] Data released at beginning of school year.

SOURCE OF DATA: *Statisztikai évkönyv 1966* (Statistical Yearbook 1966). Budapest: Központi Statisztikai Hivatal, 1967. p. 344.

attend continuation schools (*továbbképző iskolák*). Established by local government authorities, these schools operate under the same jurisdictional principles as the elementary schools. The continuation schools are 2-year institutions offering a course basically agricultural or industrial (table 21). The former type is in session for 5 months, November through March; the latter, for 10 months, September through June.

The continuation schools' basic elements were formulated in 1956;[55] its organization was effected in 1959 under Government Decree No. 36 of 1959.[56]

[55] "A Magyar Népköztársaság Ministertanácsának 1.082/1956. (VIII.25.) számú határozata a fiatalok munkalehetőségeinek és továbbtanulásának biztositásáról" (Resolution No. 1, 082/1956. (VIII.25.) of the Council of Ministers of the Hungarian People's Republic Assuring the Further Education and Working Opportunities of Young People). *Magyar Közlöny*, No. 72, August 25, 1956. p. 452.

[56] "A Magyar Forradalmi Munkás-Paraszt Kormány 36/1959 (VII.19.) számú rendelete a továbbképző iskolákról" (Decree No. 36/1959. (VII.19.). of the Hungarian Revolutionary Worker-Peasant Government Concerning the Continuation Schools). *Magyar Közlöny*, No. 77, July 19, 1959. p. 638-40. See also Decree No. 9/1959. (X.9.) MM of the Minister of Culture implementing Government Decree No. 36/1959. Ibid, No. 101, October 9, 1959. p. 875–82.

Table 17.—Number of 8-year elementary schools, classrooms, teachers, pupils, and class sections: 1966–67 [1]

Type of school	Schools	Class-rooms	Teach-ers	Pupils	Class sec-tions	Pupils per— Teach-er	Pupils per— Class	Pupils per— Class-room	Class sec-tions per class-room
Full 8 grades [2]	2,352	23,820	50,977	1,134,089	33,957	22.2	33.4	47.6	1.43
Partial 8 grades	1,011	4,312	7,220	151,876	5,417	21.0	28.0	35.2	1.26
Low enrollment with:									
Three sections [3]	164	403	558	13,367	492	24.0	27.2	33.2	1.22
Two sections	1,030	1,748	2,072	50,966	2,090	24.6	24.7	29.2	1.18
One section	1,397	1,397	1,414	29,988	1,397	21.2	21.5	21.5	1.00

[1] Data released at beginning of school year.

[2] Schools operating with all 8 grades with class teachers in the lower grades and separate subject teachers in the upper grades.

[3] The sections are organized on the basis of either grades or subjects. Rural localities usually have one- or two-teacher or one- or two-room schools.

SOURCE OF DATA: *Statisztikai évkönyv 1966* (Statistical Yearbook 1966). Budapest: Központi Statisztikai Hivatal, 1967. p. 343.

Table 18.—Number and percent of pupils in the 8-year elementary schools, by grade and type of school: 1966–67 [1]

Type of school	Total	Grade 1	2	3	4	5	6	7	8
	NUMBER								
Total	1,380,286	156,063	150,674	155,306	168,713	190,600	199,892	194,007	165,031
Full 8 grades [2]	1,134,089	120,133	116,492	121,794	131,563	162,727	171,223	168,151	142,006
Partial 8 grades	151,876	17,256	16,605	16,173	18,328	22,041	22,793	20,465	18,215
Low enrollment:									
Three sections [3]	13,367	1,990	1,851	1,831	1,974	1,573	1,545	1,398	1,205
Two sections	50,966	9,449	8,392	8,654	9,568	3,736	3,836	3,563	3,213
One section	29,988	7,235	6,834	6,854	7,280	473	495	425	392
	PERCENT								
Annual average	100.0	11.3	10.9	11.3	12.2	13.8	14.5	14.1	11.0
Full 8 grades	100.0	10.6	10.3	10.7	11.6	14.4	15.1	14.8	12.5
Partial 8 grades	100.0	11.4	10.9	10.6	12.1	14.5	15.0	13.5	12.0
Low enrollment:									
Three sections	100.0	14.9	13.8	13.7	14.8	11.8	11.6	10.4	9.0
Two sections	100.0	18.5	17.5	17.0	18.8	7.4	7.5	7.0	6.3
One section	100.0	24.1	22.8	22.9	24.3	1.6	1.6	1.4	1.3

[1] Data released at beginning of school year.

[2] Schools operating with all 8 grades have class teachers in the lower grades and subject teachers in the upper grades.

[3] The sections are organized on the basis of either grades or subjects. These are usually one- or two-room or one- or two-teacher rural schools.

SOURCE OF DATA: *Statisztikai évkönyv 1966* (Statistical Yearbook 1966). Budapest: Központi Statisztikai Hivatal, 1967. p. 344.

Table 19.—Number and percent of practical-education pupils in grades 5–8 of the 8-year elementary schools: 1960–61—1966–67[1]

School year	Number					Percent						Percent of total school enrollment
	Total	Grade				Grade				In industrial courses	In agricultural courses	
		5	6	7	8	5	6	7	8			
1960–61	223,634	105,592	73,273	40,961	3,808	60.0	44.7	27.6	3.0	--------	--------	36.3
1961–62	343,302	127,240	104,831	71,161	40,070	70.6	61.7	45.6	28.3	50.1	47.1	53.0
1962–63	440,266	140,137	126,527	103,023	70,579	79.5	71.8	62.7	47.0	48.3	49.8	66.0
1963–64	522,150	158,306	138,198	124,041	101,605	84.2	80.5	73.5	65.0	47.6	50.9	76.3
1964–65	587,849	179,310	154,803	134,530	119,206	86.3	84.6	82.0	74.7	47.7	51.0	82.3
1965–66	630,907	179,699	174,976	149,131	127,101	86.9	86.8	85.2	82.1	47.5	51.3	85.5
1966–67	654,243	167,778	175,799	169,603	142,063	88.0	87.4	87.4	86.1	47.8	52.2	87.3

[1] Data released at beginning of school year.

SOURCE OF DATA: *Statisztikai évkönyv 1966* (Statistical Yearbook 1966). Budapest: Központi Statisztikai Hivatal, 1967. p. 345.

Table 20.—Number of 8-year elementary schools, classrooms, teachers, pupils, and class sections, by municipality and county: 1966–67[1]

Municipalities and counties	Schools	Classrooms	Teachers	Pupils	Class sections	Pupils per—			Class sections per classroom
						Teacher	Class-section	Classroom	
Total	5,954	31,680	62,241	1,380,286	43,323	22.2	31.9	43.6	1.37
Municipalities									
Budapest	320	3,812	9,537	187,472	5,711	19.7	32.8	49.2	1.50
Debrecen	51	322	832	18,999	541	22.8	35.1	59.0	1.68
Miskolc	38	345	921	21,715	615	23.6	35.3	62.9	1.78
Pécs	37	324	853	17,363	504	20.4	34.5	53.6	1.56
Szeged	29	290	665	12,064	380	18.1	31.7	41.6	1.31
Counties									
Baranya	372	1,185	1,934	41,945	1,397	21.7	30.0	35.4	1.18
Bács-Kiskun	481	1,883	3,542	78,488	2,525	22.2	31.0	41.7	1.34
Békés	277	1,667	2,799	61,384	1,930	21.9	31.8	36.8	1.16
Borsod-Abauj-Zemplén	439	1,920	3,810	95,293	2,859	25.0	33.3	49.6	1.49
Csongrád	319	1,182	2,094	41,990	1,464	20.1	28.7	35.5	1.24
Fejér	224	1,219	2,528	58,671	1,820	23.2	32.2	48.1	1.49
Győr-Sopron	256	1,560	2,783	57,635	1,935	20.7	29.8	36.9	1.24
Hajdu-Bihar	213	1,247	2,660	62,398	1,921	23.5	32.5	50.0	1.54
Heves	167	925	2,015	44,633	1,412	22.2	31.6	48.3	1.53
Komárom	145	934	1,877	43,824	1,325	23.3	33.1	46.9	1.42
Nógrád	185	816	1,487	33,366	1,092	22.4	30.6	40.9	1.34
Pest	359	2,434	4,841	112,065	3,443	23.1	32.5	46.0	1.41
Somogy	325	1,301	2,093	48,107	1,555	23.0	30.9	37.0	1.20
Szabolcs-Szatmár	400	2,045	4,114	103,401	3,201	25.1	32.3	50.6	1.57
Szolnok	246	1,427	2,844	64,282	1,950	22.6	33.0	45.0	1.37
Tolna	194	1,045	1,714	36,582	1,192	21.3	30.7	35.0	1.14
Vas	260	1,176	1,874	39,722	1,324	21.2	30.0	33.8	1.13
Veszprém	330	1,577	2,702	60,852	1,953	22.5	31.2	38.6	1.24
Zala	287	1,044	1,722	38,035	1,274	22.1	29.9	36.4	1.22

[1] Data released at beginning of school year.

SOURCE OF DATA: *Statisztikai évkönyv 1966* (Statistical Yearbook 1966). Budapest: Központi Statisztikai Hivatal, 1967. p. 415.

Gymnasiums (academic and art), vocational secondary schools, and secondary *technikums* provide secondary education. All are 4-year institutions offering both theoretical and practical training. The gymnasiums operate under the overall jurisdiction of the Ministry of Culture; the secondary vocational schools and *technikums* under that of the various ministries within whose framework the particular vocational training falls. On the local level, however, all these schools are operated, maintained, and directed by the education sections of the people's councils.

Although many vocational schools and *technikums* have their own shops, the gymnasiums normally carry out their practical training programs through cooperative agreements with agricultural and industrial enterprises or institutions.

The increased importance of secondary education may be gauged from the growing number of secondary institutions and the increase in teachers and enrollment. As opposed to the 174 gymnasiums—128 boys' and 46 girls' [57]—and a few dozen vocational secondary schools that operated at the time of the country's liberation in 1945, the total number of secondary schools had already reached 419 by 1960-61 (table 22). Enrollment steadily increased until 1964-65, when it reached a peak of 417,-446 students in 593 schools. After that date, owing to the declining birth rate, secondary school enrollments declined, although classroom size and student-teacher ratios improved.

Despite great progress, secondary education is still far from universal in Hungary. One of the reasons is the still relatively high dropout rate towards the end of elementary school.[58] Also involved are a number of sociological factors, including negative family relations, the tendency of peasant and worker families to enroll their children in nonsecondary vocational (continuation) schools,[59] and a high dropout rate in the secondary schools themselves, especially the day sessions. In 1966-67, for example, the percent of children of secondary school age actually attending the day session of secondary school was 33.6 percent (table 22). Although no breakdown by year of study is available, it is fair to assume that a disproportionate number of secondary school students are in the first years.

The following tabulation shows the number of secondary school teachers, by type of school, in the 1966-67 day sessions and the percent increase over the number in 1965-66:[60]

	Number in 1966–67	*Percent increase over number in 1965–66*
Total	*12,317*	2.2
Academic gymnasium	8,281	1.2
Vocational secondary	1,462	67.1
Technikum	2,574	13.9

[57] Simon and Szarka, op. cit. p. 130.

[58] In 1948–49, for example, only 50 percent of students who had started the first year of elementary school went as far as grade 6, and only less than a third graduated from grade 8. Ibid. p. 117. Although the situation has improved since then, the problem persists, especially in the case of the children of manual workers, only 62.4 percent of whom completed elementary education, as opposed to 94.2 percent of the children of intellectuals. *East Europe*, New York. 16:2:49–50, February 1967.

[59] *East Europe*, 15:12:50–51, December 1966.

[60] *Report on Educational Progress in the 1966/67 Academic Year*, op. cit. p. 25.

Table 21.—Number of schools, class sections, and pupils in the 2-year continuation schools: 1960–61—1966–67 [1]

[—Indicates that source did not show any figures]

School year	Schools	Class sections	Pupils				Pupils engaged in part-time work
			Total	In industrial courses	In agricultural courses	Percent of girls	
1960–61	660	960	23,609	—	—	67.2	—
1961–62	885	1,255	30,264	5,102	24,836	68.9	5,521
1962–63	880	1,216	27,539	4,736	22,464	71.0	5,033
1963–64	779	1,016	21,543	3,308	17,921	72.3	4,565
1964–65	702	860	18,613	2,885	15,430	77.1	3,895
1965–66	647	815	19,659	3,644	15,678	75.9	3,354
1966–67	620	754	19,617	2,915	16,389	76.7	3,548

[1] Data released at beginning of school year.

SOURCE OF DATA: *Statisztikai évkönyv 1966* (Statistical Yearbook 1966). Budapest: Központi Statisztikai Hivatal, 1967. p. 345.

Table 22.—Number of secondary schools, classrooms, teachers, and students; percent of students who are girls and percent which total enrollment constitutes of the secondary school-age population: 1966–67 [1]

School year	Schools	Classrooms	Teachers [2]	Students				
				Total	Per teacher [2]	Per classroom [2]	Percent of girls [2]	Percent of secondary school-age children [2] in the population
1960–61	419	4,427	8,778	241,036	17.7	35.1	54.4	26.4
1961–62	425	4,592	9,232	283,747	18.5	37.2	55.1	28.5
1962–63	441	4,760	9,619	333,747	19.5	39.4	56.2	30.7
1963–64	530	5,081	10,631	385,419	19.8	41.5	56.7	33.6
1964–65	593	5,310	11,561	417,446	20.0	43.6	57.3	34.6
1965–66	591	5,597	12,049	407,485	19.6	42.3	57.5	34.6
1966–67	589	5,803	12,317	375,734	18.7	39.7	57.7	33.6

[1] Data released at beginning of school year.
[2] Day session only.

SOURCE OF DATA: *Statisztikai évkönyv 1966* (Statistical Yearbook 1966). Budapest: Központi Statisztikai Hivatal, 1967. p. 346.

The Gymnasiums

Until 1951, for all practical purposes the gymnasiums operated under Law No. XI of 1934, which was abrogated by Decree No. 14/1951 concerning general gymnasiums.

The subject, in the early years of the people's democratic regime, of various reforms affecting the student body's composition and the subject also of a series of curriculum changes, the gymnasiums in the late 1960's are based fundamentally on the general provisions of Articles 10-17, Law No. III of 1961.[61]

The gymnasiums' primary stated goal is to educate, on the basis of a background acquired in elementary school, work-loving multilaterally cultured social beings capable of absorbing further education in the institutions of higher learning, acquiring a skill, pursuing independent study, or filling a job commensurate with secondary school training.

[61] See footnote 24 of chapter III.

Toward this end the gymnasiums are expected to—

1. Create in the students the Communist-man personality and develop in them the socialist attitudes, morality, outlook, and tastes.
2. Offer a modern general education, develop basic abilities in sciences and arts, and enhance the students' general capabilities.
3. Prepare students for life and, wherever possible, teach them a skill in a particular trade or group of trades.
4. Help develop the students' interest in a particular field of art, languages, sciences, or sport through organizing special classes and specialty and sport circles.[62]

Gymnasiums may also be maintained and operated by religious denominations on the basis of an agreement concluded by the State with the various religious communities.[63] During the 1963-64 school year there were 10 denominational academic gymnasiums with a total enrollment of 2,744. Their distribution among three denominations and the cities in which they were located was as follows:

Jewish	1	(In Budapest)
Protestant	1	(In Debrecen)
Roman Catholic	8	(2 in Budapest; 1 each in Debrecen, Esztergom, Győr, Kecskemét, Pannonhalma, and Szentendre)[64]

Also during the 1963-64 school year a number of special art gymnasiums offered a combined general and art curriculum in applied, fine, or industrial art or in music. Students graduating from these institutions with the secondary school certificate are eligible to be admitted into higher education institutions in their particular spheres of art. With the 1967-68 school year, the art gymnasiums, reorganized, began to operate as vocational secondary schools of art.[65]

The academic gymnasiums have both day and evening sessions and also correspondence courses (table 24). Their enrollment increased until 1964-65, when it reached a peak of 214,097; it has been declining each year since then, dropping to 188,666 in 1966-67. The decrease resulted from a general decline in secondary school population and from an increase in the number and proportion of students attending vocational secondary schools and *technikums*. Even with this enrollment decrease, in 1966-67 the students attending general gymnasiums represented 50.2 percent of the total number enrolled in secondary schools of all types. For the day session only, the general gymnasium enrollment accounts for 59.1 percent of the total.

The correspondence courses fall between the day and evening sessions in terms of enrollment. In 1966-67 they accounted for 38,920 students, or 38 percent of total correspondence-course secondary school students; the correspondence-course students are mostly adults or gainfully employed persons.

The number of evening-session academic gymnasium students in 1966-

[62] *Tanterv és utasitás a gimnáziumok számára. Oratervek*, op. cit. p. 5.

[63] See p. 25.

[64] Simon and Szarka, op. cit. p. 141 and 189.

[65] *Report on Educational Progress in the 1966–67 Academic Year*, op. cit. p. 28.

Table 23.—Number of secondary schools, teachers, and students, by type of school and by municipality and county: 1966–67[1]

Municipalities and counties	Schools	Teachers	Pupils							
			Total	Academic schools[2]	Vocational schools	Industrial *technikums*	Agricultural *technikums*	Economic *technikums*	Per teacher	Per classroom
1	2	3	4	5	6	7	8	9	10	11
Total	589	12,317	230,299	137,511	49,873	25,685	7,191	10,039	18.7	39.7
Municipalities										
Budapest	126	3,304	57,093	31,410	12,629	9,230	183	3,641	17.3	38.8
Debrecen	15	429	7,387	3,985	1,153	1,495	243	511	17.2	42.0
Miskolc	16	432	9,525	4,802	2,413	1,980	0	330	22.0	48.8
Pécs	13	378	6,545	3,092	1,433	1,743	0	277	17.3	42.0
Szeged	15	352	6,180	2,394	1,284	1,887	322	293	17.6	37.9
Counties										
Baranya	10	179	3,115	2,081	573	0	461	0	17.4	36.2
Bács-Kiskun	35	525	9,777	6,179	2,041	0	1,014	543	18.6	33.3
Békés	31	473	9,549	6,191	2,232	500	434	192	20.2	36.4
Borsod-Abauj-Zemplén	24	435	8,788	6,590	1,317	297	481	103	20.2	40.9
Csongrád	17	302	4,677	2,360	1,564	0	248	505	15.5	34.9
Fejér	20	366	8,371	3,906	2,790	1,399	187	89	22.9	50.7
Győr-Sopron	36	602	11,934	6,489	2,660	1,548	492	745	19.8	40.9
Hajdu-Bihar	10	258	4,185	3,051	1,134	0	0	0	16.2	37.0
Heves	13	318	6,441	4,668	1,634	0	139	0	20.3	38.8
Komárom	19	384	7,570	4,096	1,639	1,374	161	300	19.7	40.5
Nógrád	15	241	4,433	2,598	981	556	159	139	18.4	37.6
Pest	33	532	9,761	6,989	1,414	688	565	105	18.3	46.9
Somogy	17	319	6,550	4,747	1,192	325	158	128	20.5	40.2
Szabolcs-Szatmár	25	579	11,617	8,232	2,087	0	471	827	20.1	40.3
Szolnok	29	589	10,321	6,692	2,515	559	555	0	17.5	37.9
Tolna	16	276	5,242	3,940	745	0	148	409	19.0	37.2
Vas	21	350	7,284	4,549	1,376	552	293	514	20.8	37.2
Veszprém	19	376	8,030	5,162	2,005	549	314	0	21.4	44.6
Zala	14	318	5,924	3,308	1,062	1,003	163	388	18.6	36.3

[1] Data released at beginning of school year. (Pertain only to day session.)

[2] Includes enrollment of art secondary schools.

SOURCE OF DATA: *Statisztikai évkönyv 1966* (Statistical Yearbook 1966). Budapest : Központi Statisztikai Hivatal, 1967. p. 415.

67 was 13,592, or 31.7 percent of all evening-session secondary school students (table 25).

Enrollment in the art gymnasiums remained relatively stable at around 1,300 in the day session—precisely 1,357 in 1966-67, representing 0.4 percent of the entire and 0.6 of the day-session secondary school student body (table 24).

III. VOCATIONAL SECONDARY EDUCATION

Vocational secondary schools *(szakközépiskolák)* and secondary *technikums* offer vocational secondary education at the secondary level.

The Vocational Secondary Schools

According to article 14 of the 1961 basic education law, the vocational secondary schools continue the general education started in elementary school, furthering the students' general culture, socialist outlook, and moral, esthetic, and physical progress; and training them for a particular skill. Since 1965, however, the vocational secondary schools have emphasized training in a group of related skills.[66]

A 4-year institution, the vocational secondary school cooperates with a shop or plant in a particular field in order to bring about the vocational training. After completing the course, a student may take the baccalaureate examination and must take the practical examination in the particular skill which he has learned. The secondary school certificate which the vocational student receives when he has successfully completed the baccalaureate requirements entitles him, on the same basis as the gymnasium graduate, to apply for admission to any higher education institution after passing the usual entrance examinations.

The vocational secondary schools use the physical facilities of the gymnasiums and offer both day and evening courses; the overwhelming number of students attends the day session.

From 1964 through 1967, total enrollment in the secondary vocational school increased from 29,197 to 50,192 (13.3 percent of the total secondary enrollment); the 1966-67 evening enrollment was only 319, or 9.7 percent of the total evening secondary school enrollment (tables 24 and 25.)

In the fall of 1966 the National Council of Education (*Országos Oktatási Tanács*) approved general plans for organizing special 2-year "workers' vocational secondary schools" *(dolgozók szakközépiskolái)*. Envisioned to operate only with evening and correspondence sections, these schools plan to admit mature skilled workers who have graduated from a good vocational school for apprentices and are eager to acquire a baccalaureate diploma or secondary school certificate to improve their economic status or to continue their technical studies. The curriculum may be adjusted to enable them to complete their vocational secondary education in 2 years while working full time.[67]

The 4-year vocational secondary schools, according to long-range plans of the National Council of Education, will be expanded beginning with 1969,[68] when a start will be made in a gradual phaseout of the secondary-level *technikums.*

In comparison with the *technikums'* curriculum, that of the vocational secondary schools provides broader training by placing greater emphasis on classwork in mathematics and the natural and physical sciences. Also, the latter schools concentrate on only 7 trades or skills, whereas the former spread out to cover 80. As the *technikums* close down, their shop, laboratory, and classroom furnishings and equipment will be redistributed among the vocational secondary schools, thus improving even

---

[66] Pál Ilku. "Népünk általános és szakmai műveltségének emeléséért," op. cit. p. 885. For the programs and curriculums of vocational secondary schools see: *Szakközépiskolák 1964/65. tanévi óratervei* (Programs of Vocational Secondary Schools for the 1964-65 Academic Year). *Művelődésügyi Közlöny* (Educational Gazette), Budapest, No. 12, 1964, p. 1-41 (appendix); *Mezőgazdasági szakközépiskolák óratervei* (Programs of Agricultural Secondary Schools), Ibid. p. 45-57; *Közgazdasági és kereskedelmi szakközépiskolák óratervei* (Programs of Economic and Commercial Vocational Secondary Schools), Ibid. p. 59-67; *Ipari és egészségügyi szakközépiskolák 1965-66, tanévi óratervei* (Programs of Industrial and Health Vocational Secondary Schools for the 1965-66 Academic Year). *Művelődésügyi Közlöny*, No. 13, 1965. p. 1-45 (appendix).

[67] Béla Medgyes. "A dologozók szakközépiskoláiról" (Concerning the Workers' Vocational Secondary Schools). *Köznevelés*, XXIII:8:287–89, April 28, 1967.

[68] See p. 82-84.

Table 24.—Number of students in day and evening sessions and correspondence courses of secondary schools and *technikums,* by course: 1960-61 and 1964-65—1966-67; and percent which enrollment in each course constitutes of the entire enrollment in its type of school: 1966-67

Type of school and course	1960–61	1964–65	1965–66	1966–67	Percent of 1966–67 enrollment
	SUMMARY				
Grand total	241,036	417,446	407,485	375,734	100.0
Secondary					
Art	1,432	1,387	1,325	1,357	0.4
Academic gymnasium	139,616	214,097	206,963	188,666	50.2
Vocational	0	29,197	41,562	50,192	13.3
Technikums					
Agricultural	11,248	27,917	27,029	21,481	5.7
Economic	37,824	63,658	54,081	43,482	11.6
Industrial	50,916	81,190	76,525	70,556	18.8
	DAY SESSION				
Total	*155,527*	*231,308*	*236,589*	*230,299*	*100.0*
Secondary					
Art	1,432	1,387	1,325	1,357	0.6
Academic gymnasium	108,258	149,889	146,900	136,154	59.1
Vocational	0	29,124	41,220	49,873	21.7
Technikums					
Agricultural	6,247	7,089	7,348	7,191	3.1
Economic	17,730	17,343	13,461	10,039	4.4
Industrial	21,860	26,476	26,335	25,685	11.1
	EVENING SESSION				
Total	*27,237*	*55,038*	*50,463*	*42,950*	*100.0*
Secondary					
Academic gymnasium	8,368	17,571	15,561	13,592	31.7
Vocational	0	73	342	319	0.7
Technikums					
Economic	6,278	11,877	10,437	8,120	18.9
Industrial	12,591	25,517	24,123	20,919	48.7
	CORRESPONDENCE COURSES				
Total	*58,272*	*131,100*	*120,433*	*102,485*	*100.0*
Secondary					
Academic gymnasium	22,990	46,637	44,502	38,920	38.0
Technikums					
Agricultural	5,001	20,828	19,681	14,290	13.9
Economic	13,816	34,438	30,183	25,323	24.7
Industrial	16,465	29,197	26,067	23,952	23.4

SOURCE OF DATA: *Statisztikai évkönyv 1966* (Statistical Yearbook 1966). Budapest: Központi ; tatisztikai Hivatal, 1967. p. 346.

Table 25.—Number of students in day and evening sessions and correspondence course of secondary schools and *technikums,* by course: 1966–67

Type of school and course	Total	Year of study			
		First	Second	Third	Fourth
	SUMMARY				
Grand total	375,734	101,168	94,929	93,796	85,841
Secondary					
Academic gymnasium [1]	190,023	51,581	46,871	46,683	44,888
Vocational	50,192	15,574	14,627	12,600	7,391
Technikums					
Agricultural	21,481	5,382	5,470	5,484	5,145
Economic	43,482	9,896	9,385	11,645	12,556
Industrial	70,556	18,735	18,576	17,384	15,861
	DAY SESSION				
Total	*230,299*	*60,306*	*59,306*	*57,915*	*52,772*
Secondary					
Academic gymnasium [1]	137,511	34,480	34,830	34,745	33,456
Vocational	49,873	15,459	14,527	12,496	7,391
Technikums					
Agricultural	7,191	2,052	1,846	1,666	1,627
Economic	10,039	1,687	1,608	2,648	4,096
Industrial	25,685	6,628	6,495	6,360	6,202
	EVENING SESSION				
Total	*42,950*	*12,516*	*10,696*	*10,304*	*9,434*
Secondary					
Academic gymnasium	13,592	5,169	3,075	2,739	2,609
Vocational	319	115	100	104	0
Technikums					
Economic	8,120	1,844	2,193	2,127	1,956
Industrial	20,919	5,388	5,328	5,334	4,869
	CORRESPONDENCE COURSES				
Total	*102,485*	*28,346*	*24,927*	*25,577*	*23,635*
Secondary					
Academic gymnasium	38,920	11,932	8,966	9,199	8,823
Technikums					
Agricultural	14,290	3,330	3,624	3,818	3,518
Economic	25,323	6,365	5,584	6,870	6,504
Industrial	23,952	6,719	6,753	5,690	4,790

[1] Also includes enrollment of art secondary gymnasiums.

SOURCE OF DATA: *Statisztikai évkönyv 1966* (Statistical Yearbook 1966). Budapest: Központi Statisztikai Hivatal, 1967. p. 347.

more the latter's potential for quality instruction in 37 rather than 80 trades or skills.[69]

The *Technikums*

During the late 1960's, Hungary had three types of technical-vocational schools or *technikums* in operation: industrial, agricultural, and economic. *Technikums* are 4-year secondary institutions that entitle their graduates who have the technical secondary school certificate to apply for admission into the higher technical institutions in their particular fields of specialization or to hold jobs commensurate with their training. Beginning with 1969, these *technikums* are to be gradually phased out and their functions assumed by the vocational secondary schools.[70]

Industrial Technikums.—The structure and functions of the industrial *technikums (ipari technikumok)* are based on Decree No. 37 of 1955, upheld by article 17 of the 1961 education law. The stated objective of these institutions is to train cultured and patriotic skilled individuals dedicated to advancing the interests of the country and people. Toward this end, these institutions are expected to—

1. Offer intermediate practical and theoretical training in a particular area of industry, with emphasis on the nature and handling of the means of production, the factors determining the production process, and plant maintenance.
2. Provide practical training in all spheres of a particular trade or skill.
3. Assure the advancement of the students' general cultural level.

Admission to industrial *technikums* is normally restricted to graduates of the 8-year elementary ("general") schools who are between 18 and 40 years of age and have had 2 years' experience in industrial production.[71] Besides their regular practical work as part of the curriculum, students completing the first, second, and third years of the *technikum* must spend 4 weeks each summer in production.[72] When they finish the course, *technikum* graduates must work for at least 2 years in the trade or skill for which they were trained.[73]

The industrial *technikums,* originally established in 1950 under Decree No. 40/1950, for the most part used the vocational secondary schools then in operation as a basis for their development.[74]

---

[69] Sándor Vendégh. "Hol tart a szakközépiskola?" (Where Does the Vocational Secondary School Stand?) *Köznevelés*, XXIV:11:407–08, May 24, 1968.

[70] Sándor Vendégh. "Hol tart a szakközépiskola?", op. cit. p. 407.

[71] Decree No. 21/1960. (V.I.) of the Government. *Magyar Közlöny*, No. 4, May 1, 1960. p. 207.

[72] Order No. 30/1959. MM of the Minister of Culture. *Művelődésügyi Közlöny* (Educational Gazette), Budapest, No. 11, 1959. p. 218–19.

[73] Decree No. 14 of 1956 of the Presidential Council of the People's Republic. *Magyar Közlöny*, No. 53, June 23, 1956. p. 309.

[74] At the time of the liberation in 1945, Hungary had 17 industrial secondary schools and 22 intermediate industrial vocational schools, which on September 1, 1945 were placed under the jurisdiction of the Minister of Industry *(Iparügyi Miniszter)*. To advise him, a National Council for Industrial Education *(Országos Iparoktatási Tanács)* was established in 1946. The first reform in this area was made in 1947 with the establishment of the technical secondary school (*műszaki középiskola*), a 4-year institution whose graduates were allowed to enter the corresponding institutions of higher learning. The second major reform followed the nationalization of 1948, which 1 year later resulted in the transformation of the intermediate vocational institutions into gymnasiums—reflecting the ideologically motivated egalitarian tendencies of the time—and their placement under the jurisdiction of the Ministry of Culture. The industrial *technikums* proper, established by Decree No. 40/1950, were placed under the jurisdiction of the corresponding ministries by Decree No. 16/1951. To assist in the development and synchronization of vocational education, the Council of Ministers (Resolution No. 2074/21/1952)

In 1963–64 the industrial *technikums* numbered 67 (table 24).[75] In 1966–67 the 70,556 *technikum* students constituted 18.8 percent of the entire secondary school enrollment (table 25).

Agricultural Technikums.—Decree No. 10 of 1956 of the Presidential Council, upheld by Article 17 of the Education Law of 1961, governs the operation of the agricultural *technikums*. According to article 1 of the 1956 decree, the primary function of these institutions is to train cultured, patriotic, and socially skilled workers for the needs of agriculture. Towards this end, they are to—

1. Provide intermediate practical and theoretical training in specific areas of agriculture, the structure and handling of the means of production, the processes of cultivation, and the maintenance of agricultural crops.
2. Enable the students to acquire the most modern techniques in their fields of specialization.
3. Provide the students with a general cultural background.[76]

Like the industrial *technikums*, the agricultural *technikums* (*Mezőgazdasági technikumok*) are 4-year institutions admitting graduates of 8-year elementary schools who have not reached age 18 by the time they register. (Older persons may enter only the correspondence sections of *technikums*.) Operating under the immediate jurisdiction of the Minister of Agriculture (*Földművelésügyi Miniszter*), the *technikums* are subordinated to the Ministry of Culture with regard to curriculum, examinations, and similar matters. Students completing the course are expected to take a qualifying examination in skill. After passing this examination, they receive a diploma—the "agricultural technical diploma" (*Mezőgazbasági technikusi oklevlé*)—entitling them to be admitted to a higher education institution in the same field of study or to get a job commensurate with their training.

Originally established in 1950,[77] the agricultural *technikums* have undergone a number of structural and curricular reforms.[78] By 1963–64 they numbered 40.[79]

Enrollments reached their height in 1964–65, with 27,917 students. In 1966–67, the enrollment was 21,481 (5.7 percent of total secondary school enrollment) (table 24). Of the 21,481, day students numbered 7,191 (3.1 percent of total secondary day-session enrollment) and correspondence students, 14,290 (13.9 percent of total secondary correspondence enrollment) (table 25).

Economic Technikums.—The structure and functions of economic *technikums* (*közgazdasági technikumok*) are based on Decree No. 38

established a *Technikum* Council (*Technikumi Tanács*) in 1952. Following the curriculum reforms of 1955, which involved mainly a decrease in the number of areas of specialization and an increased emphasis on theoretical studies, Decree No. 37/1955 laid the foundation of the structure of the industrial *technikums* as operating in the late 1960's. Simon and Szarka, op. cit. p. 143–49.

[75] Ibid. p. 151.

[76] "A Népköztársaság Elnöki Tanácsának 1956. évi 10. számú törvényerejű rendelete a mezőgazdasági technikumokról" (Decree No. 10 of 1956 of the Presidential Council of the People's Republic Concerning the Agricultural *Technikums*). *Magyar Közlöny*, No. 42, May 20, 1956. p. 246–48.

[77] Decree No. 246/1950. M.T. of the Council of Ministers.

[78] At the time of the liberation in 1945, Hungary had 23 agricultural secondary schools. They were placed under the jurisdiction of the Minister of Agriculture in the same year; to advise him on educational matters, a Council for Agricultural Vocational Education (*Mezőgazdasági Szakoktatási Tanács*) was established. The reforms instituted after the Nationalization Act of 1948 affected agricultural education similarly as it did industrial vocational education (see footnote 74).

[79] Simon and Szarka, op. cit. p. 163.

of 1955. According to this decree, the primary functions of the *technikums* are to—

1. Provide solid theoretical and economic training for the performance of the duties required by various economic positions in State or public administration and enterprise management.
2. Supply practical training in all areas of interest to economic experts in a specific field of specialization.
3. Provide a general cultural background for the students.

Like the industrial and agricultural *technikums*, the economic ones have dual administration, operating under the immediate jurisdiction of economic ministries or agencies subordinated to the Council of Ministers, but with the Ministry of Culture providing academic guidance. Before they were reorganized in 1955, the economic secondary institutions were subject to the same reform measures that affected all secondary vocational institutions.[80]

During 1963-64, 57 economic *technikums* were operating.[81] Total enrollment reached an all-time high of 63,658 in 1964-65; by 1966-67 it gradually declined to 43,482 (table 24), representing 11.6 percent of the entire secondary school student body. Well over half of these students were registered in correspondence courses, representing 24.7 percent of the students registered in such courses (table 25).

IV. EDUCATION FOR MINORITY NATIONALITIES

One of the first measures adopted by the National Provisional Government in 1945 was to abrogate the discriminatory laws concerning minority nationalities, especially Jews. As a result of the 1919 and 1947 peace treaties, Hungary has emerged as a basically homogeneous country with relatively small minorities of Germans, Jews, Romanians, Serbs, and Slovaks.

Under a 1946 decree,[82] establishing schools for minority nationalities was made dependent on demographic rather than political criteria. According to the decree, the parents or guardians of at least 10 children of compulsory school age have the right to request that they be assigned to a special school for the particular nationality. Besides the regulation concerning compulsory elementary education for children of minority nationalities, measures were also taken to establish special schools at the secondary and higher education levels.

Following the 1948 nationalization of educational establishments, schools for nationalities were also transformed into State institutions, and their rights and privileges were protected by constitutional as well

---

[80] In 1945, Hungary had 58 commercial secondary schools—16 State, 27 communal, 12 denominational, and 3 sponsored by social organizations. In that year, they were placed under the jurisdiction of the Minister of Trade and Transportation (*Kereskedelem-és Közlekedésügyi Miniszter*), who was to be advised in educational matters by a Council on Trade Vocational Education (*Kereskedelmi Szakoktatási Tanács*). In 1949–50 these schools were transformed into economic gymnasiums, and 1 year later, by Decree No. 41/1950, were changed back into economic secondary schools. In 1952 they were converted to economic *technikums* (Decree No. 10/1952). Simon and Szarka, op. cit. p. 152–54.

[81] Simon and Szarka, op. cit. p. 156.

[82] Decree No. 1200/1946. (II.20) VKM of the Ministry of Culture.

as educational-legal provisions.[83] With the change in the political nature of the people's democratic regime, however, these rights in education, like those in other cultural spheres, were to be exercised in accordance with the principle, "national in form, socialist in content." The content of education, consequently, became standardized according to the political objectives of the regime, only the language of instruction being different in the schools for the nationalities.

During the 1963-64 school year, 1.9 percent of elementary pupils attended schools for minority nationalities in which instruction was given in their native language rather than in Hungarian. Many of these children were in 21 elementary schools expressly set up for minority nationalities (8 Serbo-Croatian, 6 Romanian, 6 Slovak, and 1 German). Others were in five Hungarian schools having separate sections for other nationalities—four schools with Romanian sections and one with a German section. In addition, 290 elementary schools taught minority nationality languages. These schools were distributed as follows: [84]

119	German	9	German and Serbo-Croatian
104	Slovak	6	Slovenian
41	Serbo-Croatian		
11	Romanian		

Besides the elementary schools, minority nationalities are served by a few gymnasiums. In 1959 they could attend five such gymnasiums—one each for the German, Romanian, and Serbo-Croatian nationalities, and two for the Slovak. Three Hungarian-language gymnasiums had separate German sections. By 1968, Hungary had seven nationality gymnasiums enrolling 733 students. Of these, 158 attended the German gymnasiums of Baja, Budapest, and Pécs, 96 the Serbo-Croatian gymnasium of Budapest, and 79 the Romanian gymnasium of Gyula.[85] The two Slovakian gymnasiums are located in Békéscsaba and Budapest.

The Jewish community, which before the war had a well-developed network of all types of schools,[86] has been reduced to only two educational institutions. One of these is the National Theological Seminary (*Országos Rabbiképző Intézet*) of Budapest—the only institution of this type in the entire Communist world—with a 1967-68 enrollment of 14 students, including two from Czechoslovakia and one from East Germany.[87] The other is a coeducational secondary school, also in Budapest, with a total 1967-68 enrollment of about 80. The language of instruction

[83] Paragraph 3 of Article 49 of the Constitution of August 20, 1949, for example, states: "The Hungarian People's Republic insures to all nationalities living within its borders the possibility of education in their native tongue and the possibility of developing their national culture." *Constitution of the Hungarian People's Republic.* Budapest: Athenaeum, 1949, 20 p. The basic elements of these provisions were also included in paragraph 2, article 2, of the fundamental education act of 1961 cited above. In addition, each major education decree or law contains provisions to this effect.

[84] Simon and Szarka, op. cit. p. 126.

[85] Aurél Hencz. *A művelődési intézmények és a művelődésigazgatás fejlődése, 1945–1961* (The Evolution of Educational Institutions and Administration, 1945–1961). Budapest: Közgazdasági és Jogi Könyvkiadó, 1962. p. 98; László Kővágó. "Népköztársaságunk nemzetiségi politikájáról" (On the Nationality Policy of Our People's Republic). *Társadalmi Szemle* (Social Review), Budapest. XXIII:11:29–38, November 1968.

[86] For a detailed account of the Jewish educational system in Hungary before 1948, see Aron Moskovits. *Jewish Education in Hungary (1848–1948).* New York: Bloch Publishing Company *for* The Dropsie College for Hebrew and Cognate Learning, 1964. 357 p. For material on Jewish education in Transylvania (under Hungarian jurisdiction until 1918; the northern half of it between 1940 and 1944), see Moshe Carmilly-Weinberger- "Jewish Education in Transylvania in the Days of the Holocaust." *Yad Vashem Bulletin*, Jerusalem, No. 21, November 1967. p. 3–8.

[87] Henry Kamm. "Hungary's Jews Live in Comfort." *The New York Times*, May 2, 1968.

is Hungarian, with the curriculum also including Hebrew and Jewish subjects. Once the seat of world-renowned *Yeshivas* and *Talmud Torahs*,[88] Hungary now has only a few small community-organized and community-maintained educational establishments for religious instruction, with a total registration of about 500.[89] Most of these are also located in Budapest, which contains the overwhelming majority of the 80,000 to 100,000 Jews in Hungary.

To assure a supply of teachers for the nationality schools, some higher education institutions, including teacher-training institutes and universities, have established special sections or departments. Thus, kindergarten and elementary teachers for the Serbo-Croatian schools are trained in two teacher-training institutes: the Teachers College of Pécs,[90] and the department of education at Eötvös Loránd University of Budapest.[91] The latter also has a Slavic Philological Institute *(Szláv Filológiai Intézet)* serving Serbo-Croatian cultural interests.

The Romanian schools draw their teaching staffs primarily from the graduates of two teacher-training institutes that offer specialization in Romanian and from the Teachers College of Szeged, which has a department of Romanian studies. Students interested in Romanian studies can also avail themselves of the facilities of the Romanian Philological Institute *(Román Filológiai Intézet)* of Eötvös Loránd University.

The German minority schools have a relatively easier recruitment task, since every university offers specialized training in German language and literature. In addition, two teacher-training institutes provide a special German curriculum.

The Slovak minority schools draw their teachers from two teacher-training institutes and from the Teachers College of Szeged, which offers specialization in Slovak studies. The Slovak schools are also assisted by the Slovak Philological Institute *(Szlovák Filológiai Intézet)* of the Eötvös Loránd University.[92]

Health and Health Services

Hungarian educational authorities pay considerable attention to protecting children's health. Although supervision over health matters for both students and employees of the educational system is entrusted to State, district, or school physicians and subordinate auxiliary personnel, primary responsibility for organizing the system of health services lies with the school principal and his assistant. They must provide space for a school infirmary and waiting room, place first-aid kits in all areas where accidents might occur (such as shops, gymnasiums, and laboratories), and see that posters calling attention to possible dangers are displayed in all areas where they might be useful.

---

[88] The *Yeshiva* is an institution offering Jewish talmudic subjects at advanced level. The *Talmud Torah* (Study of the Law) is a community-maintained Jewish school employing one or several teachers for the instruction of religious subjects, normally at a lower level.

[89] Henry Kamm. "Hungary's Jews Live in Comfort," op. cit.

[90] For material on the teachers' colleges, see p. 149-50.

[91] See p. 111-12.

[92] Aurél Hencz. *A művelődési intézmények és a művelődésigazgatás fejlődése*, op. cit. p. 98–99. See also *Tájekoztató a magyar felsőoktatási intézményekről, 1965* (Guide to the Hungarian Institutions of Higher Learning, 1965). Budapest: A Művelődésügyi Minisztérium Kiadványa, 1965. p. 75–81, 85–89.

Under a yearly plan, which must be ready by August 31, health measures are carried out jointly by the school physician and the principal. School employees must have yearly health check-ups; pupils are expected to report regularly for general, eye, dental, and other checkups as required. Special measures are also taken to prevent the spread of infectious diseases. Special classes in the elementary schools teach traffic safety, emphasizing rules affecting pedestrians and cyclists.[93] Official school regulations provide detailed instructions as to what teachers and others in the school system must do in case of an accident.[94]

Employment and Further Education of Graduates

In pursuing the dual aim of preparing technically well-trained and politically reliable individuals, Hungarian educational authorities, in conjunction with the mass organizations, especially trade union and youth associations, have taken a series of measures to guide elementary and secondary school graduates in selecting their careers. A primary objective is to direct elementary school graduates toward the agricultural and industrial vocational schools or the technical schools; and to provide adequate job opportunities for those who are unwilling or unable to continue formal education.[95]

Only about one-third of the elementary school graduates enter secondary school (table 22) and even fewer actually graduate. About half of the secondary students are in academic ("general") gymnasiums (table 24), and most of the students in those gymnasiums are from an intellectual social background.[96] About half of the secondary school students view secondary education as a stepping stone towards entering a higher education institution and through it eventually getting a non-manual desk job (table 26). As a result of a nationwide survey covering 98.6 percent of third-year secondary school students, the University Computation Center (*Egyetemi Számitóközpont*), in a study prepared for the Ministry of Culture, concluded that of the approximately 55,000 secondary school graduates in 1968, a total of 26,443 (table 27), including 18,129 gymnasium graduates, intended to pursue their studies in institutions of higher education.[97]

---

[93] Report on Educational Progress in the 1966/67 Academic Year, op. cit. p. 33.

[94] *Rendtartás az általános iskolák és a gimnáziumok számára*, op. cit. p. 91–97.

[95] "A Magyar Forradalmi Munkás-Paraszt Kormány 1.024/1959. (VII.19.) számú határozata az iskoláit végző fiatalkorúak munkábaállításáról" (Resolution No. 1,024/1959. (VII.19.) of the Hungarian Revolutionary Worker-Peasant Government Concerning the Employment of Minors, Graduates of School). *Magyar Közlöny*, No. 77, July 19, 1959. p. 640–41.

The career guidance system was formalized in December 1961, when the government called for the establishment of a Career Guidance Council (*Pályaválasztási Tanács*) operating under the general direction of the Ministry of Labor, the Ministry of Culture, and the National Planning Office. "A Magyar Forradalmi Munkás-Paraszt Kormány 1.027/1961. (XII.30.) számú határozata az ifjuság pályaválasztási tanácsadásról" (Resolution No. 1,027/1961. (XII.30.) of the Hungarian Revolutionary Worker-Peasant Government Concerning the Career Guidance of Youth). *Magyar Közlöny*, No. 101, December 30, 1961. p. 1,032.

[96] See p. 75. In regard to children of manual workers, the situation of Hajdú-Bihar county and its county seat Debrecen is illustrative. Of 2,858 first-year secondary school students in 1966-67, a total of 56.2 percent were such children. In the Debrecen gymnasiums, however, the percent was only 37.4.

In regard to children with a peasant background, they numbered only 105 of the Debrecen gymnasiums' 910 students, and only 266 of the Hajdú-Bihar county gymnasium's 738 students. By contrast, peasants constituted 42.7 percent of the county population. József Bényei. "Falusi gyerekek a középiskolában" (Peasant Children in Secondary Schools). *Köznevelés*, XXIII:3:85–86, February 10, 1967.

[97] Ferenc Vati Papp. "Középiskolások—válaszút előtt" (Secondary School Students—At the Crossroads). *Köznevelés*, XXIV:3:85–87, February 9, 1968.

The aspirations of many of these students to attend a higher education institution are bound to be frustrated, since the fall 1968 admission quota was established at 8,000 day-session students. Of these, from 3,800 to 4,300 were expected to be assigned to persons who had acquired their secondary-school certificate or baccalaureate diploma at an earlier date. Thus, for the nation as a whole, the number of applicants is about three times as large as the number of places. Even more frustrating to the applicants is the fact that many of them have received high grades in secondary school. Of 26,443 applying for admission to higher education in 1968, a total of 14,500 received grades of Excellent, Very Good, or Good.

Table 26.—Percent of 3d-year secondary school students indicating certain career objectives, by type of secondary school: 1968

Career objective	All secondary schools	Gymnasiums	Vocational schools	*Technikums*
Continue studies	*70.8*	*88.1*	*42.7*	*48.8*
Higher education	47.9	55.3	31.2	44.0
School for skilled workers	9.0	12.3	6.1	2.0
Other education	13.9	20.5	5.4	2.8
Seek employment	*26.0*	*9.1*	*53.1*	*47.6*
Unwilling to study or work; or undecided	*3.2*	*2.8*	*4.2*	*3.6*

SOURCE OF DATA: Ferenc Vati Papp. "Középiskolások—válaszút előtt" (Secondary School Students—At the Crossroads). *Köznevelés* (Public Education), XXIV:3:86, February 9, 1968. Budapest.

The ratio between applicants and vacancies varies from field to field. For example, in the School of Philosophy at Eötvös Loránd University applications for the Hungarian-foreign language specialization are 600 percent larger than the available number of places; for the history-foreign language specialization, 800 percent; and for the psychology-biology specialization, 3,200 percent. The situation is similar in most nontechnical areas of specialization and in teacher-training institutes and colleges. In some highly technical fields, on the other hand, things are different: for example, the power mechanics specialization at the Polytechnical University of Budapest received only 52 applications for 73 places, and the chemical mechanics specialization field showed a 54-percent ratio of applications to available places.[98]

The white-collar aspirations of secondary school students are also clearly indicated in their applications for admission to schools for training skilled workers that admit only students who hold a secondary school certificate.

For fall 1968, the schools for skilled workers established an admission quota of 8,000; however, only about 5,000 secondary school students applied. About 4,000 of these were gymnasium students. Another basic problem of the schools for skilled workers is an imbalance in the number of applications among the various skills, which obviously have varying prestige values in the minds of young people. For example, while the number of applicants for electrical mechanics was 1,552 and for engine mechanics 679, foundry workers and smiths recruited only 4 applicants each and welding only 3. A new trend, however, is seen in

[98] Ibid. p. 85–86.

Table 27.—Number and percent of 3d-year secondary students indicating certain career objectives; percent of these students who are girls and percent whose parents are manual workers: 1968

Item	Total	Will continue study				Will seek employment	Unwilling to work	Undecided
		Total	Higher education	School for skilled worlers	Other education			
Total	55,252	39,104	26,443	4,997	7,664	14,384	109	1,655
Girls	31,576	22,290	13,800	1,702	6,788	8,147	104	1,035
Children of manual workers	31,483	21,197	12,622	3,412	5,163	9,180	70	1,036
	PERCENT							
Total	*100.0*	*70.8*	*47.9*	*9.6*	*13.9*	*26.0*	*0.2*	*3.0*
Girls	100.0	70.6	43.7	5.4	21.5	25.8	0.3	3.3
Children of manual workers	100.0	67.4	40.1	10.8	16.5	29.1	0.2	3.3

SOURCE OF DATA: Ferenc Vati Papp. "Középiskolások—válaszút előtt" (Secondary School Students—At the Crossroads). *Köznevelés* (Public Education), XXIV: 3:86, February 9, 1968.

the number of admissions from applicants who have attended secondary vocational schools and *technikums*. In 1966 only 230 graduates of such schools were admitted; according to plans, about 1,000 were to be admitted in 1968.

A concern of the planning authorities is revealed by figures relating to secondary school graduates seeking employment. In 1968, as opposed to the 39,104 students (70.8 percent) who wanted to pursue further studies, only 14,384 (26 percent) expressed a desire to seek employment (tables 26 and 27). Approximately 60 percent of the 14,384, wanted to find white-collar employment. But only about 20 to 25 percent of the projected new jobs in the national economy each year are white-collar jobs, and, as in the past, most of them will be filled by graduates of higher education institutions.[99]

On the basis of their studies, the Hungarian educational authorities have started a campaign for intensified vocational guidance in the secondary schools that will direct all but the most highly gifted students into training in areas of great importance for the national economy.[100]

---

[99] Ibid. p. 86–87.

[100] For further details on Hungary's school guidance system, see *Report on Educational Progress in 1965-66 Presented at the XXIXth Session of the International Conference on Public Education in Geneva,* July 1966. p. 20–23.

VI. Vocational and Technical Education

Evolution and Scope

Although the network of vocational schools in prewar Hungary was relatively well developed, it probably represented the weakest link in the pre-Communist educational system. The shortcomings of vocational education were not so much quantitative as qualitative. The number of agricultural, industrial, and commercial lower and intermediate vocatonal institutions was relatively high. The institutions were considerably diversified, offering training in a variety of occupations. For example, special agricultural institutions offered training in agriculture, dairying, forestry, viniculture, and viticulture. In 1941-42, the industrial schools for apprentices provided vocational training in a multitude of fields for 98,782 students.[1]

From the qualitative point of view, however, the vocational secondary schools were rather inferior, lagging considerably behind the academic secondary schools. The qualitative difference between these schools were recognized and accepted, whether consciously or inadvertently, by both official educational policy and public opinion.[2] Aside from neglecting theoretical aspects of the sciences and humanities, the schools for apprentices, for example, offered primarily rudimentary practical shop training of interest to small-scale industry or artisans, neglecting the requirements of both modern industrial technology and general education. The commercial vocational schools, on the other hand, had a student population basically geared to the pursuit of routine white-collar bureaucratic jobs as accountants, bookkeepers, or salespersons, with little or no knowledge of the world of banking and finance.

After World War II (especially following the political transformation of Hungary along "socialist" lines in 1947), vocational-technical education experienced a development unmatched in the prewar era. The nationalization of banking, industry, and transportation, the gradual collectivization of agriculture, and the subsequent introduction of centralized planning required a swift and successful solution to the problem of producing a professionally competent and politically reliable pool of skilled or semiskilled manpower. The new regime was consequently compelled by its political and economic objectives to pay ever-greater

[1] See p. 15.

[2] This was true in spite of the fact that Law No. XIII of 1938 stipulated that the vocational secondary schools were coequal with the gymnasiums. See, for example, Gyula Simon *and* József Szarka. *A magyar népi demokrácia nevelésügyének története* (History of the Educational System of the Hungarian People's Republic). Budapest: Tankönyvkiadó, 1965. p. 142.

attention to the development and expansion of vocational-technical education. Consequently in Hungary (as in the other peoples and socialist democracies), vocational education has emerged to a large extent as training for a specific job or function in industry or agriculture, with the educational programs (including their curriculums, syllabuses, and enrollment quotas) reflecting the various and constantly changing occupational needs of the country as determined by the upper echelons of the Party and Government.

The scope of vocational education was defined in Article 9 of the fundamental education act of 1961.[3] Accordingly, the primary function of the agricultural, commercial, forestry, industrial, and transportation vocational schools is to provide training for their students in a particular trade or profession, hand-in-hand with strengthening the basic education and the ideological and moral concepts which the students acquired in the elementary schools.

Structure

Vocational-technical education in the Hungarian People's Republic is offered at three clearly differentiated levels: lower vocational schools for apprentices, intermediate or vocational secondary schools, and higher vocational-technical schools.[4]

The prewar structure of vocational schools for apprentices *(tanonciskolák)* remained in effect until 1949, when under the general provisions of Law No. IV it was incorporated as a link in the general system of education. Identified officially since 1961 as "schools for skilled workers" *(szakiskolák)*, these institutions are basically of three types: industrial (*ipari*), agricultural (*mezőgazdasági*), and commercial (*kereskedelmi*).

Industrial Vocational Schools for Apprentices

The industrial institutions for apprentices (*iparitanuló-intézetek*) were originally under the jurisdiction of the Minister of Culture.[5] In 1945, by a decision of the Provisional Government they were placed under the direction of the Minister of Industry *(Iparügyi Miniszter)* under the immediate control of the National Manpower Office *(Országos Munkaerőgazdálkodási Hivatal*). Following the adoption of Law No. IV of 1949, which specified unified direction of vocational schools, the industrial institutions for apprentices were placed under the direction of the Office of Manpower Reserves (*Munkaerőtartalékok Hivatala*). In 1916, the Office assumed responsibility for maintaining and directing apprentice institutions that belonged to or served the interests of co-operative enterprises, local industry, and small private industrial enterprises.

[3] "1961. évi III. törvény a Magyar Népköztársaság oktatási rendszeréről" (Law No. III of 1961 Concerning the Educational System of the Hungarian People's Republic). *Magyar Közlöny* (Hungarian Gazette), Budapest, No. 74, October 17, 1961. p. 567.

[4] This chapter deals exclusively with the various types of lower and higher vocational schools. See p. 78-84 for intermediate vocational education.

[5] See footnote 37, chapter III.

After the Office of Manpower Reserves was dissolved in the late 1950's the Ministry of Labor (*Munkaügyi Minisztérium*) assumed jurisdiction over most of the vocational schools.[6] Some of the schools that were organized within the framework of factories came under the jurisdiction of the ministry exercising control over the particular factory. In addition, certain vocational institutions for apprentices operated under the immediate control of appropriate sections of the executive committees of local, district, or county people's councils.[7]

The admission of students into the various programs for training skilled workers is based on age, education aptitude, and medical status. Theoretically, the industrial schools for apprentices admit only graduates of the 8-year elementary school between the ages of 14 and 17. Exception is made for secondary school graduates who have the baccalaureate (*érettségi*) diploma: they may be admitted up to age 25. Training lasts from 1 to 3 years, depending upon the skill to be learned; for secondary school graduates it is reduced to 1 to 2 years.

The curriculum provides for both theoretical and practical training, coupled with some subjects of general education depending upon the particular skill pursued. In vocational training as such, the curriculum generally provides a 4:1 ratio in favor of the practical over the theoretical. The last year is devoted entirely to practical work in the factories or plants.

The practical part of the training consists of four differentiated phases: introductory, basic, transition to independent work, and work in production. During the first three phases there is a close relation between the theoretical and practical aspects, with theoretical instruction on any topic presumably given 1 week before the corresponding practice. During the first two phases, the practical part of the training takes place in school shops (or in special workshops attached to the large plants), where students work in groups of 6 to 15; in the last two phases, usually during the second or third year of the 3-year program, the practical training is given on either individual or a collective basis in the workshops of the large plants. During the first 2 years practical training takes up 4 days each week and theoretical studies 2 days (13 class hours). Third-year students and students holding baccalaureate diplomas from secondary schools spend 5 days a week on practical training and only one on theoretical work.[8]

The students are employed by factories or plants as apprentices, under conditions specified by law. The laws relating to this field of education specify the conditions for contracting apprentices, employer

---

[6] Aurél Hencz. *A művelődési intézmények és a művelődésigazgatás fejlődése, 1945-1961* (The Evolution of Educational Institutions and Administration, 1945-1961). Budapest: Közgazdasági és Jogi Könyvkiadó, 1962. p. 73-74.

[7] During the 1958-59 school year, for example, 39,218 of the 101,561 lower-vocational school students were working in institutions controlled by the Ministry of Labor; 44,352 in the local industries or cooperatives under the control of the people's councils; and 17,991 in establishments of factories controlled by a variety of economic ministries. UNESCO. *World Survey of Education—III: Secondary Education*. Paris, 1961. p. 636.

[8] Graduates of secondary schools holding the baccalaureate or equivalent degree and registered in the vocational schools for the acquisition of a skill are known as "technical students" (*műszaki tanuló*). The scope and length of their training is specified in Government Resolution No. 1,002/1956. (I.7.). *Magyar Közlöny*, No. 2, January 7, 1956, p. 13-15. See also Ferenc Abent, "A Magyar Népköztársaság közoktatásügye" (The Public Educational System of the Hungarian People's Republic). *In*: *A közoktatásügy Európa szocialista országaiban* (Public Education in the Socialist Countries of Europe). Budapest: Tankönyvkiadó *for the* Országos Pedagógiai Intézet, 1965. p. 298.

and apprentice responsibilities, hours and wages, apprentice benefits, and conditions for terminating their contracts.[9]

Depending on the progress of their studies, apprentices are paid either by the hour or by the amount of their production. In 1964, for example, the hourly rate ranged from 0.45 to 2.70 forints.[10] Students are also supplied with textbooks, work-clothes, and meals for a nominal fee. In 1964, approximately 15.9 percent of the students lived in special dormitories, where they paid from 20 to 120 forints monthly for room and board, depending on their year of study.

The admission quotas of the industrial schools for apprentices are determined on the basis of skilled-labor requirements of the various enterprises. The skills in which these schools offer training are listed in the National Register for Training Skilled Workers (*Országos Szakmunkásképzési Jegyzék*). In 1964 the Register listed 293 separate skills.[11]

When they finish their course, students take the skilled-worker examination (*szakmunkásvizsga*) that tests both their theoretical and practical knowledge. Students who pass this examination before a State-appointed committee are given a skilled-worker certificate (*szakmunkásbizonyitvány*).[12]

Normally in a given school year, training will not be offered in all the Register-listed skills, for usually a labor shortage does not exist in all skills at any one time. Skills in very short supply at a given time, however, may offer retraining and upgrading courses for older workers at the discretion and under the supervision of enterprise managers.[13]

The vocational schools for apprentices are terminal. However, students interested in continuing their education may enter the evening or correspondence sections of secondary schools and after 2 years earn a secondary school certificate or baccalaureate diploma.

Agricultural Vocational Schools

With the land collectivized, the cooperative system expanded, and agriculture increasingly mechanized and specialized, the need for a greater number of educated and skilled farm workers has grown tremendously in recent years. The program adopted by the Hungarian regime to satisfy the skilled-manpower needs of agriculture, forestry, and other related fields involved a two-pronged approach: training new cadres seeking a career in agriculture and retraining older workers in new techniques.

The lower vocational agricultural schools were first systematically

[9] See, for example, "A város-és községgazdálkodási miniszter, a földművelésügyi miniszter és az állami gazdaságok minisztere 1/1956. (VII.24.) V.K.G.M. számú rendelete a helyiipari tanulóképzésről" (Decree No. 1/1956. (VII.24.) V.K.G.M. of the Minister of Urban and Village Affairs, the Minister of Agriculture and the Minister of State Farms Concerning the Training of Local Industry Apprentices). *Magyar Közlöny*, No. 63, July 24, 1956. p. 389-95.

[10] The official exchange rate in 1964 was 11.74 forints to the U.S. dollar. (See footnote 54, chapter III.)

[11] Ferenc Ábent. "A Magyar Népköztársaság közoktatásügye," op. cit. p. 298-99.

[12] The procedural details of the skilled workers' examination were outlined in Decree No. 2/1959. (IV.10.) Mü.M. of the Minister of Culture.

[13] See, for example, Resolution No. 1,043/1956. (V.30.) concerning the organization of retraining and upgrading courses for industrial workers in *Magyar Közlöny*, No. 41, May 30, 1956. p. 273-74; or Decree No. 6/1959 (X.24.)Eü.M. of the Minister of Health for the organization of a course for dental technicians in *Magyar Közlöny*, No. 104, October 24, 1959. p. 892-94.

organized in 1958, when Law No. IV of 1949 relating to the industrial schools for apprentices was taken as a model for the agricultural schools' structure and functions. After the Hungarian educational system was reorganized in 1961, the agricultural vocational schools were also revamped. In the late 1960's they continued to operate on the basis of a 1965 decree.[14]

From the structural point of view, the agricultural vocational schools (*mezőgazdasági szakmunkástanuló iskolák*) reflect the jurisdictional competence of the ministries or agencies exercising direct control over them. Consequently, in the sphere of agriculture proper, schools can be organized only by the Ministry of Agriculture or by the corresponding section of the executive committee of the county people's council, with the concurrence of the Ministry. The National Association of Cooperatives (*Szövetkezetek Országos Szövetsége*) has the exclusive responsibility for establishing and dissolving apicultural schools; the National Forestry Directorate (*Országos Erdészeti Főigazgatóság*), for establishing and dissolving forestry schools.

The organization of schools or courses for further training or for retraining of workers is the exclusive responsibility of the people's councils acting in cooperation with the interested or affected cooperatives or collectives.

The admission procedures and the employment conditions are basically similar to those of the industrial schools for apprentices. The length of the course varies from 2 to 3 years, depending on the requirements of the skill as specified in the National Register for Training Skilled Workers. The course involves both theoretical and practical training, the former normally offered during the winter months. The practical part of the course is offered within the framework of the agricultural, forestry, or related enterprise with which the students enter into a formal contractual employment arrangement whose details are regulated by law.[15]

Upon completing certain examinations, graduates of the agricultural vocational schools may continue their training in the correspondence sections of the agricultural *technikums*.[16]

Commercial Vocational Schools

Law No. IV of 1949 provided for the establishment of commercial or merchant (salesperson) training schools (*kereskedőképző iskolák*). Normally, these schools are 2-year institutions preparing socialist salespersons. Their importance and number have consistently declined as their role in the teaching of more technical economic subjects has been taken over by the intermediate and higher economic *technikums*.[17]

[14] "A földművelésügyi miniszter és a munkaügyi miniszter 1/1965. (II.21.) FM-MüM számú együttes rendelete a mező-és erdőgazdasági szakmunkás és betanitott munkás képzésről" (Joint Decree No. 1/1965. (II.21.) FM-Mü.M of the Minister of Agriculture and the Minister of Labor Concerning Further Training of Forestry and Agricultural Skilled Workers and the Further Training of Workers). *Magyar Közlöny*, Budapest, No. 13, February 21, 1965. p. 145-46.

[15] Ibid.

[16] Ferenc Ábent. "A Magyar Népköztársaság közoktatásügye," op. cit. p. 301. For information on the agricultural *technikums*, see p. 83.

[17] See p. 83-84.

Besides these schools for training socialist salespersons, there are schools for training stenographers, typists, and office workers (*Gépíró-, gyorsíró- és irodakezelői szakiskolák*). Graduates of such schools who wish to become qualified for better paying jobs may take a special examination before the National Committee for Examining Steno-Typists (*Gyorsírókat és Gépírókat Vizsgáztató Orszgágos Bizottság*).[18]

Enrollment

Of the 183,599 vocational-school students in 1966-67 (table 29), a total of 91,639 were trained in large-scale enterprises under the direction of the Ministry of Labor, 49,746 in local industrial establishments (of these, 14,363 in small private units), and 42,214 in enterprises operating under the jurisdiction of various economic ministries.[19] The 11,114 students in the commercial vocational schools specialized in salesmanship for various kinds of endeavors. Of these, 3,011 were acquiring skills for selling food products.[20]

The 20,829 agricultural vocational students in 1966-67 were distributed among 16 different vocations. In descending order of enrollment, the distribution was as follows:

5,527	agricultural mechanics	859	irrigation mechanics
3,929	vegetable production mechanics	847	flower growing
2,260	vegetable production	203	sheep raising
1,057	pomiculture	158	forestry
1,643	poultry farming	156	pig farming
1,177	cattle raising	83	fishing
1,088	agricultural blacksmithing	44	apiculture
869	viticulture	29	hunting[21]

The industrial vocational schools in 1966-67 had 151,656 students in 30 different trades.[22] That same year the schools for steno-typists, with 12,420 students (mostly girls), experienced an enrollment decline of 0.4 percent from their 1965-66 total.[23]

Higher *Technikums* and Higher Technical Schools

Established in the early 1960's, the higher *technikums* (*felsőfokú technikumok*) and the higher technical schools (*felsőfokú szakiskolák*) are identified as "new types" of higher education institutions "dedicated to training technicians who will be highly skilled and equipped with the most advanced theoretical and practical knowledge to serve the various

[18] Aurél Hencz. *A művelődési intézmények és a művelődésigazgatás fejlődése, 1945–1961*, op. cit. p. 71.
[19] *Statisztikai évkönyv 1966* (Statistical Yearbook 1966). Budapest: Központi Statisztikai Hivatal, 1967. p. 354.
[20] Ibid. p. 357.
[21] Ibid.
[22] For details on enrollment in the various branches of the 30 industrial vocational fields, see Ibid. p. 355-57.
[23] *Report on Educational Progress in the 1966/67 Academic Year Presented at the XXXth Session of the International Conference on Public Education, Geneva, July 1967.* [Budapest, 1967] p. 26.

Table 28.—Number of vocational schools, student homes, and teachers: 1960–61—1966–67[1]

School year	Schools	Branch schools	Student homes	Teachers in—		
				Classrooms	Student homes	School shops
1960–61	212	121	140	1,582	[3] 474	3,472
1961–62	215	113	157	1,647	[3] 536	3,682
1962–63	232	119	[2] 202	1,788	[3] 559	3,966
1963–64	224	112	[2] 206	2,006	356	[4] 5,100
1964–65	229	97	[2] 208	2,248	380	[4] 5,642
1965–66	259	95	164	2,446	379	4,713
1966–67	254	95	159	2,442	393	4,404

[1] Data released at beginning of school year.

[2] Forty of the homes were located at the agricultural and construction sites.

[3] Includes the workers entrusted with supervision of vocational school students at the sites.

[4] Includes shop or plant instructors.

SOURCE OF DATA: *Statisztikai évkönyv 1966* (Statistical Yearbook 1966). Budapest: Központi Statisztikai Hivatal, 1967. p. 354.

branches of industry, construction, transportation, agriculture, trade, and public health." [24]

Cooperating with appropriate factories, shops, and scientific organizations, these institutions are directed by the ministries having immediate jurisdiction over them and by the Ministry of Culture, each exercising its legally assigned responsibilities.[25]

The *technikum* or technical school on this higher level has a director and is staffed by ideologically and professionally competent instructors who hold a university degree. Its day session offers 2- to 3-year courses. Its evening session and correspondence sections require at least 6 months longer.

It is important to distinguish higher *technikums* as postsecondary specialized schools rather than higher educational institutions. Unlike higher educational institutions, which normally require 12 years of elementary-secondary academic schooling, higher *technikums* admit applicants with less formal training: students who have completed 8 years of general school and 3 years of industrial school for apprentices and workers who are skilled in some specialty and who hold "skilled-worker certificates" (*szakmunkás bizonyitvány*). Such students and workers would not have sufficient academic background to be admitted to regular higher education institutions. Graduates from higher *technikums* may apply for admission to undergraduate, regular higher education institutions, where they may or may not be given advanced credit, depending upon how the specific program is related to their academic and training background. In essence, higher *technikums* are postsecondary schools training skilled technicians, as distinguished from polytechnical universities, which are higher educational institutions training engineers.

The age limit for admission is 35 for the day session and 45 for the evening session and correspondence sections.

[24] "A Magyar Forradalmi Munkás-Paraszt Kormány 12/1962. (V.5.) számú rendelete a felsőfokú technikumokról" (Decree No. 12/1962. (V.5.) of the Hungarian Revolutionary Worker–Peasant Government Concerning the Higher *Technikums*). *Magyar Közlöny*, No. 30, May 5, 1962, p. 264-67. See also Articles 18 and 20 of Law No. III of 1961 cited above.

[25] See p. 30-31, 33.

Table 29.—Number of students in vocational schools, by trade: 1960–66, 1965–66, and 1966–67; and number under miscellaneous categories, by trade: 1966–67[1]

Trade	1960–61	1965–66	1966–67	Miscellaneous categories, 1966–67					
				In first year	Girls	High school graduates	Living in homes	Trained in— School shop	Trained in— Plant shop
Total	125,343	172,383	183,599	75,483	40,343	11,348	25,513	15,868	40,670
Agriculture	7,590	20,382	20,829	8,318	6,321	47	8,397	4,503	4,518
Automechanics	4,056	6,546	7,594	3,064	1	587	87	438	1,549
Blacksmith	1,750	1,181	1,306	562	0	0	549	145	372
Chemical, rubber and synthetics	418	1,905	2,216	992	840	147	619	502	744
Clothing	5,727	4,942	6,518	3,220	5,938	217	12	306	740
Construction materials	650	440	489	218	240	139	21	0	73
Construction mechanics	540	1,404	1,355	442	0	22	769	348	335
Draftsmanship	0	14	0	0	0	0	0	0	0
Electrician	7,409	11,378	12,118	4,695	483	543	562	215	3,296
Electro-technician	3,081	5,594	5,983	2,635	920	4,034	93	229	1,183
Food industry	1,716	2,017	2,338	1,111	963	109	512	492	459
Fur and leather	3,435	3,518	4,034	1,644	2,240	95	159	438	1,163
General construction	3,555	6,191	6,663	2,761	25	31	2,904	0	957
Iron and metal industry	721	959	881	420	293	122	164	25	206
Locksmith	20,437	28,314	29,628	11,595	76	606	1,377	3,883	7,527
Lumber industry	6,987	5,049	5,297	2,140	32	90	221	130	747
Masonry	9,961	10,730	11,481	4,397	1	28	3,285	0	954
Mechanic technician	2,974	4,929	5,471	2,287	1,253	1,605	44	500	1,214
Metal cutting	9,548	12,603	13,339	5,283	1,007	264	553	2,571	3,643
Metallurgy	1,222	869	820	286	16	1	500	151	147
Mining	4,546	3,621	3,016	1,030	0	0	2,086	193	1,624
Painting	3,886	6,148	6,315	2,234	12	16	736	0	270
Paper industry	169	312	259	94	72	1	50	0	76
Pattern-making	367	296	297	112	1	9	24	51	52
Plumbing	1,982	4,676	5,340	2,256	0	49	1,035	143	1,163
Polishing	727	702	773	471	32	7	56	14	94
Printing	1,533	1,747	1,567	482	587	361	8	143	0
Restaurant work	3,214	5,663	5,956	2,267	2,835	759	154	196	2,379
Small handicrafts	5,810	5,771	6,376	2,805	4,544	857	6	21	80
Textiles	1,405	2,611	2,909	2,663	2,793	12	0	0	1,068
Trade (Sales)	9,062	10,649	11,114	4,213	8,771	587	371	193	3,525
Welding	865	1,222	1,317	786	47	3	159	38	512

[1] Data released at beginning of school year.

SOURCE OF DATA: *Statisztikai évkönyv 1966* (Statistical Yearbook 1966). Budapest: Központi Statisztikai Hivatal, 1967. p. 354.

Students who successfully complete the course and pass the State examination are entitled to a "skilled technician diploma" (*szaktechnikusi oklevél*), if they graduated from a *technikum;* or to a "technical school diploma" (*szakiskolai oklevél*), if they graduated from a higher technical school. Graduates of these two types of institutions may, within 10 years of their graduation, pursue their specialty by registering in the correspondence courses of a university. They must complete those courses in not fewer than four and not more than 10 semesters. If they do so and if they pass the State examination and meet the dissertation requirements they are entitled to a university degree equal to that awarded to full-time day-session university students.[26]

Two types of *technikums*—industrial (*ipari*) and agricultural (*mezőgazdasági*) —train skilled technicians for various branches of industry and agriculture. The higher technical schools primarily train account-

[26] *Tájékoztató a magyar felsőoktatási intézményekről 1965*, op. cit. p. 65. See also p. 66-75 concerning the *technikums* and higher technical schools.

ing and finance specialists for finance and banking organizations and domestic and foreign trade institutions and enterprises (table 30).

Although in existence for only a few years, the higher *technikums* and the higher technical schools have gained students rapidly. Most of the students are graduates of vocational secondary schools and intermediate *technikums*.[27] Some are those who have been unable to fulfill requirements for admission to a university.

During 1966-67, higher *technikums* and higher technical schools had 20,201 students—about 22.5 percent of all students enrolled in all higher education institutions. This total number was divided as follows: industrial *technikums*—12,173; agricultural *technikums*—5,060; higher technical schools—2,968 (table 31).

Table 30.—Number of required years of study in courses at the higher agricultural *technikums* and industrial *technikums* and at higher technical schools, by course; and cities where the courses are given: 1966–67

Course and *technikum* or school	Required years of study	City
HIGHER AGRICULTURAL *TECHNIKUMS* (*Felsőfokú Mezőgazdasági Technikumok*)		
Agricultural mechanics	3	Körmend, Mezőtúr, and Szekszárd
Animal husbandry	2	Debrecen, Kaposvár, and Hódmézővásárhely
Animal husbandry and health	2	Budapest
Fodder production	2	Hódmezővásárhely
Horticulture	2	Fertőd
Horticulture and viniculture	2	Kecskemét and Nyiregyháza
Irrigated plant production	2	Szarvas
Management	2	Zsámbék
Plant production	2	Karcag, Kiskunhalas, Körmend, Nagykanizsa, Putnok, Székesfehérvár, and Szekszárd
Poultry farming	2	Gödöllő-Pécel
Vegetable production	2	Gyöngyös
Viniculture	2	Do.
HIGHER INDUSTRIAL *TECHNIKUMS* (*Felsőfokú Ipari Technikumok*)		
1. Higher *Technikum* for Chemical Industrial Mechanics (*Felsőfokú Vegyipari Gépészeti Technikum*)		
Chemical industrial mechanics	3	Esztergom and Pécs
Measurement-control techniques	3	Kazincbarcika
Mine mechanics	3	Esztergom
2. Higher *Technikum* for Constructions and Construction Machines Industry (*Felsőfokú Épitő-és Épitőanyagipari Gépsézeti Technikum*)		
Construction electrification	3	Budapest
Construction mechanics	3	Do.
Silicate industry	3	Do.
3. Higher *Technikum* for Electric Machines Industry (*Felsőfokú Villamosgépipari Technikum*)		
Manufacture of electrical machines	3	Do.
4. Higher *Technikum* for Food Industry (*Felsőfokú Élelmiszeripari Technikum*)		
Food technology	3	Budapest and Szeged
Mechanization and automation	3	Budapest

[27] See p. 78-84.

5. Higher *Technikum* for Light Industry (*Felsőfokú Könnyűipari Technikum*)		
Clothing industry	3	Do.
Leather industry	3	Do.
Printing	3	Do.
6. Higher *Technikum* for Machine Industry (*Felsőfokú Gépipari Technikum*)		
Machine manufacturing technology	3	Budapest and Kecskemét
7. Higher *Technikum* for Machine and Telecomunication Industries (*Felsőfokú Gépipari és Hiradásipari Technikum*)		
Machine manufacturing technology	3	Székesfehérvár
8. Higher *Technikum* for Metallurgy (*Felsőfokú Kohászati Technikum*)		
Machine manufacturing technylogy	3	Dunaújváros
Metallurgy	3	Do.
9. Higher *Technikum* for Motor Vehicles and Traffic (*Felsőfokú Gépjármű-Közlekedési Technikum*)		
Technical management and supplies	3	Budapest
Traffic and trade	3	Do.
10. Higher *Technikum* for Rail Traffic (*Felsőfokú Vasutforgalmi Technikum*)		
Rail traffic	3	Szeged
11. Higher *Technikum* for Surveying (*Felsőfokú Földmérési Technikum*)		
Surveying	3	Székesfehérvár
12. Higher *Technikum* for Telecommunications (*Felsőfokú Távközlési Technikum*)		
Wire telecommunication technology	3	Budapest
Wireless telecommunication technology	3	Do.
13. Higher *Technikum* for Telecommunications and Instruments (*Felsőfokú Hiradás és Müszeripari Technikum*)		
Telecommunications	3	Do.
Wireless telecommunications technology	3	Do.
14. Higher *Technikum* for Water Supplies (*Felsőfokú Vizgazdálkodási Technikum*)		
General and agricultural water supplies	3	Baja
Water supplies and sewerage	3	Do.

HIGHER TECHNICAL SCHOOLS
(*Felsőfokú Szakiskolák*)

1. Higher Technical School of Finance and Accounting (*Felsőfokú Pénzügyi és Számviteli Szakiskola*)		
Accounting	3	Budapest
Finance	3	Do.
2. Higher Technical School for Foreign Trade (*Felsőfokú Külkereskedelmi Szakiskola*)		
Foreign language correspondence on foreign trade	2½	Do.
3. Higher Technical School for General and Catering Trades (*Felsőfokú Kereskedelmi és Vendéglátóipari Szakiskola*)		
Catering trade	3	Do.
General trade	2½	Do.

SOURCE OF DATA: *Tájékoztató a magyar felsőoktatási intézményekről, 1965* (Guide to the Hungarian Institutions of Higher Learning, 1965). Budapest: A Művelődésügyi Minisztérium Kiadványa, 1965. p. 65-75.

Table 31.—Number of students in day and evening sessions and correspondence courses of higher agricultural and industrial *technikums* and technical shools: 1966–67; and number of 1966 graduates[1]

Higher *technikum* or technical school	Day session			Evening session			Correspondence courses		
	Total	Girls	1966 graduates	Total	Girls	1966 graduates	Total	Girls	1966 graduates
Total	9,143	2,123	2,123	4,783	1,177	938	6,275	1,151	1,540
Higher agricultural *technikums* (*Felsőfokú mezőgazdasági technikumok*)	2,859	532	1,177	0	0	0	2,201	203	971
Higher industrial *technikums* (*Felsőfokú ipari technikumok*)	5,321	1,021	761	3,919	661	740	2,933	473	410
Higher technical schools (*Felsőfokú szakiskolák*)	963	570	185	864	516	198	1,141	475	159

[1] Data released at beginning of academic year.

SOURCE OF DATA: *Statisztiaki évkönyv 1966* (Statistical Yearbook 1966). Budapest: Központi Statisztikai Hivatal, 1967. p. 351.

VII. Higher Education

Post-World War II Evolution

Higher education in Hungary, like education at all other levels in that country, has undergone qualitative, structural, and institutional changes since 1945.

During the transitional years 1945-48, the changes involved primarily dismissal of some of the arch-reactionary faculty members who openly and vocally had identified themselves with the Nazi regime, revision of the curriculum, and adoption of a more liberal admission policy, favoring especially those who had been disadvantaged during the Horthy era.

The institutions of higher learning continued to operate basically under the same organizational-structural principles in effect before the war. Each university operated as a self-governing unit which elected its own administrative officials, regulated administrative and disciplinary matters, controlled faculty appointments and dismissals, selected the curriculum, and set qualifications for degrees.

The 1948 educational reform produced a radical change in the scope and goals of higher education and in the composition of the faculty and student body. Education in general, but especially higher education, was increasingly identified as a social instrument for the "construction of socialism."

With the Communist assumption of power completed, higher education took on a dual task of preparing the highly competent and skilled technical-scientific personnel needed by the planned economic system and of creating an ideologically and politically reliable intelligentsia responsive to the requirements of the regime.

By 1950, the higher education institutions had been stripped of their traditional autonomy. As State institutions, they were placed under the leadership of Government-appointed administrators, and the powers of rectors, directors, and deans were greatly expanded. Together with representatives of the Teachers Union,[1] the Communist Party, and youth organizations operating at the institutional, faculty, and class levels, the institutions were instrumental in and responsible for implementing the particular policies which the regime stipulated at any given time.

The Party-State's political objectives required that to begin with the student body be purified, the faculty subordinated, technical training advanced, and the entire system be reoriented ideologically.

After education had been nationalized, the Communists acquired con-

[1] See p. 167-68.

trol over which students would be admitted to higher education and how many assigned to each school and department. These powers were formally exercised by the Admissions Division of the Ministry of Culture. Social background and class origin became the primary criteria for admission, and applicants were divided into five groups: worker, peasant, middle-class intelligentsia, kulak, and "X". The term kulak was normally applied not only to large landowners, but also, regardless of the size of their holdings, to those who in any way resisted the regime's collectivization drive. The "X" group included the sons and daughters of the former aristocracy and of those who had held various positions in the governmental and army apparatus of the pre-Communist regimes.[2]

To assure a sufficient number of properly qualified students of peasant and working-class origin, the Government adopted a plan under which young people of the right social background who had not completed secondary school, but were of university age, could enroll in an intensive 1-year course entitling them to a so-called "express secondary school certificate." The holders of this certificate became eligible for admission to a higher education institution without having to take the normally required admittance examination. As a result of these measures, students of peasant and working-class background came to constitute about 66 percent of the student body by the beginning of academic year 1949-50. The required change in the composition of the student body, however, had a negative effect on the quality of both the students and the teaching process. At the Polytechnical University of Budapest *(Budapesti Műszaki Egyetem)*, for example, 35 to 45 percent of the holders of "express" secondary school certificates failed their course work.[3]

Faculty subordination was assured through a prescribed curriculum, a vertical system of control and supervision, and dismissals. The new curriculum differed radically from the old one, de-emphasizing the humanities and social sciences in favor of the technical and natural sciences. The change was assured by a concomitant structural reorganization of existing institutions and the establishment of new, primarily technical, colleges.

In 1949-50, a separate school of natural sciences[4] was established at the Eötvös Loránd University of Budapest (*Eötvös Loránd Tudományegyetem*). In 1951 the schools of medicine were separated from their original institutions and transformed into independent medical universities (*orvostudományi egyetemek*), and a number of polytechnical universities and colleges were established, including the Polytechnical University of Heavy Industry (*Nehézipari Műszaki Egyetem*) at Miskolc and the Polytechnical University of Construction and Transportation (*Építőipari és Közlekedési Műszaki Egyetem*) at Budapest.[5]

The ideological reorientation of the higher education system involved introduction of Marxism-Leninism as a required subject in each school

---

[2] Elinor Murray. "Higher Education in Communist Hungary, 1948–1956." *The American Slavic and East European Review*, New York. XIX:3:399, October 1960.

[3] Ibid. p. 402.

[4] The terms "school" and "faculty" as a separate division of an institution of higher learning are used interchangeably throughout this publication.

[5] For a succinct review of the changes introduced in higher education after 1945, see Aurél Hencz. *A művelődési intézmények és a művelődésigazgatás fejlődése, 1945–1961* (The Evolution of Educational Institutions and Administration, 1945–1961). Budapest: Közgazdasági és Jogi Könyvkiadó, 1962. p. 76–94.

and department, compulsory dialectical-materialist interpretation of all natural and social phenomena, and a vast Russification program to enrich the curriculum with the Russian language, as well as Russian history, literature, and science; and to emphasize Russian contributions to all fields of learning.

Following Stalin's death and the subsequent introduction of the "New Course" line into the regime's political objectives, certain adjustments had to be made in the educational system as well. Although social origin remained an important factor for admission to higher education, the institutions reverted more and more to standard professional criteria: talent, potential, secondary school grades, and grades on admission examinations. The Government initiated new administrative and structural changes that laid the foundation for the present system of higher education.

Aims and Principles

The general provisions concerning the aims and principles of higher education were outlined in Articles 18 to 23 of Law III Concerning the Educational System of the Hungarian People's Republic.[6] According to Article 19, higher education's primary objective is to take students who are familiar with the basic teachings of Marxism-Leninism and who are capable of applying these teachings in the practice of their professions or specialties. Another major objective is to assure that the most outstanding students who fulfill this primary objective are trained to become the leading researchers and scientists in their respective fields.

Organization and Structure

Jurisdiction

The requirements of the planned economic system and the highly centralized character of the Government produced a complex jurisdictional set-up in higher education. Jurisdiction over establishing higher education institutions and over organizing and structuring individual institutions is exercised by the Presidential Council of the People's Republic (*A Népköztársaság Elnöki Tanácsa*), the Ministry of Culture and various other ministries with educational responsibilities, the National Planning Office (*Országos Tervhivatal*), and the Hungarian Academy of Sciences (*Magyar Tudományos Akadémia*).

Learning from its experience during the first 8 years after the 1948 educational reforms,[7] the Government in 1956 passed a decree regulating the organization and structure of higher education.[8]

According to the Presidential Council's Decree No. 4 of 1956 and the

[6] *Magyar Közlöny* (Hungarian Gazette), Budapest. No. 74, October 17, 1961, p. 568. See also p. 28-29 of the present publication.

[7] The general direction of higher education was entrusted in 1951 to the National Council of Higher Education (*Országos Felsőoktatási Tanács*) which shared its responsibilities with the Ministry of Higher Education (*Felsőoktatási Minisztérium*) (established in 1952). Both were dissolved, however, in 1953, and jurisdiction was basically resumed by the ministries exercising educational responsibilities.

[8] "A Népköztársaság Elnöki Tanácsának 1956. évi 4. számú törvényerejű rendelete a felsőoktatási intézmények szervezeti kérdéseiről" (Decree No. 4 of 1956 of the Presidential Council of the People's Republic Concerning the Organization of the Institutions of Higher Learning). *Magyar Közlöny*, No. 10, February 9, 1956. p. 57-58.

Government's Decree No. 35/1962. (IX.16.),[9] only the Presidential Council can establish and dissolve universities, colleges and, until the early 1960's, academies.[10]

Karok (schools), *technikums,* and institutes[11] are established and dissolved by the Council of Ministers acting on the advice of the minister having jurisdiction over the particular institution, the president of the Hungarian Academy of Sciences and, until 1967, the president of the Council of Science and Higher Education (*Tudományos és Felsőoktatási Tanács*).[12] Jurisdiction over establishing and dissolving departments (*szakok*) is exercised by the minister in charge of the particular institution, together with the Minister of Finance, the presidents of the National Planning Office and the Hungarian Academy of Sciences and, until 1967, the president of the Council of Science and Higher Education. Specialty areas (*tanszékek*) are established, consolidated, and dissolved by the minister having jurisdiction over the particular institution, together with the Minister of Finance and the president of the Academy. To establish and dissolve departments and specialty areas not under the jurisdiction of the Minister of Culture also requires his concurrence.

University rectors (chancellors or presidents) and deans of universities with only one school, as well as directors of colleges and academies and university professors, are appointed by the Council of Ministers. College and academy deans and professors and department chairmen are appointed by the minister having jurisdiction over the particular institution.[13]

The curriculum (*tanterv*) of universities, colleges, and higher institutes is approved by the minister having jurisdiction over the particular institution. The number of years of study for evening sessions and correspondence sections of all higher institutions requires the Minister of Culture's approval.

The functions and responsibilities of the ministers who exercise jurisdiction over the institutions and those of the Minister of Culture are clearly delineated by law. Thus, they are required to:

1. Organize, direct, and supervise the institutions' work in accordance with the by-laws.
2. Set specialization and degree requirements.
3. Provide necessary materials and personnel for the institutions' effective operation.

---

[9] *Magyar Közlöny*, Budapest, No. 70, September 16, 1962. p. 581–83. Government Decree No. 35/1962 was amended on June 20, 1969 by Decree No. 25/1969. (VI.20.). For details see footnote 16.

[10] The academies, mostly agricultural and pedagogical, were later transformed into higher agricultural *technikums* and teacher-training institutes, respectively.

[11] Paragraph 2, Article 18 of Law No. III cited above.

[12] The Council of Science and Higher Education was established by Government Decree No. 32/1957. (VI.5.) of June 5, 1957. (*Magyar Közlöny*, No. 63, June 5, 1967. p. 355–56) to coordinate all scientific and research work and higher education. It was dissolved in 1967 by Government Resolution No. 1010/1967 (V.28.) (*Magyar Közlöny*, No. 33, May 28, 1967. p. 301–02). Its functions in establishing and dissolving departments and specialty areas were taken over by the National Council of Education (*Országos Oktatási Tanács*) in accordance with Government Resolution No. 1022/1967. (XIII.2.) (*Magyar Közlöny*, No. 52, August 2, 1967. p. 391); its research-coordinating responsibilities were assigned to the ministries having jurisdiction over the particular areas in accordance with Government Resolution No. 1010/1967 cited above.

The Council of Science and Higher Education functions relating to financing study trips abroad and centralizing and evaluating the studies conducted on such trips were transferred to the Institute for Cultural Relations (see p. 32) under Government Resolution No. 1023/1968. (VIII.6.), published in *Magyar Közlöny*, No. 64, August 6, 1968. p. 635–36.

[13] Decree No. 4 of 1965 cited above.

4. Approve organizational and operational regulations.
5. Regulate the appointive power of the institutions' directors.
6. Determine how programs and textbooks shall be approved.[14]

The Minister of Culture, in conjunction with the minister who exercises jurisdiction, is empowered to:

1. Establish general principles and techniques for the teaching-process.
2. Direct the teaching of Marxism-Leninism.
3. Determine general regulations for organizing and operating higher education institutions, the examination system, State examinations, dissertations, and discipline.
4. Determine, in conjunction with the Minister of Finance, a system of financial assistance and rewards for students.
5. Regulate the conditions and processes governing admissions.
6. Regulate the conditions for appointing tenured university professors *(cimzetes egyetemi tanár)* and associate professors *(docens)* and determine their rights and duties.
7. Determine the competitive process for appointing lecturers and instructors.
8. Regulate the awarding of university doctoral degrees.[15]

The Ministry of Culture has jurisdiction over the regular universities (*Tudományegyetemek*), polytechnical universities (*Műszaki egyetemek*), art colleges (*Művészeti főiskolák*), and the teacher-training colleges (*Tanárképző főiskolák*) and institutes (*Tanitóképző és óvónőképzö intézetek*). The medical universities *(Orvostudományi egyetemek)* operate under the jurisdiction of the Ministry of Health (*Egészségügyi Minisztérium*); and the College of Physical Education (*Testnevelési főiskola*) under the Hungarian Association of Physical Education and Sports (*Magyar Testnevelési és Sportszövetség*).[16]

Administration

Each university and institution of university status is headed by a rector (chancellor or president). The colleges and the teacher-training institutes are each headed by a director (*igazgató*).[17] The rectors and directors guide, administer, and supervise the operations of their respective institutions; and their instructions and orders are binding on all administrative employees, teaching personnel, and students. In ac-

---

[14] Decree No. 35/1962. (IX.16.) cited above.

[15] Ibid.

[16] *World Survey of Education IV: Higher Education.* New York: UNESCO, 1966. p. 586. For a list of the higher education institutions operating under the jurisdiction of the various ministries, see appendix to Decree No. 22 of 1962 of the Presidential Council of the People's Republic Concerning the Institutions of Higher Learning. *Magyar Kölöny*, No. 70, September 16, 1962. p. 573-77.

During summer 1969, three decrees were issued amending Government Decree No. 22 of 1962 just indentified, as well as Government Decree No. 35/1962. Among other things, these three decrees concerned (1) the Minister of Culture's jurisdiction over higher education, (2) the administrative setup's structure and functions, (3) the faculty's responsibilities, (4) curriculums and syllabuses, (5) students' rights and responsibilities, and (6) the place and role of the Communist Youth League (*Kommunista Ifjúsági Szövetség*) and of trade union organizations in higher education institutions. (See Decree No. 14 of 1969 of the Presidential Council of the People's Republic amending Decree No. 22 of 1962. *Magyar Közlöny*, No. 46, June 20, 1969. p. 445-46; Decree No. 25/1969. (VI. 20.) of the Hungarian Revolutionary Worker-Peasant Government concerning universities and university-type colleges. Ibid. p. 447-50; Decree No. 3/1969. (VII.4.) MM of the Minister of Culture concerning the organization and function of universities and university-type colleges. Ibid. No. 51, July 4, 1969. p. 494-506.)

[17] See Decree No. 22 of 1962 cited above.

cordance with the one-man-rule principle employed in the management of any socialist enterprise or institution, the rectors and directors are top Government-appointees responsible for implementing given State and Party directives.

The rectors and directors are assisted in their work by deputy rectors (*rektorhelyettesek*) and deputy directors (*igazgatóhelyettesek*) and by the university college, institute, etc. council (*egyetemi, főiskolai, intézeti, stb. tanács*). Institutes operating with only one school (faculty) are headed by a dean (*dékán*).[18]

Normally, a university has several schools, each headed by a dean, who is assisted by deputy or assistant deans (*dékánhelyettesek*) and a faculty council (*kari tanács*). The dean's office (*dékáni hivatal*) is in charge of admissions, registration, management of grade books, scholarships and fellowships, and board and dormitories.

Each school is divided into departments (*szakok; tanszékek*), the basic unit engaged in the teaching, research, and scientific process. The department chairmen (*tanszékvezetők*) are responsible for implementing the department program, the curriculum, and the professional and political-ideological development of the members of their respective departments.

Like all Hungarian governmental organizations, higher education is administered in a highly centralized manner. In view of worldwide student unrest (an unrest which to some extent also engulfed the students of the people's democratic and socialist countries), the Hungarian Government adopted some small but meaningful measures to ease the rigidities of over-centralization. According to the plan outlined by Károly Polinszky, Deputy Minister of Culture, at a national conference of university and college leaders held on September 17, 1968, in Budapest, the Ministry of Culture will in the future restrict itself to determining the main principles of educational policy rather than issuing detailed and comprehensive directives as it did in the past.

The principles to be determined by the Ministry, however, are envisioned to establish the curriculum's content (especially that of ideological indoctrination), the extent of basic and specialized instruction, the maximum number of lectures per week for a teacher, and the examination requirements. Within this general framework, the university and college authorities (such as rectors, deans, and councils) will have the power to determine the form of the instruction and the methods of examination in a more flexible manner by taking into consideration the views of the students. In this new decisionmaking process in higher education, the Communist Youth League[19] and the Party organizations in the institutions of higher learning will also participate, thus assuring compliance with a particular Party line regarding education and student affairs.[20]

---

[18] Until 1962, exception was made for medical universities operating with only one school each, like those of Debrecen and Pécs (see p. 115) which, under Government Decree No. 65/1957 (X.24.), were headed by rectors. *Magyar Közlöny*, No. 114, October 24, 1957. p. 748.

[19] For details on the Communist Youth League, see p. 182-89.

[20] The statutes on the reforms in higher education are planned to be published in January 1969, while those of the universities and colleges by June 30, 1969. The reforms are to go into effect on September 1, 1969. *Népszabadság* (People's Freedom), Budapest, September 18, 1968; *Magyar Nemzet* (Hungarian Nation), Budapest, October 23, 1968; *Magyar Hirlap* (Hungarian News Journal), Budapest, October 30, 1968.

Admissions

Requirements

The institutions of higher learning admit applicants within the limit of the number of places determined by the National Planning Office in accordance with the economic and cultural requirements of the country. Theoretically, applications for admission are evaluated by taking into consideration the following four factors: aptitude, talent, training, and attitudes.[21] Applicants seeking admission to the day session must be under age 35, have the necessary educational background (including the secondary school certificate or its equivalent), and be in satisfactory health. The age limit is waived for applicants to evening sessions or correspondence courses who have spent at least 1½ years in production or in an agricultural cooperative. Military service is considered equivalent to time spent in production. The higher *technikums* and technical schools admit workers who are skilled in some specialty and who hold skilled-worker certificates (*szakmunkás bizonyitvány*).[22] Students with foreign secondary or higher education diplomas are admitted only after an evaluation (*honositás*) of their records.

Procedures

Applications for admission must be submitted to the applicant's secondary school if they are still attending the school or have left it within 2 years and are not employed; otherwise, the applications are to be submitted to the employer. The school or the employer will forward the application together with an evaluation and recommendation. The application must be accompanied by the secondary school certificate or its equivalent, a medical certificate issued within 30 days and, in the case of applicants to the day session, the secondary school records. Civil servants and members of the armed forces must also submit the approval of the Minister of the Interior or Defense, respectively.

Applicants who have fulfilled all requirements are informed in writing and are instructed to report to the examination authorities no later than 8 days before the examinations begin.

Examinations

The examinations consist of written, oral and, in some cases, practical parts. The examination material must not be at a higher level than the material covered in the secondary schools, and the subjects and general

---

[21] There is a considerable literature on the difficulties involved in evaluating these factors objectively and on the shortcomings or failures of the secondary institutions to develop these qualifications in their students. See, for example, Lajos Somos. "A főiskolai felvételekről" (Concerning Admissions to College). *Köznevelés*, XXII:8:289–90, April 22, 1966.

[22] The system of admissions was at first regulated by the following decree: "A művelődésügyi miniszter 3/1963. (V.19.) MM számú rendelete a felsőoktatási intézményekbe való felvétel szabályozásáról" (Decree No. 3/1963. (V.19.) MM of the Minister of Culture Concerning Admissions to Institutions of Higher Learning). *Magyar Közlöny*, No. 34, May 19, 1963. p. 227–30. This was superseded in 1968 as follows: "A művelődésügyi miniszter 3/1968. (V.26.) MM számú rendelete a felsőoktatási intézményekbe való felvétel szabályozásáról" (Decree No. 3/1968. (V.26.) MM of the Minister of Culture Concerning Admissions to the Institutions of Higher Learning). *Magyar Közlöny*, No. 44, May 26, 1968. p. 481–86.

specifications are normally published in guides issued by the Ministry of Culture.[23] Exempt from admission examinations are the first 10 winners of the National Secondary School Studies Competition (*Országos Középiskolai Tanulmányi Verseny*), the Kürschák József Mathematics Competition (*Kürschák József matematikai verseny*), and the Eötvös Loránd Physics Competition (*Eötvös Loránd fizikai verseny*).[24]

Also exempt from admission examinations are the first- and second-place winners in the "Who Is a Scientist in What Field?" (*Ki miben tudos?*) television program. To take advantage of any of these exemptions, an applicant must have graduated no longer than 3 years before the admission date or must have won the competition no longer than 3 years before that date.[25]

Secondary school graduates relaxing in the main hall of Kossuth Lajos University between scheduled admission examinations of the university

The admission examinations for the day session are normally held in June and July, while those for admission to the evening sessions and correspondence courses are held between October and January. The written examinations take 2 hours for each subject; the oral ones, approximately half an hour.

To process the admission applications and to evaluate and examine the applicants, the school or institution must select each year a suitable number of examination committees (*vizsgabizottságok*) and one admis-

[23] The general requirements for the admission examination offered in 1965 by subject and area of specialization are given for example, in *Tájékoztató a magyar felsőoktatási intézményekről*, op. cit. p. 117-46.

[24] Article 14 of Decree No. 3/1968. (V.26.) MM cited above and Decree No. 3/1964. (VI.28.) MM of the Minister of Culture. For the latter decree, see *Magyar Közlöny*, No. 41, June 28, 1964. p. 274–75.

[25] Ibid.

sion committee (*felvételi bizottság*). The chief function of the former is to evaluate academic background and achievement; of the latter, to make the final decision by evaluating those same factors in addition to others.

The applicants are graded according to a point system ranging from "0" to "5," with "0" standing for failure. The composite score also includes the grades received in secondary school, the grades received on examinations for the secondary school certificate, and a point value for attitudes. Admissions are granted according to rank in the composite scores. An exception is made for children of "martyrs of the workers' movement" and for holders of the "Hungarian Freedom Award" (*Magyar Szabadság Érdemrend*) and the "For Worker-Peasant Power" (*Munkás-Paraszt hatalomért*) award. Priority is also given to children of peasants and workers and to former members of the armed forces within 2 years from their discharge, and applicants who have spent at least 1 year in production.

An applicant who has been rejected may appeal to the head of the institution, and if again rejected, to the Minister exercising immediate jurisdiction over the institution.

Some institutions of higher learning use the so-called "conditional admission" (*feltételes felvétel* or *előfelvétel*) for applicants who did well on the composite scores but who could not be admitted for lack of space. This procedure entitles the applicants to be admitted the following year. One of the objectives is to induce these applicants to work in production in the meantime, and enter the institution with a record of 2 years of practical work. Such conditionally admitted students must pursue short courses organized under the auspices of the evening sessions or correspondence courses of higher education institutions. The applicants are then admitted to the first year of the university course without having to take another admission examination.

To help students prepare for the admission examinations, many institutions of higher learning, in cooperation with the education sections of the county peoples' councils, organize special evening preparatory courses. Those covering more than one subject begin in December and cost 450 forints, while those for a single subject begin in March and cost 230 forints.[26]

Types of Institutions

Hungarian higher education experienced considerable development during the post-World War II period. Spearheaded by a greater interest in and concern for education in general and by the primary goal of the regime to train a sufficient number of politically reliable specialists, this development was marked by both a quantitative increase in the number of institutions, teachers, and students and an expansion in the character and types of institutions (tables 32 and 33).

Some highlights of Hungarian higher education's growth between 1937-38 and 1960-61 follow:[27]

---

[26] Concerning the value of the forint, see footnote 54 of chapter III.

[27] *Statistical Pocket Book of Hungary 1967.* Budapest: Publishing House for Economics and Law, 1967. p. 182.

	1937–38	1960–61[1]
Institutions	16	92
Instructors	1,724	5,635
Students	11,747	44,585
Percent of students who were women	14.5	37.9

[1] Include higher *technikums* and technical schools.

Hungarian higher education institutions may be divided into six types: universities, medical universities, polytechnical universities, agronomic universities and colleges (*agrártudományi egyetemek és főiskolák*), teacher-training colleges and institutes, and special colleges (including colleges of fine arts, a physical education college, and military schools).[28]

Table 32.—Number of higher education institutions, by type and location: 1960–61—1966–67[1]

Academic year	Total	Universities and colleges	Higher *technikums* and technical schools	Training institutes for kindergarten and elementary teachers	Location: Budapest	Location: Provinces
1960–61	43	29	0	14	15	28
1961–62	60	29	17	14	17	43
1962–63	87	30	43	14	28	59
1963–64	89	30	46	13	28	61
1964–65	91	[2] 31	47	13	29	62
1965–66	92	[2] 31	48	13	29	63
1966–67	92	[2] 31	48	13	29	63

[1] Data released at beginning of academic year.

[2] Includes the evening division of the Institute for Training Instructors of Motor-Disorder Victims *(Mozgássérültek Nevelőképző és Nevelőintézete)*, located in Budapest.

SOURCE OF DATA: *Statisztikai évkönyv 1966* (Statistical Yearbook 1966). Budapest: Központi Statisztikai Hivatal, 1967. p. 348.

Table 33.—Total number of instructors in higher educational institutions; number of students in these institutions, by type of institution; and total number of students in these institutions, day and evening sessions and correspondence courses: 1960–61—1966–67[1]

Academic year	Instructors[2]	Students: Total	Universities and colleges	Higher *technikums* and technical schools	Training institutes for kindergarten and elementary teachers	Day session	Evening session	Correspondence courses
1960–61	5,635	44,585	42,186	--------	2,399	29,344	1,341	13,900
1961–62	5,865	53,302	48,284	1,325	3,693	34,526	4,595	14,181
1962–63	6,702	67,324	56,523	6,336	4,465	40,253	7,970	19,101
1963–64	7,278	82,280	64,816	12,449	5,015	45,236	12,067	24,977
1964–65	7,938	91,923	[3] 69,724	17,115	5,084	48,810	[3] 14,405	28,708
1965–66	8,444	93,957	[3] 69,263	20,148	4,546	51,002	[3] 14,721	28,234
1966–67	8,889	89,544	65,621	20,201	3,722	52,327	13,244	23,973

[1] Data released at beginning of academic year.

[2] Includes physical education instructors.

[3] Includes 26 and 23 evening-session students of the Institute for Training Instructors of Motor-Disorder Victims *(Mozgássérültek Nevelőképző és Nevelőintézete)* during the 1964-65 and 1965-66 academic years, respectively.

SOURCE OF DATA: *Statisztikai évkönyv 1966* (Statistical Yearbook 1966). Budapest: Központi Statisztikai Hivatal, 1967. p. 348.

[28] See appendix B for a listing of Hungarian higher education institutions of university or college caliber and appendix C for a listing of Hungarian institutions primarily specializing in training technicians or lower-elementary and kindergarten teachers. See chapter VIII for a discussion of teacher-training colleges and institutes.

Hungary has five regular academic universities: the Eötvös Loránd University in Budapest, the Karl Marx University of Economics in Budapest, the Kossuth Lajos University in Debrecen, the József Attila in Szeged, and the University of Pécs in Pécs.

The number of years of study at these institutions varies from 4 years at Karl Marx (except for its degree in planning and mathematics, which requires 5 years) and at the other four universities' schools (faculties) of law and political science to 5 years at these four universities' schools of natural science and philosophy. At all five universities the admission requirements are basically the same except those concerning examinations, which normally are given in the subjects of a student's intended specialization.[29]

After a student has successfully completed his course requirements, he may in some schools (faculties)—for example, Eötvös Loránd University's School of Political Science and Law—be required to take an additional 6 months of "end-training" (*záróigyakorlat*). During those 6 months he prepares a thesis, studies for the State examination, and attends courses or consultations specified by the dean. When he completes all these requirements, he receives a certificate (*abszolutórium*) entitling him to take the State examination, and after passing this examination, he is awarded a diploma (*oklevél*) in his special field.[30]

Eötvös Loránd University

By far the most prestigious institution of higher learning, the Eötvös Loránd University (*Eötvös Loránd Tudományegyetem*) was originally founded in 1561 as a Jesuit college. In 1635 the college was changed into a university by Archbishop Péter Pázmány, whose name it bore until 1949, when it acquired the present name. Its inner structure was changed in 1957, when the following three schools were established: [31] School of Natural Science (*Természettudományi Kar*), formed by consolidating the School of Mathematics, Physics, and Chemistry and the School of Biology and Geology; School of Philosophy (*Bölcsészettudományi Kar*),[32] formed by consolidating the School of Languages and Literature and the School of History; and School of Political Science and Law (*Állam- és Jogtudományi Kar*). On September 1, 1957, the School of Philosophy also absorbed the Lenin Institute (*Lenin Intézet*), a formerly independent institution of higher learning established in 1954 to advance Marxist-Leninist and Russian studies.[33] The university also supervises the activities of the Center for Further Training in For-

[29] For further details on the universities, especially admission requirements and organizational structure. see *Tájékozta ó a magyar felsőoktatási intézményekről 1965* (Guide to the Institutions of Higher Learning 1965), Budapest: A Művelődésügyi Minisztérium Kiadványa, 1965. p. 21–23.

[30] For further details on examinations and grading, see p. 127.

[31] "A Népköztársaság Elnöki Tanácsának 1957. évi 33. számú törvényerejű rendelete az Eötvös Loránd Tudományegyetem szervezetének modositásáról" (Decree No. 33 of 1957 of the Presidential Council of the People's Republic Concerning the Change in the Structure of the Eötvös Loránd University). *Magyar Közlöny*, No. 62, June 2, 1957. p. 345.

[32] The School of Philosophy is basically the same as the School of Liberal Arts in the United States.

[33] *Magyar Közlöny*, No. 71, June 25, 1957. p. 422.

eign Languages (*Idegen Nyelvi Továbbképző Központ*) in Budapest.[34]

Specialization in languages, including the major modern Western ones—English, French, German, Italian, and Spanish—is offered under the auspices of various departments of the School of Philosophy. This is also true of the other universities. By far the most extensive training is offered within the framework of the department of education preparing language teachers or teachers with a dual specialization, one being a foreign language.

In addition to the language training offered at the Center associated with the Eötvös Loránd University, extensive modern foreign language training is offered under the auspices of the Karl Marx University of Economics.[35]

The university's 1966-67 enrollment consisted of 5,235 students in the day session, 2,201 in the evening session, and 1,563 in the correspondence courses (table 34) . Total enrollment was 8,999.

József Attila University

Formerly known as the University of Szeged (*Szegedi Tudományegyetem*), the József Attila University (*József Attila Tudományegyetem*) traces its history to 1872, when the Franz-Joseph University was established at Kolozsvár (Cluj), currently in Romania. Following the absorption of Transylvania into Romania in 1918, the university was transferred to Szeged. Reorganized, it began operations in 1921. It has three schools—Natural Science, Philosophy, and Political Science and Law—the School of Medicine having become a separate institution in 1951. In 1966-67, József Attila had 2,170 day-session students, 216 evening-session students, and 1,176 correspondence-course students (table 34) . Its total enrollment was 3,562.

Karl Marx University of Economics

Founded in 1948 to train economic specialists steeped in Marxism-Leninism, the Karl Marx University of Economics (*Marx Károly Közgazdaságtudományi Egyetem*) offers a 4-year program under the auspices of the following three schools: General Economics (*Általános Közgazdasági Kar*) , Industry (*Ipari Kar*) , and Trade (*Kereskedelmi Kar*) .

During the first year of their study, all students have a basic prescribed program composed of economic geography, history of economics, Marxism-Leninism, mathematics, and political economy. They normally take their specialized courses during the last 2 years. The School of General Economics also has a special department to train economics teachers for the vocational secondary schools of trade and commerce.

The university offers a rigorous foreign language program under the auspices of its Foreign Language Institute. Language teaching differs for each major field, with students normally required to take two foreign languages during the 4 years: Russian and either English, French, Ger-

[34] *Magyar Közlöny*, No. 91, December 3, 1967. p. 930.
[35] See section this page, on Karl Marx University.

man, or Spanish. Students majoring in foreign trade or communications have 8 hours of language per week: 4 in Russian and 4 in one of the Western languages. International relations majors must take 12 hours of

Table 34.—Number of students in day and evening sessions and correspondence courses of five universities, by university and faculty (school): 1966–67; and number of 1966 graduates[1]

University, city and faculty (school)	Day session			Evening session			Correspondence courses		
	Total	Girls	1966 graduates	Total	Girls	1966 graduates	Total	Girls	1966 graduates
Grand total	11,831	6,843	1,855	4,418	2,270	623	4,591	1,773	1,024
Eötvös Loránd University *(Eötvös Loránd Todományegyetem) Budapest* *Total*	*5,235*	*3,199*	*783*	*2,201*	*1,100*	*341*	*1,563*	*602*	*426*
Natural science[2]	2,378	1,318	375	298	142	14	225	106	65
Philosophy[3]	2,127	1,472	303	1,109	632	180	931	388	254
Political science and law[4]	730	409	105	794	326	147	407	108	107
József Attila University *(József Attila Tudományegyetem) Szeged* *Total*	*2,170*	*1,411*	*309*	*216*	*80*	*48*	*1,176*	*465*	*232*
Natural science[2]	1,089	682	174	0	0	0	163	57	42
Philosophy[3]	722	532	73	8	4	0	594	271	119
Political science and law	359	197	62	208	76	48	419	137	71
Karl Marx University of Economics[5] *(Marx Károly Közgazdaságtudományi Egyetem) Budapest* *Total*	*2,151*	*1,201*	*398*	*1,790*	*998*	*218*	*784*	*290*	*126*
General economics	846	501	125	364	226	59	236	100	70
Industry	666	383	120	851	396	96	300	118	34
Trade	639	317	153	575	376	63	248	72	22
Kossuth Lajos University *(Kossuth Lajos Tudományegyetem) Debrecen* *Total*	*1,979*	*1,274*	*308*	*53*	*34*	*0*	*684*	*300*	*76*
Natural science[2]	1,080	646	176	0	0	0	289	148	43
Philosophy[3]	899	268	132	53	34	0	395	152	33
University of Pécs[6] *(Pécsi Tudományegyetem) Pécs* *Total*	*296*	*158*	*57*	*158*	*58*	*16*	*384*	*116*	*64*

[1] Data released at beginning of academic year.

[2] Five-year program.

[3] Five-year program.

[4] Four-year program.

[5] Four-year program.

[6] Only one faculty (school)—political science and law.

SOURCE OF DATA: *Statisztikai évkönyv 1966* (Statistical Yearbook 1966). Budapest: Központi Statisztikai Hivatal, 1967. p. 351-52.

language per week: 6 in Russian and 6 in the selected Western language. During the first three terms, language instruction is concentrated on improving the students' ability to understand, speak, read, and write the foreign language.

Customarily, the Institute's staff prepares the foreign language texts. In English, for example, students use the Institute's *An Intermediate English Practice Book* and *Advanced Practice Book*. Towards the end of the third term and during the fourth term they use *Readings for Intermediate and Advanced Students of English About Great Britain and the United States*. These readings are coupled with a great variety of grammar exercises and the use of language tapes.[36]

In 1966-67, Karl Marx had 2,151 students in its day session, 1,790 in its evening session, and 1,790 in its correspondence courses (table 34). Total enrollment was 4,725.

Kossuth Lajos University

Originally founded in 1912, when it incorporated the schools of the Reformed College of Debrecen (founded in 1538), the Kossuth Lajos University has two schools—Natural Science and Philosophy, both offering 5-year programs. Its earlier Schools of Medicine and Theology became separate institutions soon after the 1948 educational reform, and its School of Law was discontinued.

The second smallest of the five regular universities, Kossuth Lajos in 1966-67 had 1,979 students in its day session, 53 in its evening session, (all in the School of Philosophy), and 684 in its correspondence courses (table 34). Total enrollment was 2,716.

As with all other Hungarian higher education institutions, this one normally accepts only a given number of students, determined by its capacity and by admission quotas set by the National Planning Office and other interested central governmental organs. In 1965, for example, 796 students applied for admission to the School of Philosophy, which had only 180 places available.[37]

University of Pécs

The smallest of Hungary's regular universities, the University of Pécs (*Pécsi Tudományegyetm*) is also Hungary's oldest university. Founded by King Louis I in 1367, it became an academy of law in 1785. Its present university form was established in 1923. Pécs operates only with a School of Political Science and Law. The university's 1966-67 day session had 296 students, its evening session 158, and its correspondence courses 384 (table 34). Total enrollment was 838.

---

[36] Lilian O. Feinberg and Jeno Tarjan. "Foreign Language Study in Budapest." *International Educational and Cultural Exchange*. IV:1:27–30. Summer 1968.

[37] István Szendrey. "A felvételi munka tapasztalatai a Kossuth Lajos Tudományegyetemen" (Experiences in the Admission Procedures at the Kossuth Lajos University). *Felsőoktatási Szemle* (Review of Higher Education), Budapest, XV:6:336–40, June 1966.

The present system of medical-pharmaceutical education in Hungary is based on reforms worked out in 1950 and implemented beginning with the 1951-52 academic year. In accordance with the reforms, the medical schools were separated from their parent universities and transformed into independent medical universities operating under the immediate jurisdiction of the Ministry of Health, with the Ministry of Culture exercising certain prerogatives in academic matters.

In 1966-67, Hungary had four medical universities located in Budapest, Debrecen, Pécs, and Szeged; and a University of Veterinary Medicine (*Állatorvostudomanyi Egyetem*), located in Budapest.[38]

The medical universities in Budapest and Szeged operate with three schools each—General Medicine (*Általános Orvostudományi Kar*), Pharmacy (*Gyógyszerésztudományi Kar*), and Stomatology (*Fogorvostudományi Kar*). The other two medical universities each operate with only a School of General Medicine.

During the first 3 years of their studies, medical students devote most of their time to general basic medical subjects emphasizing theory; during the next 2 years, to practical clinical subjects. During the summer, fourth- and fifth-year students also work as hospital interns usually in the counties associated with the particular medical university.[39]. Sixth-year students spend the entire year as interns, working 3 months in each of the following four departments: *Internal Medicine,* with 2 weeks devoted to outpatient clinics in neurology; *Surgery,* with 1 month devoted to traumatology and 2 weeks each to otorhinolaryngology and stomatology; *Obstetrics and Gynecology;* and *Pediatrics,* with 2 weeks devoted to infectious diseases.[40]

Examinations are both oral and practical, with a *colloquium* at the end of the semester and a *rigorosum* at the end of the academic year. Sixth-year students are required to take four examinations, one after each of the four 3-month periods mentioned above. These examinations are offered under the auspices of the university. For the doctor's diploma, the State examination covers forensic medicine, hygiene and epidemiology, philosophy, and social medicine; it is attended by a representative of the State.

Successful candidates are awarded the degree of Doctor of Medicine (*Orvosdoktori oklevél*) entitling them to practice general medicine. For 2 years, however, in accordance with the education or scholarship contract which admitted them to the medical university, they must practice in an assigned place, usually a provincial hospital or an epidemiological-public health station. This requirement is also in effect for dentistry and pharmacy graduates.

Doctors who wish to obtain the title "Specialist" (*Szakorvos*) must pass

---

[38] Hungarian sources classify the University of Veterinary Medicine as part of the agronomic system of higher education.

[39] Territorially, the counties of Pest, Fejér, Győr- Sopron, Komárom, Nógrád and Veszprém and the municipality of Budapest belong to the Medical University of Budapest; those of Borsod-Abaúj-Zemplén, Hajdú-Bihar, Szabolcs-Szatmár, and Heves, and the municipalities of Debrecen and Miskolc to the Medical University of Debrecen; the counties of Baranya, Tolna, Somogy, Vas, and Zala and the municipality of Pécs to the Medical University of Pécs; and those of Csongrád, Bács-Kiskun, Békés, and Szolnok and the municipality of Szeged to the Medical University of Szeged.

[40] *World Directory of Medical Schools.* Geneva: World Health Organization, 1963. p. 132.

Table 35.—Number of hours per week, per subject, in the first and second semesters at the medical university schools of general medicine, by year of study: 1965-66

Subject	Theoretical		Practical	
	First semester	Second semester	First semester	Second semester
First Year				
Anatomy	4	2	4	4
Histology	0	2	0	2
Latin [1]	----------	0	----------	0
Medical biology	3	[2] 2	2	2
Medical chemistry	[3] 5	[2] 4	4	4
Medical physics	2	[2] 2	3	2
Philosophy	[3] 3	[3] 2	0	1
Physical education	0	0	1	1
Russian	0	0	2	2
Second Year				
Anatomy	[3] 2	[2] 2	4	5
Biochemistry	2	[2] 2	2	2
Histology	2	[2] 2	2	2
Philosophy	[3] 1	0	1	0
Physical education	0	0	1	1
Physiology	[3] 6	[2] 4	4	4
Russian	0	0	2	2
Third Year				
General surgery	3	0	2	0
Introduction to internal medicine [4]	[3] 3	3	2	2
Microbiology and parasitology	3	[2] 2	2	2
Morbid anatomy	[3] 4	[2] 5	4	4
Pathological physiology	[3] 3	[2] 3	2	2
Political economy	[3] 2	[3] 1	0	1
Radiology	0	[3] 2	0	1
Special surgery	0	3	0	2
Fourth Year				
Dermatology and venereal diseases	2	[2] 2	1	1
Obstetrics and gynecology	4	4	1	2
Orthopedics	[3] 1	0	2	0
Pharmacology and toxicology	[3] 4	[2] 3	2	2
Scientific socialism	[3] 2	[3] 1	0	1
Special internal medicine (Infectious diseases)	[3] 5	5	3	3
Special surgery	4	4	1	2
Surgical anatomy and surgical techniques [5]	1	[2] 1	2	2
Fifth Year				
Forensic medicine	2	1	1	2
Health organizations (History of medicine)	2	[2] 0	1	0
Neurology and psychiatry	3	[2] 3	2	2
Ophthalmology	[2] 3	0	2	0
Otorhinolaryngology	0	[3] 2	0	2
Pediatrics	3	3	2	2
Public health and epidemiology	3	4	3	3
Scientific socialism	[3] 1	0	1	0
Special internal medicine (Infectious diseases)	[3] 5	5	2	2
Stomatology	0	[3] 1	0	2
Tuberculosis	0	[3] 1	0	2
Urology	[3] 1	0	2	0
Sixth Year				
Twelve-months' clinical practice with 3 months in each of the following departments: internal medicine, obstetrics and gynecology, pediatrics, and surgery.				

[1] For those who did not take Latin in secondary school.

[2] *Rigorosum* (year-end) examination.

[3] *Colloquium* (semester-end)) examination.

[4] Four weeks during the summer of compulsory training in a hospital for infectious diseases.

[5] Four weeks of compulsory surgical practice in a hospital.

SOURCE OF DATA: *World Survey of Education*—IV: Higher Education. New York: UNESCO, 1966 p. 589. *World Directory of Medical Schools*. Geneva: World Health Organization, 1964. p. 132.

Table 36.—Number of students and number of years of study at the five medical universities, by university and faculty (school): 1966–67; and number of 1966 graduates [1]

University and faculty (school)	Total	Girls	1966 graduates	Years of study
Grand total	8,353	5,154	1,295	
Medical University of Budapest (*Budapesti Orvostudományi Egyetem*)				
Total	*3,961*	*2,168*	*663*	
General medicine	2,603	1,284	370	6
Pharmacy	480	386	138	4½
Stomatology	878	498	155	4½
Medical University of Debrecen [2] (*Debreceni Orvostudományi Egyetem*)				
Total	*1,076*	*481*	*149*	*6*
Medical University of Pécs [2] (*Pécsi Orvostudományi Egyetem*)				
Total	*1,135*	*560*	*155*	*6*
Medical University of Szeged (*Szegedi Orvostudományi Egyetem*)				
Total	*1,597*	*877*	*228*	
General medicine	1,101	518	153	6
Pharmacy	385	305	75	4½
Stomatology	111	54	0	4½
University of Veterinary Medicine (*Állatorvostudományi Egyetem*) [3]				
Total	*584*	*68*	*100*	*5*

[1] Data released at beginning of academic year.

[2] The medical universities of Debrecen and Pécs each have only one faculty (school) of general medicine.

[3] Located in Budapest.

SOURCE OF DATA: *Tájékoztató a magyar felsőoktatási intézményekről* (Guide to the Hungarian Institutions of Higher Learning). Budapest: A Művelődésügyi Minisztérium kiadványa, 1965, p. 33-37, 62; *Statisztikai évkönyv 1966* (Statistical Yearbook 1966). Budapest: Központi Statisztikai Hivatal, 1967. p. 352.

a special examination before a National Examination Committee for the Qualification of Medical Specialists (*Országos Szakorvosképesítő Vizsgabizottság*) in one of the following 30 specialties: [41]

- Anesthesiology
- Childhood tubercular diseases
- Child psychiatry
- Child surgery
- Eye diseases
- Hygiene and epidemiology
- Hygienical and epidemiological laboratory examinations
- Infants' and children's diseases
- Infectious diseases
- Internal medicine
- Lung and tubercular diseases
- Lung surgery
- Medical laboratory examinations
- Medical organization
- Neurology
- Neuro-surgery

[41] "Az egészségügyi miniszter 7/1960. (VIII.24.) Eü.M. számú rendelete a szakorvosi képesitésről" (Decree No. 7/1960. (VIII.24.) Eü.M. of the Minister of Health Concerning the Qualification of Medical Specialists). *Magyar Közlöny*, Budapest, No. 72, August 24, 1960. p. 522-24. This Decree was amended in April 1968, providing for the following additional specialization areas: (31) Forensic medicine; (32) Forensic psychiatry; (33) Occupational or plant medicine; and (34) Aviation medicine. "Az egészségügyi miniszter 1/1968. (IV.9.)EüM. számú rendelete a szakorvosi képesitésről szóló 7/1960. (VIII.24.)EüM számú rendelet kiegészitéséről" (Decree No. 1/1968. (IV.9.)EüM of the Minister of Health Ameding Decree No. 7/1960. (VIII.24.)EüM Concerning the Qualification of Medical Specialists). *Magyar Közlöny*, No. 30, April 9, 1968. p. 325-26.

Obstetrics and gynecology
Oncoradiology
Orthopedics
Otorhinolaryngology
Pathological and histological examinations
Psychiatry
Radiology
Rheumatology and physical therapy
Skin and veneral diseases *or*
Venereal diseases and cosmetology
Sport medicine
Surgery
Tooth and mouth diseases
Traumatology
Urology

Examination committees operate in the four medical university cities of Budapest, Debrecen, Pécs, and Szeged.

As compared with pre-World War II medical enrollment, that during the 1960's shows a startling increase in the number of girls, a phenomenon characteristic of medical-pharmaceutical education in all the socialist countries. Medical and veterinary institutions in 1966-67 had 8,353 students, of whom 5,154 were girls. Their percent was greatest in pharmacy and lowest in veterinary medicine.

Total medical enrollment has had a general increase. As against only 1,451 students in the Schools of General Medicine and Stomatology in 1937-38, there were 6,904 in 1966-67. Because of the general increase in the number of engineering and polytechnical students in the postwar years, however, the percent of medical-stomatological students in the total student body decreased from 12.3 percent in 1937-38 to 7.7 percent in 1966-67.[42] Of the total of 1,295 graduates in 1966, 827 were in general medicine, 155 in dentistry, 213 in pharmacy,[43] and 100 in veterinary medicine.

With the exception of the medical personnel actively engaged in teaching, all physicians practicing in Hungary are required by law to attend a 5-month refresher course every 3 to 5 years.[44] These courses are organized under the auspices of the Institute for the Further Training of Physicians (*Orvostovábbképző Intézet*) and are offered, conducted, and guided by the State Hospital of Budapest located in Szabolcs Street. Like the medical universities, the Institute operates under the jurisdiction of the Ministry of Health.[45]

[42] *Statistical Pocket Book of Hungary 1967*, op. cit. p. 182. In 1960, the number of medical graduates was 795. During the same year Hungary had 14,398 physicians and about 1,300 doctors of dental medicine providing a ratio of 690 inhabitants per physician. *World Survey of Medical Schools*, op. cit. p. 131.

[43] Pharmaceutical studies in Hungary are pursued also under the auspices of the National Pharmaceutical Institute *(Országos Gyógyszerészeti Intézet)* of Budapest, which was established by Decree No. 2/1962. (III.22.) Eü.M. of the Minister of Health in March 1962. The primary function of the Institute is like that of the Food and Drug Administration in the United States. For text of Decree No. 2/1962, see *Magyar Közlöny*, No. 19, March 22, 1962. p. 202.

[44] "A Magyar Népköztársaság Minisztertanácsának 1.013/1956. (11.9.) számú határozata az orvostovábbképzés szervezetéről" (Resolution No. 1,013/1956. (II.9.) of the Council of Ministers of the Hungarian People's Republic Concerning the Organization of the Further Training of Physicians). *Magyar Közlöny*, No. 11, February 9, 1956. p. 63.

[45] For more details on medical education, see *Tájékoztató a magyar felsőoktatási intézményekről 1965*, op. cit. p. 33-37.

With the priority development of industry in postwar Hungary, polytechnical education acquired a special importance for training the politically reliable engineers and technicians needed by the socialist enterprises.[46] As compared with 1937-38, when there were only 1,052 students in technical higher education (representing 9 percent of the total higher education student body), in 1966-67 there were 32,404 (representing 36.2 percent). Of these 10,890 were in polytechnical universities, 13,074 in *technikums,* and 8,440 in other forms of technical higher education.[47]

Polytechnical University of Budapest

In 1966-67, Hungary had four polytechnical institutions of university status (table 37). Of these, by far the best known is the Polytechnical University of Budapest (*Budapesti Műszaki Egyetem*), founded in 1782. During 1966-67 its day session had 5,580 students, its evening session 3,350, and its correspondence courses 1,370 (table 37). Total enrollment was 10,300.

In June 1967 the university absorbed the Polytechnical University of Construction and Transportation (*Épitőipari és Közlekedési Műszaki Egyetem*) in Budapest.[48]

[46] For a revealing article on the importance attached to the appointment of politically reliable and professionally competent faculty for the training Communist-oriented engineers, see Pál Bátkai. "A káderfejlesztés elvei a Budapesti Műszaki Egyetemen" (The Principles Underlying the Training of Cadres at the Polytechnical University of Budapest). *Felsőoktatási Szemle*, Budapest. XV:3:135-39. March 1966. For a good summary of some of the most important features of higher technical education in Hungary, see L. Gillemot. "The Present Situation of Technical Higher Education in Hungary." *Hungarian Heavy Industries*, Budapest, First Quarter 1969.

[47] *Statistical Pocket Book of Hungary 1967*, op. cit. p. 182. See also tables 6 and 12.

[48] Decree No. 14 of 1967 of the Presidential Council of the People's Republic and Government Decree No. 15/1967. (VI.11.). *Magyar Közlöny*, No. 37, June 11, 1967. p. 318-19.

Table 37.—Number of students in day and evening sessions and correspondence courses of the four polytechnical universities, by university and faculty (school): 1966–67; and number of 1966 graduates[1]

Polytechnical university and faculty	Day session			Evening session			Correspondence courses		
	Total	Girls	1966 graduates	Total	Girls	1966 graduates	Total	Girls	1966 graduates
Grand total	10,890	2,187	1,813	6,026	752	422	2,572	268	310
Polytechnical University of Budapest (*Budapesti Műszaki Egyetem*) *Total*	*5,580*	*1,008*	*915*	*3,350*	*576*	*313*	*1,370*	*97*	*147*
Chemical engineering	734	389	146	460	238	73	0	0	0
Electrical engineering	2,620	352	415	1,425	164	84	939	72	59
Mechanical engineering	2,226	267	354	1,465	174	156	431	25	88
Polytechnical University of Construction and Transportation[2] (*Épitőipari és Közlekedési Műszaki Egyetem*) *Total*	*2,476*	*742*	*399*	*623*	*174*	*72*	*565*	*71*	*101*
Construction engineering	701	301	121	308	104	47	106	17	35
General engineering	1,301	394	205	198	58	8	335	46	46
Transportation engineering	474	47	73	117	12	17	124	8	20
Polytechnical University of Heavy Industry[3] (*Nehézipari Műszaki Egyetem*) *Total*	*2,171*	*230*	*366*	*53*	*2*	*0*	*389*	*17*	*62*
Mechanical engineering	1,370	128	265	53	2	0	162	3	22
Metallurgy	359	59	39	0	0	0	97	10	19
Mining	442	43	62	0	0	0	130	4	21
University of Chemical Industry of Veszprém (*Veszprémi Vegyipari Egyetem*) *Total*	*663*	*207*	*133*	*0*	*0*	*37*	*248*	*83*	*0*

[1] Data released at beginning of academic year.

[2] Located in Budapest.

[3] Located in Miskolc.

SOURCE OF DATA: *Statisztikai évkönyv 1966* (Statistical Yearbook 1966). Budapest: Központi Statisztikai Hivatal, 1967, p. 351.

The Polytechnical University of Construction and Transportation itself was formed in 1955 through consolidation of the Polytechnical University of Transportation (*Közlekedési Műszaki Egyetem*) and the Polytechnical University of Construction (*Építőipari Műszaki Egyetem*).[49]

The Polytechnical University of Heavy Industry (*Nehézipari Műszaki Egyetem*) of Miskolc was founded in 1949. In 1959, it absorbed the

[49] Aurél Hencz. *A művelődési intézmények és a művelődésigazgatás fejlődése, 1945-1961*, op. cit. p. 82-83.

School of Mining and Metallurgy (*Bánya- és Kohómérnöki Kar*) of the Polytechnical University of Budapest which operated at Sopron.[50]

The University of Chemical Industry of Veszprém (*Veszprémi Vegyipari Egyetem*) was established in 1951 through the transformation of the School of Industrial Chemistry (*Vegyipari Kar*) of the Polytechnical University of Budapest that operated in Veszprém into an independent institution of university status.

In March 1963, the Presidential Council provided for the establishment of a polytechnical university in Győr envisioned to begin its operations during the 1968-69 academic year.[51]

The university day session offers a 5-year program leading to a diploma in engineering (*mérnöki oklevél*). The first year is devoted to science-mathematics: chemistry, descriptive geometry, mathematics, mechanics, and physics; the third and fourth years to specialties.[52] First-, fourth-, and fifth-year students are expected to put in 30 weeks of practical work in their specialties.[53]

The Training of Engineer-Economists

The introduction and utilization of new technology and the need for organized planning and for increasing economic effectiveness (especially in construction, transportation, and the machine-building industry) induced the Government to introduce the training of engineer-economists. Launched in 1956, the program is offered under the auspices of the polytechnical universities of Budapest and the Karl Marx University of Economics. It involves an intensive four semester correspondence course in economics for engineers already holding the State diploma. When they graduate from this correspondence course they receive the engineer-economist diploma *(Mérnök-Közgazdász oklevél)*.[54]

The Further Training of Engineers

To increase the efficiency of engineering through enabling practicing engineers to keep abreast of scientific and technical developments in their field, the Government in 1960 organized the further training of engineers on a systematic basis. Such further training can take the form of individual study, organized lectures, specialized engineering training,

[50] *Ibid.* In 1952, the university was named after Mátyás Rákosi, then Secretary General of the Hungarian Communist Party (Decree No. 8 of 1952); In October 1956, its name was changed back to the original one by virtue of Decree No. 20 of 1956 of the Presidential Council. *Magyar Közlöny*, No. 91, Oct. 18, 1956. p. 562.

[51] "A Népköztársaság Elnöki Tanácsának 1963. évi 5. számú törvényerejű rendelete a Győri Műszaki Egyetem létesitéséről" (Decree No. 5 of 1963 of the Presidential Council of the People's Republic Concerning the Establishment of the Polytechnical University of Győr). *Magyar Közlöny*, No. 18, March 23, 1963. p. 101. In July 1966, the Government adopted Resolution No. 1012/1966. (VII.17.) reaffirming the establishment of a polytechnical institution of higher learning in Győr. *Magyar Közlöny*, No. 48, July 17, 1966. p. 485-86. In June 1968, under Decree No. 16, the Presidential Council announced the establishment of a Polytechnical Transportation and Telecommunications College (*Közlekedési és Távközlési Műszaki Főiskola*) at Győr. Placed under the jurisdiction of the Ministry of Culture, the 3-year college was scheduled to function with 4 faculties or schools. *Magyar Közlöny*, No. 46, June 4, 1968. p. 505. See also Resolution No. 1018/1968. (VI.4.) of the Government, Ibid. p. 506-07.

[52] For the detailed curriculum of the schools of electrical engineering, for example, see *World Survey of Education*. VI. *Higher Education*, op. cit. p. 590.

[53] *Tájékoztató a magyar felsőoktatási intézményekről 1965*, op. cit. p. 37.

[54] "A Magyar Népköztársaság Minisztertanácsának 1.035/1956. (V.19.) számú határozata a mérnökök közgazdasági képzéséről" (Resolution No. 1,035/1956. (V.19.) of the Council of Ministers of the Hungarian People's Republic Concerning the Training of Engineers in Economics). *Magyar Közlöny*, No. 41, May 19, 1956. p. 240.

and study abroad. The various programs are organized under the auspices of the Institute for the Further Training of Engineers (*Mérnöki Továbbképző Intézet*). Originally established in 1936 and reorganized in 1949, the Institute is under the control of the Ministry of Education and operates through a number of provincial branches. Its primary task is to organize lectures and courses and to issue publications. The correspondence course for specialized engineer training requires from three to five semesters.[55] Program participants are granted special paid leave.

IV. AGRONOMIC UNIVERSITIES AND COLLEGES

Just as the nationalization of the industrial enterprises and the subsequent introduction of planning led to the development of polytechnical institutions, the expropriation of the estates and the establishment of State and collective farms gave an impetus to agronomic-agricultural education in Hungary. Unevenly developed, agronomic higher education was periodically confronted with problems.[56]

Before the liberation in 1945, agricultural higher education was provided under the auspices of the School of Agriculture and Veterinary Medicine (*Mezőgazdasági és Állatorvosi Kar*) of the József Nádor University of Technology and Economics (*József Nádor Műszaki és Gazdaságtudományi Egyetem*). Within the framework of this school the present Agronomic University (*Agrártudományi Egyetem*) was established in 1945 in Budapest and Gödöllő.[57] The university began its operations with four schools—Veterinary Medicine (*Állatorvostudományi Kar*), Forestry (*Erdőmérnöki Kar*), Horticulture and Viticulture (*Kert- és Szőlészettudományi Kar*), and Agriculture (*Mezőgazdaságtudományi Kar*). The first three constituted the nucleus for separate universities in 1953.[58]

During the 1966-67 academic year, agronomic higher education was offered under the auspices of two universities and four colleges (table 38).[59] The program varies from 4½ to 5 years and leads to a degree in engineering. Operating under the jurisdiction of the Ministry of Agriculture, these institutions admit graduates of the agricultural vocational secondary schools and of the higher agricultural *technikums*. The latter are admitted without having to take the required admittance examination. As with all other Hungarian higher education institutions, those for agronomic training have more applicants than number of places assigned under a quota system by the National Planning Office acting in conjunction with the institutions.[60]

---

[55] "A Magyar Forradalmi Munkás-Paraszt kormány 1023/1964. (VIII.30.) számú határozata a mérnöktovábbképzés és a szakmérnökképzés továbbfejlesztéséről" (Resolution No. 1023/1964. (VIII.30.) of the Hungarian Worker-Peasant Government Concerning the Further Training of Engineers and the Program of Specialized Engineering). *Magyar Közlöny*, No. 55, August 30, 1964.

[56] László Fábián. "A mezőgazdasági szakemberképzés és problémái" (The Training of Agricultural Specialists and Its Problems). *Agrártudomány* (Agronomic Science), Budapest, 12:11:1-3, 1950. Aladár Kovács. "Változások a mezőgazdasági felsőoktatásban" (Changes in Agricultural Higher Education). *Felsőoktatási Szemle*, 6:1-2:67-68, 1957.

[57] László Szekeres. "Az Agrártudományi Egyetem" (The Agronomic University). *Felsőoktatási Szemle*, 7:10:606-10, 1958.

[58] Aurél Hencz. *A művelődési intézmények és a művelődésigazgatás fejlődése*, op. cit. p. 87.

[59] Although Hungarian sources identify the University of Veterinary Medicine as part of the agronomic institutions of higher learning, in this text it is treated as part of the medical universities. See p. 115.

[60] Gyula Szabó. "Gondolatok a mezőgazdasági és erdészeti egyetemek és főiskolák 1965/66. tanévi benépesítési munkájáról" (Thoughts on Enrollment in the Agricultural and Forestry Universities and Colleges During the 1965-66 Academic Year). *Felsőoktatási Szemle*, 15:6:347-50. June 1966.

Table 38.—Number of students in the day session and correspondence courses of the higher agronomic institutions, by institution and faculty (school): 1966–67; and number of 1966 graduates[1]

Institution, city and faculty (school)	Day session			Correspondence courses		
	Total	Girls	1966 graduates	Total	Girls	1966 graduates
Grand total	4,192	935	796	2,554	425	386
Agronomic Colleges[2] *(Agrartudomanyi Főiskolak)* *Debrecen* *Keszthely* *Mosonmagyaróvár*						
Total	*1,405*	*324*	*278*	*977*	*122*	*155*
Agronomic University *(Agrártudományi Egyetem)* *Gödöllő-Budapest*						
Total	*1,573*	*243*	*299*	*1,033*	*162*	*150*
Agricultural mechanical engineering	754	30	122	371	29	46
General agriculture	819	213	177	662	133	104
College of Horticulture and Viniculture[3] *(Kertészeti és Szőlészeti Főiskola)* *Budapest*						
Total	*695*	*264*	*131*	*346*	*117*	*45*
University of Forestry and Lumber Industry *(Erdészeti és Faipari Egyetem)* *Sopron*						
Total	*519*	*104*	*88*	*198*	*24*	*36*
Forest engineering	324	42	64	91	13	17
Lumber engineering	195	62	24	107	11	19

[1] Data released at beginning of academic year.

[2] The source did not show separate figures for the three agronomic colleges.

[3] The college was transformed into a horticulture university *(kertészeti egyetem)* under Decree No. 25 of 1968, issued by the Presidential Council of the People's Republic. *Magyar Közlöny* (Hungarian Gazette), No. 70, p. 669. September 1, 1968. Budapest.

SOURCE OF DATA: *Statisztikai évkönyv* 1966 (Statistical Yearbook 1966). Budapest: Központi Statisztikai Hivatal, 1967. p. 351.

By far the largest and most prestigious of these institutions is the Agronomic University of Budapest and Gödöllő, with a total 1966-67 enrollment of 2,606. Of these, 1,573 were in the day session and 1,033 in the correspondence section. The university also has an Institute for the Further Training of Skilled Workers *(Szakember Továbbképző Intézet)* offering accelerated and refresher courses.[61]

V. ART AND SPORT INSTITUTIONS[62]

Hungary has a few outstanding art institutions of higher learning, which admit only highly talented secondary or special-school graduates who are recommended by their teachers and who fulfill the other standard requirements for university admission. The length of study varies from institution to institution. The Hungarian College of Fine Arts *(Magyar Képzőművészeti Főiskola)*, founded in 1871, offers a 7-year course, the last 3 years of which are devoted to the mastery of a particular art, such as sculpture and painting. The Hungarian College of Indus-

[61] Aurél Hencz. *A művelődési intézmények és a művelődésigazgatás fejlődése*, op. cit. p. 87.

[62] The military schools for officers, which are also classified as institutions of higher learning are discussed in chapter IX.

trial Arts (*Magyar Iparművészeti Főiskola*) offers a 4-year program for training decorators and designers of textile, jewelry, ceramics, etc. The College of Dramatic and Cinematographic Art (*Szinház- és Filmművészeti Főiskola*) established as a college in 1948 through reorganization of the Hungarian National Academy of Dramatic Arts (*Országos Magyar Szinművészti Akadémia*), it offers a 4-year course for training actors and film operators and a 5-year course for training stage and film directors. The Liszt Ferenc College of Music (*Liszt Ferenc Zeneművészeti Főiskola*), founded in 1875, admits only talented graduates of music vocational schools and offers a 5-year course for training musicians and music teachers.

The organizational structure and general scope of the higher art institutions were established in 1949.[63] They operate under the auspices of the Ministry of Culture.

Table 39.—Number of students in the day session and correspondence courses of the art, music, and physical education higher institutions: 1966–67; and number of 1966 graduates[1]

Institution and city	Day session			Correspondence courses		
	Total	Girls	1966 graduates	Total	Girls	1966 graduates
Grand total	1,480	690	234	473	137	107
College of Dramatic and Cinematographic Art (*Szinház- és Filmművészeti Főiskola*) Budapest						
Total	*96*	*24*	*35*	*0*	*0*	*0*
Hungarian College of Fine Arts (*Magyar Képzőművészeti Főiskola*) Budapest						
Total	*148*	*59*	*23*	*29*	*13*	*0*
Hungarian College of Industrial Arts (*Magyar Iparművészeti Főiskola*) Budapest						
Total	*206*	*109*	*45*	*0*	*0*	*0*
Hungarian College of Physical Education (*Magyar Testnevelési Főiskola*) Budapest						
Total	*377*	*175*	*70*	*444*	*124*	*107*
Liszt Ferenc College of Music (*Liszt Ferenc Zeneművészeti Főiskola*) Budapest						
Total	*653*	*323*	*61*	*0*	*0*	*0*

[1] Data released at beginning of academic year. According to the Hungarian source, only the Hungarian College of Industrial Arts had an evening session. Its total enrollment of 17 included 14 girls.

SOURCE OF DATA: *Statisztikai évkönyv 1966* (Statistical Yearbook 1966). Budapest: Központi Statisztikai Hivatal, 1967. p. 352.

The Hungarian College of Physical Education (*Magyar Testnevelési Főiskola*) operates under the guidance of the Hungarian Council of Physical Education and Sport (*Magyar Testnevelési és Sport Tanács*). Its program is based to a large extent on findings and recommendations of the

[63] For references to decrees relating to the organizational structure of the art institutions of higher learning, see Aurél Hencz. *A művelődési intézmények és a művelődésigazgatás fejlődése*, op. cit. p. 374.

Scientific Research Institute of the Hungarian College of Physical Education (*Magyar Testnevelési Főiskola Tudományos Kutató Intézete*), which was established under Government Resolution No. 1004/1959. (I.25.) as amended by Government Resolution No. 1005/1969 (II.27.).

Both art and sport institutions on the higher education level train secondary school teachers. The teacher-training program normally lasts for only 4 years in contrast to the training program for sculptors and painters, which lasts 7 years.[64] Before they can be assigned to a school, graduates of the teacher-training programs in either art or sport must pass a State examination.[65]

During the 1966-67 academic year, these institutions had 1,480 students in the day session and 473 in the correspondence courses (table 39). By far the largest institution is the Liszt Ferenc College of Music, many of whose graduates have emerged as leading concert performers and conductors throughout the world.

Financing

Budgetary Allocations

The State budget provides funds for operating higher education institutions. Their expenditures comprise both operational costs (including salaries of the administrative personnel and of the faculty) and capital expenditures for construction, equipment, and furnishing new buildings. Expenditures must stay within the limits prescribed by directives of the National Economic Plan.

Tuition and Fees

Order No. 159/1963.(M.K.14.)MM of the Minister of Culture[66] regulates tuition. In accordance with that order, day-session students with excellent, outstanding, or good grade averages are exempt from any tuition payments. Those with a fair grade average or below pay tuition geared to the income of their parents or guardians, calculated per family member. Per semester, that scale is the following:

	Average income in forints[1] *per family member*		
Average grade	*Under 1,100*	*Between 1,100 and 1,800*	*Above 1,800*
Fair *(közepes)*	150	250	350
Passing *(elégséges)*	250	350	450
Unsatisfactory *(elégtelen)*	500	500	500

[1] Concerning the value of the forint, see footnote 54 of chapter III.

The student's first-year tuition is set according to the rank he obtained in the composite scores for all students taking the admittance examination.

[64] "A Magyar Forradalmi Munkás-Paraszt Kormány 1020/1964. (VIII.19.) számú határozata a Képzőművészeti Főiskola, valamint az Iparművészeti Főiskola képzési idejéről" (Resolution No. 1020/1964. (VII.19.) of the Hungarian Worker-Peasant Government Concerning the Length of Study in the College of Fine Arts and the College of Industrial Arts). *Magyar Közlöny*, No. 45, July 19, 1964. p. 304.

[65] For details on training teachers and instructors of physical education see p. 151-52.

[66] *Tájékoztató a magyar felsőoktatási intézményekről*, op. cit. p. 14-15.

Except for those enrolled in teacher-training colleges and institutes, evening-session and correspondence-course students also pay tuition. The range is 80 to 350 forints per semester, depending upon the student's income and his scholastic achievement. If his average grade is excellent or outstanding and his monthly income is under 1,600 forints, he is exempt from tuition payment.

Scholarships and Grants

Hungary has a liberal scholarship and student welfare program. Day session students may receive two basic types of State assistance: social benefits and scholarships.

Social assistance to students consists of dormitory rooms, meals at discount prices, and regular and emergency financial aid. Priority in dormitory assignment is given to students who live at long distances from the institution. For social assistance, students are grouped into three categories, depending on the per capita income (in forints) of their families or guardians, as follows:

Forints

1. Under 800
2. Between 800 and 1,100
3. Above 1,100

Scholarships are of two types: general and People's Republic scholarships *(Népköztársasági Tanulmányi Ösztöndij)*. Administered by the dean's or director's office and awarded for one semester, general scholarships are for students whose grades are "Good" or better. Their value ranges from 100 to 300 forints per month: "Excellent" students receive 300, "Outstanding" students 250, and "Good" students 150. The People's Republic scholarships, of two grades, yield 1,000 and 700 forints per month, respectively, for "Outstanding" students. First-year students are not eligible.

So-called "social" scholarships are awarded to students by cooperatives, enterprises, and social organizations. Priority is given especially to children of workers performing physical work; the intention is to stimulate enrollment of workers in the villages and provincial towns. The qualifications for such scholarships are relatively easy: applicants must show unimpeachable attitudes and have at least average grades.

These scholarships are awarded on the basis of a contract under which the recipients undertake to work after graduation for a period of time and at a location set forth in the contract. Normally, the service is for the same number of years as the number during which the recipent held the scholarship. The scholarship itself consists of three parts: a base amount ranging from 200 to 450 forints per month, a bonus for those who agree to work in rural areas after graduation, and a supplement for those who have distinguished themselves in their studies.

Evening-session and correspondence-course students, especially those enrolled in polytechnical institutes, are given special paid leaves of absence to prepare for their course or State examinations and are assigned to types of work and shifts that will not interfere with their academic responsibilities.[67]

Examinations and Grading

Basically, examinations are of three kinds: colloquiums at the end of a semester, *rigorosa (szigorlatok)* at the end of a scholastic year or the completion of a subject, and State at the end of the university course.[68]

Academic-scholastic achievement is measured and recorded in higher education the same way as in elementary and secondary: *5*—outstanding or excellent; *4*—good; *3*—average; *2*—passing; *1*—failure. Two kinds of grades (those expressed in figures and those expressed in adjectives) appear in the student's "course book" (*leckekönyv*).

Students who have an outstanding academic record, who show special achievement in a particular field, and who also have a history of exemplary attitude and behavior are awarded the Higher Education Studies medal (*Felsőoktatási Tanulmányi Érdemérem*) in the presence of the minister exercising jurisdiction over the school. Medal recipients are given special privileges when positions are being filled and postgraduate scholarships awarded.[69]

Scientific Degrees and Their Requirements

Hungary awards two types of higher scientific degrees: Candidate-in-Science (*Tudományok kandidátusa*) and Doctor of Science (*Tudományok doktora*). The first step in the acquisition of the Candidate-in-Science degree is taken in the aspirature system.

The stated objective in training candidates and doctors in science is (a) to assure a supply of university and college instructors and scientific resarchers imbued with a Marxist ideology; and (b) to stimulate scientific research work in the service of socialist construction.

The Scientific Qualification Committee

Candidates for higher degree work under the supervision and direction of the Scientific Qualification Committee (*Tudományos Minösitő*

---

[67] For details see "A művelődésügyi miniszter 6/1963. (XI.6.)MM számú rendelete a társadalmi tanulmányi ösztöndij szabályozásáról szóló 22/1963. (IX.21.) Korm. számú rendelet végrehajtásáról (Decree No. 6/1963. (XI.6.)MM of the Minister of Culture Concerning the Implementation of Decree No. 22/1963. (IX.21) Korm. Concerning the Regulation of Social Scholarships). *Magyar Közlöny*, No. 78, November 6, 1963. p. 584-92. The appendix to the Decree includes a sample of the contract form.

See also "A művelődésügyi miniszter 6/1968. (VIII.11.)MM számú rendelete a nappali tagozaton iskolai képzésben résztvevőkkel köthető tanulmányi szerződésekről" (Decree No. 6/1968. (VIII.11.)MM of the Minister of Culture Concerning the Study Contracts That Can be Concluded with Those Enrolled in the Day Session). Ibid. No. 66, August 11, 1968. p. 650-54.

In July 1969 the Minister of Culture issued a new decree abrogating Decree No. 6/1968. (VIII.11.)MM. The new one altered somewhat the provisions concerning study contracts with day session students. See Decree No. 5/1969. (VII.27.)MM of the Minister of Culture. *Magyar Közlöny*, No. 57, July 27, 1969. p. 573-76.

[68] For details concerning the bar examination and the practical work requirements of law students see Decree No. 6/1949. (VI.11.)I.M. of the Minister of Justice in *Magyar Közlöny*, No. 65, June 11, 1959. p. 541-46.

[69] "A Népköztársaság Elnöki Tanácsának 1958. évi 1-7. számú határozata a kiváló egyetemi (főiskolai, akadémiai) hallgatók kitüntetéséről" (Resolution No. 1-7 of 1958 of the Presidential Council of the People's Republic Concerning the Decoration of Outstanding University (College, Academy) Students). *Magyar Közlöny*, No. 18, February 23, 1958. p. 166-67.

Bizottság) in accordance with general directions outlined by the Government.[70]

The Committee operates under the guidance and supervision of the presidential board of the Hungarian Academy of Sciences *(Magyar Tudományos Akadémia)*. The president, secretary, and members of the Committee are appointed by the Government on recommendation by the Academy's president. The members and officials of the Committee normally hold higher degrees and include some representatives from the ministries. To implement its responsibilities, the Committee establishes special committees for various scientific fields. Appeals from Committee decisions may be filed with the president of the Academy.

Table 40.—Number of persons holding science degrees, by degree level: 1961–66

Year	Doctor of science	Candidate in science	Aspirature in science
1961	303	1,806	1,714
1962	307	1,996	1,663
1963	340	2,212	1,300
1964	371	2,403	970
1965	384	2,518	584
1966	418	2,776	558

SOURCE OF DATA: *Statisztikai évkcnyv 1966* (Statistical Yearbook 1966). Budapest: Központi Statisztikai Hivatal, 1967. p. 361.

The Aspirature

The first step in earning the degree of Candidate-in-Science is the aspirature, which may be obtained either through a scholarship or through correspondence courses. The participants are selected by the Scientific Qualification Committee through public competitions and admittance examinations. To be eligible for the aspirature, candidates must have completed a university or college course must have worked at least 3 years following graduation, must have acquired specialized knowledge in a specific area, must show an inclination toward scientific research, and must be under 35 years of age. Exemptions from some of these requirements may be granted by the Committee.

The "scholarship aspirature" students receive a State scholarship and prepare for their Candidate-in-Science degree at an assigned scientific organization for 3 years. The "correspondence aspirature" students continue to work at their regular jobs but are given special paid time off and leaves of absence to prepare for the degree.[71]

All aspirature students work under the guidance of an "aspirature leader" appointed by the Scientific Qualification Committee, in cooperation with the university departments in the various areas. Preparation of the candidates in philosophy and languages is the responsibility of the universities.

[70] "A Népköztársaság Elnöki Tanácsának 1963. évi 19. számú törvényerejű rendelete a tudományos minösitésről és a tudományos fokozatokról" (Decree No. 19. of 1963 of the Presidential Council of the People's Republic Concerning the Scientific Qualification System and the Scientific Degrees). *Magyar Közlöny*, No. 57, August 14, 1963, p. 413-16, as amended by Decree No. 19 of 1967 of the Presidential Council and implemented by Government Decree No. 20/1963. (VIII.14.). See *Magyar Közlöny*, cited above. p. 416-24.

[71] "A munkaügyi miniszter 4/1965. (X.3.)MuM számú rendelete az ösztöndijas aspiránsok és ösztöndijas doktorjelöltek munkaviszonyával és társadalom-biztositásával kapcsolatos egyes kérdések szabályozásáról" (Decree No. 4/1965. (X.3.)MuM of the Minister of Labor Concerning the Regulation of Certain Questions Relating to the Social Security and Employment of Aspirature Students and Doctoral Candidates with Scholarships). *Magyar Közlöny*, No. 56, October 3, 1965. p. 520-22.

The Candidate-in-Science Degree

The degree of Candidate-in-Science may be awarded to scholarship and correspondence-course aspirature students, as well as to others not participating in this form of training who fulfill certain conditions. These latter must have graduated from a university or college, must have engaged in scientific work, must have prepared and defended a dissertation that reveals new scientific results in the service of social progress, and must have passed special examinations.

Given by special scientific committees appointed by the Scientific Qualifying Committee in cooperation with the universities, the examinations cover the candidate's fields, philosophy, and foreign languages. Permission to defend one's dissertation is granted only after it has been dicussed by the candidate's colleagues at his place of work. Normally, the defense is public; either the entire text or excerpts from it are published in a specialized journal. When he has successfully defended his dissertation, the candidate is qualified to receive the degree of Candidate-in-Science.

There are no age limits for either the candidate-in-science or doctoral candidates as there are for candidates for the aspirature. Moreover, there are no definite legal requirements as to the number of years a candidate may take to complete the degree rquirements except that the Scientific Qualification Committee may demand that the candidate-in-science again take the degree examinations if he submits his dissertation 5 years after first taking them.[72]

The Doctorate

Candidates for the degree of Doctor of Science enjoy special scholarships or paid leaves to prepare for the degree at an institution to which they are assigned for this purpose by the Committee.

Candidates for the doctoral degree must fulfill the following conditions: (a) have earned the degree of Candidate-in-Science, unless exempted by the Scientific Qualification Committee; (b) have worked for at least 3 years after receiving the Candidate-in-Science degree in some branch of science, with significant scientific results; and (c) prepare and defend a doctoral dissertation that is based on independent scientific work, sets forth new scientific results, and serves social progress. Conditions and procedures for the dissertation's defense are similar to those applying to the Candidate-in-Science dissertation. Doctoral candidates who have an outstanding secondary school and university record and who pass the doctoral examination *summa cum laude* are awarded a special doctoral degree and diploma, "Promotio sub auspiciis Rei Publicae Popularis," given together with a gold ring bearing the emblem of the People's Republic.[73]

Holders of higher scientific degrees (table 40) have special advantages

---

[72] Article 13 of Decree No. 19 of 1963 of the Presidential Council cited above.

[73] "A Népköztársaság Elnöki Tanácsának 1958. évi 1-6 számú határozata a kitüntetéses doktorráavatásról" (Resolution No. 1-6 of 1958 of the Presidential Council of the People's Republic Concerning the Awarding of Doctoral Degrees with Honors). *Magyar Közlöny*, No. 18, February 23, 1958. p. 166. For information on the medical doctorate, see p. 115-18.

when jobs are being filled and grants awarded. In return, they are obligated to pursue scientific work, help maintain the supply of trained scientific workers, and serve the cause of social progress.

Under government-established conditions, foreigners may also earn Hungarian scientific degrees.

Evaluation of Foreign Degrees

Foreigners permanently settled in Hungary and Hungarians who have studied and earned a degree abroad may have their records evaluated and their diplomas equated with those granted by Hungarian institutions of higher learning.

The procedure is relatively simple: An applicant must submit his foreign diploma, a copy of his transcript, and his citizenship or residency papers to the faculty or institution of his particular specialty. In the absence of such a faculty or institution, the applicant must send his documents to the Ministry of Culture. If a faculty (school) renders an unfavorable decision, the applicant may appeal to the rector (if the university has several faculties) or (in the case of all other institutions) to the minister who exercises direct control over the particular faculty.[74]

Enrollment

In order to satisfy the requirements of Hungary's increasingly industrialized economy, the Government laid more and more stress after World War II on training engineers and technicians. They were of course to be trained in such a manner as to become not only professionally competent but also ideologically and politically reliable.

The pre-War (1937-38) figures for higher education contrast sharply with the post-War ones (1966-67), as shown below:

	1937–38	*1966–67*
Institutions	16	92
Instructors	1,724	8,889
Students	11,747	89,544

Of the entire 11,747 students in 1937-38, only 14.5 percent were women; but of the entire 89,544 in 1966-67, the day session alone (52,327 students) was 43.3 percent women.[75]

Of the 92 institutions identified in 1966-67 as offering higher education, 48 were in fact higher *technikums*—that is, technical schools that

[74] "A művelődésügyi miniszter 8/1963. (XII.30.)MM rendelete a külföldi felsőoktatási intézmények által kiállitott oklevelek honositásáról" (Decree No. 8/1963. (XII.30.)MM of the Minister of Culture Concerning the Evaluation of Diplomas Issued by Foreign Institutions of Higher Learning). *Magyar Közlöny*, No. 94, December 30, 1963. p. 733-34, as amended by Decree No. 1/1966. (V.7.)MM of the Minister of Culture. For the latter decree see *Magyar Közlöny*, No. 30, May 7, 1966, p. 274.

The conditions under which Hungarians may study abroad are carefully regulated by law. See "A Magyar Forradalmi Munkás-Paraszt Kormány 1020/1968. (VI.19.) számú határozata magyar állampolgároknak külföldi tanintézetekben folytatandó tanulmányairól" (Resolution No. 1020/1968. (VI.19.) of the Hungarian Revolutionary Worker-Peasant Government Concerning the Studies by Hungarian Citizens in Foreign Educational Institutions). *Magyar Közlöny*, No. 49, June 19, 1968. p. 532.

Of the entire 11,747 students in 1937-38, only 14.5 percent were women; but of the entire 89,544 in 1966-67, the day session alone (52,327) students was 43.3 percent women.[75]

[75] *Statistical Pocket Book of Hungary 1967*, op. cit. p. 182.

might most accurately be termed specialized postsecondary schools.[76] The total enrollment count for 1966-67 (89,544) must therefore take cognizance of the fact that these *technikums* alone accounted for three large segments of that enrollment: 4,159 students in agriculture, 2,968 in economics, and 13,074 in polytechnical (industrial) classes (table 41). These segments totaled 20,201.

Table 41.—Number of students in higher education institutions, by specialized field: 1960–61 and 1964–65—67, and percent which enrollment in each field constitutes of the entire enrollment: 1966–67

Field of specialization	1960–61	1964–65	1965–66	1966–67	Percent of entire 1966–67 enrollment
Total	44,585	91,923	93,957	89,544	100.0
Agriculture	3,308	9,834	10,112	9,063	10.1
[*In technikums*	*0*	*4,983*	*5,061*	*4,159*	*4.6*]
Art	831	873	858	1,149	1.3
Economics	2,390	6,718	7,486	7,693	8.6
[*In technikums*	*0*	*2,174*	*2,670*	*2,968*	*3.3*]
Law	3,827	4,332	3,936	3,755	4.2
Medicine	5,744	6,652	6,776	6,904	7.7
Natural sciences	2,964	6,070	5,779	5,522	6.2
Pharmacy	865	912	909	865	1.0
Philosophy	3,905	7,399	7,164	6,838	7.6
Physical education	486	904	885	821	0.9
Polytechnical education	12,349	30,408	32,854	32,404	36.2
[*In technikums*	*0*	*9,958*	*12,417*	*13,074*	*14.6*]
Remedial education	330	[3] 713	[3] 694	668	0.7
Teacher-training colleges	4,561	11,414	11,338	9,556	10.7
Teacher-training institutes	1,687	3,899	3,422	2,838	3.1
Teacher-training institutes for kindergarten teachers	712	1,185	1,124	884	1.0
Veterinary medicine	626	610	620	584	0.7

[1] Figures cover day and evening sessions and correspondence courses.

[2] Data relesed at beginning of academic year.

[3] Includes data of the Institute for Training Instructors of Motor-Disorder Victims (*Mozgássérültek Nevelőképző és Nevelőintézete*).

SOURCE OF DATA: *Statisztikai évkönyv 1966* (Statistical Yearbook 1966). Budapest: Központi Statisztikai Hivatal, 1967. p. 348.

The 1937-38—1966-67 enrollment contrasts carry over into figures for specialized fields, as disclosed below:

	1937–38		*1966–67*	
	Number	*Percent of total enrollment*	*Number*	*Percent of total enrollment*
Architecture and engineering	1,052	9.0	32,404	36.2
Law	4,671	39.8	3,755	4.2

Placement of Graduates

According to a decree adopted in 1961,[78] higher education graduates were to undergo a compulsory 2-year probation (only 1 year if they

[76] See p. 96.

[77] *Statistical Pocket Book of Hungary 1967*, op. cit. p. 182.

[78] "A Magyar Forradalmi Munkás-Paraszt Kormány 21/1961. (V.25.) számú rendelete a felsőiskolák nappali tagozatán végzők foglalkoztatásáról" (Decree No. 21/1961. (V.25.) of the Hungarian Revolutionary Worker-Peasant Government Concerning the Employment of the Day-Session Graduates of the Institutions of Higher Learning). *Magyar Közlöny*, No. 39, May 25, 1961. p. 332-33.

had already had 1 year of practical training) at enterprises or organizations specified by the ministries. The sphere and conditions of employment were restricted by the decree.

In November 1967, the Council of Ministers adopted a new system for placing and employing college graduates, stipulating that they "can be employed without restrictions and according to the general regulations."[79] Under this new system, graduates will find employment according to three methods: (1) looking for their own jobs, (2) entering competitions conducted by enterprises, and (3) seeking employment-agency help. If a graduate holds an enterprise- or organization-granted scholarship that obligates him to work for the grantor after his graduation, he would not look for a job.

Placing medical-university graduates (i.e., pharmacists and physicians), and graduates of agronomic universities and teacher-training colleges and institutes will continue to be the responsibility of the ministry having jurisdiction over the particular institution.

This new system for placing and employing college graduates was adopted in accordance with the principles of "economic mechanization" ("Libermanism"), also introduced in 1967, which welds to the socialist economy the price-and-market mechanism that is characteristic of a capitalist economy.

Table 42.—Number of students in the first and last years of their studies in day and evening sessions and correspondence courses of higher education institutions, by specialized field: 1960–61 and 1964–65—1966–67[1]

Field of specialization	1960–61		1964–65		1965–66		1966–67	
	First year	Last year	First year	Last year	First year	Last year	First year	Last year
	DAY SESSION							
Total	8,369	4,350	14,112	9,538	14,154	10,669	14,389	11,896
Agriculture	719	360	2,090	1,725	2,075	1,719	1,943	1,764
[*In technikums*	*0*	*0*	*1,315*	*1,145*	*1,283*	*1,091*	*1,194*	*1,106*]
Art	163	166	207	174	157	166	299	202
Economics	358	184	770	494	909	640	945	832
[*In technikums*	*0*	*0*	*243*	*121*	*360*	*201*	*406*	*277*]
Law	278	0	370	254	346	275	426	321
Medicine	1,108	814	1,249	1,053	1,242	977	1,171	1,154
Natural sciences	791	279	1,075	644	1,052	749	1,060	777
Pharmacy	242	209	232	218	228	227	227	226
Philosophy	538	255	860	446	788	523	662	709
Physical education	92	44	114	92	105	81	74	108
Polytechnical education	2,269	1,138	4,616	2,497	5,031	3,155	5,364	3,738
[*In technikums*	*0*	*0*	*1,850*	*646*	*2,259*	*1,047*	*2,729*	*1,352*
Remedial education	66	43	56	59	56	67	65	78
Teacher-training colleges	612	489	1,314	677	1,128	923	990	925
Teacher-training institutes	724	0	730	812	632	763	719	678
Teacher-training institutes for kindergarten teachers	269	255	292	276	275	280	324	265
Veterinary medicine	140	114	137	117	130	124	120	119

[79] *Népszabadság* (People's Freedom), Budapest, November 3 and 4, 1967.

Field of specialization	1960–61 First year	1960–61 Last year	1964–65 First year	1964–65 Last year	1965–66 First year	1965–66 Lasr year	1966–67 First year	1966–67 Last year
	EVENING SESSION							
Total	965	49	4,806	961	3,685	2,230	2,730	2,505
Agriculture	0	0	0	0	0	0	0	0
Art	9	0	0	14	18	0	0	0
Economics	0	0	759	329	881	450	790	457
[*In technikums*	*0*	*0*	*284*	*0*	*293*	*0*	*337*	*183*
Law	0	0	430	223	283	181	239	236
Medicine	0	0	0	0	0	0	0	0
Natural sciences	44	10	137	7	111	25	64	21
Philosophy	0	0	410	164	279	187	138	222
Physical education	0	0	0	0	0	0	0	0
Polytechnical education	912	39	3,044	224	2,113	1,364	1,499	1,569
[*In technikums*	*0*	*0*	*1,507*	*26*	*1,209*	*818*	*1,152*	*1,066*
Remedial education [2]	0	0	26	0	0	23	0	0
Teacher-training colleges	0	0	0	0	0	0	0	0
Teacher-training institutes	0	0	0	0	0	0	0	0
Teacher-training institutes for kindergarten teachers	0	0	0	0	0	0	0	0
	CORRESPONDENCE COURSES							
Total	5,285	1,032	11,079	4,332	8,081	6,603	5,029	6,810
Agriculture	483	132	1,740	693	1,394	1,255	845	1,153
[*In technikums*	*0*	*0*	*1,161*	*383*	*893*	*912*	*384*	*814*]
Art	0	0	0	0	17	0	10	0
Economics	461	144	610	173	657	307	741	317
[*In technikums*	*0*	*0*	*392*	*87*	*445*	*178*	*519*	*166*]
Law	954	352	478	256	348	277	224	218
Medicine	0	0	0	0	0	0	0	0
Natural sciences	118	0	1,093	60	397	156	183	204
Philosophy	540	[3] 132	1,141	275	519	470	340	558
Physical education	71	32	178	122	146	104	98	110
Polytechnical education	677	240	2,039	616	2,322	1,019	1,803	1,043
[*In technikums*	*0*	*0*	*1,185*	*217*	*1,513*	*584*	*1,276*	*638*]
Remedial education	55	0	129	48	76	51	79	79
Teacher-training colleges	1,467	0	2,860	1,342	1,595	2,072	500	2,528
Teacher-training institutes	271	0	458	483	340	593	145	366
Teacher-training institutes for kindergarten teachers	188	0	353	264	270	299	61	234

[1] Data released at beginning of academic year.

[2] Figures of the Institute for Training Instructors of Motor-Disorder Victims *(Mozgássérültek Nevelőképző és Nevelőintézete)*.

[3] Does not include enrollment of extension department *(szakosító tagozat)*.

SOURCE OF DATA: *Statisztikai évkönyv 1966* (Statistical Yearbook 1966). Budapest: Központi Statisztikai Hivatal, 1967. p. 349-50.

The Teaching Faculty

Ranks and Titles

Aside from physical education instructors and teaching fellows (trainees), the teaching faculty in higher education includes the ranks of professor (*tanár*), *docens* or *docent* (equivalent to the American associate professor), assistant professor (*adjunktus*), and assistant (*tanársegéd*).

University professors are appointed by the Council of Ministers;[80]

[80] The Council of Ministers exercises this prerogative through the minister having direct jurisdiction over the particular institution. "A Magyar Forradalmi Munkás-Paraszt Kormány 1008/1968. (III.24.) számú határozata az egyetemi tanárok kinevezéséről" (Resolution No. 1008/1968. (III.24.) of the Hungarian Revolutionary Worker-Peasant Government Concerning the Appointment of University Professors). *Magyar Közlöny*, No. 25, March 24, 1968. p. 286.

professors at *technikums,* colleges, and institutes and *docents* at universities and colleges, by the minister exercising jurisdiction over the particular institution.[81]

In selecting professors, the Council of Ministers or the appropriate minister engages in competitive bidding and requests the President of the Hungarian Academy of Sciences to give his recommendation. If the minister making the appointment is not the Minister of Culture, he also requests the latter's advice. Dismissal of a professor is the exclusive responsibility of the minister exercising direct jurisdiction over the institution where the professor is employed.[82]

In addition to the faculty members just described, there are the so-called titular (*cimzetes*) professors and *docents,* all of whom are appointed by the minister exercising jurisdiction over the school(s) where they are to be employed. He appoints them on the recommendation of the institution's rector or director and of the faculty council. In an institution having several schools, the deans of these schools initially make their recommendations to the rector.

The rank of titular professor or *docent* can be awarded to persons who have already earned the degree of Candidate-in-Science or Doctor of Science and who—

1. Show a capacity for pursuing independent study in one of the sciences taught at the university.
2. Have served at least 2 years as visiting lecturer at a university.
3. Are not employed as part of the regular teaching faculty at any higher education institution.[83]

The minister who has jurisdiction normally appoints a titular professor or a *docent* as department chairman to direct and supervise the department's activities. The chairman's duties also require him to approve the departmental work plan for lectures and practical class work.

Recruitment of teaching faculty is conducted on a competitive basis. Young members in a department who are interested in receiving a permanent appointment, instructors at other higher education institutions, and qualified persons employed in fields other than teaching may apply for vacant positions. Recent graduates may apply for a position as assistant.

Work Load and Salary

Theoretically, members of the teaching faculty lecture (or conduct practical classes) for only 8½ hours a week.[84] Their work load, however, includes not only lecture hours but also standard departmental responsibilities. In addition, they (especially ones of high rank) are expected to devote much of their spare time to research and writing for publication.

Teaching faculty are entitled to a salary raise every 3 years. At a

[81] Article 9 of Decree No. 22/1962 cited above.

[82] Article 4 of Resolution No. 1008/1968 cited above.

[83] "A művelődésügyi miniszter 1/1963. (II.24.)MM számú rendelete a cimzetes egyetemi (főiskolai) tanárokról és docensekről" (Decree No. 1/1963. (II.24.)MM of the Minister of Culture Concerning the Titular University (College) Professors and Docents). *Magyar Közlöny,* No. 10, February 24, 1963. p. 58-59.

[84] The teaching system in higher education is rather rigid, instructors being bound to follow the programs, curriculums, and syllabuses prescribed by the central educational authorities. see Articles 10-14 of Decree No. 22/1962, cited above.

regular university, the 1965 beginning salary of a professor without previous teaching experience was 3,350 forints per month. The highest monthly salary for a full professor was 4,650 forints. At teacher-training colleges, the teaching faculty that year had a somewhat lower salary scale: from 2,750 to 4,050 forints per month; at teacher-training institutes, from 1,900 to 3,450. The 1965 supplementary monthly forint allowances were scaled as follows: *rector*—1,900; *university dean*—1,200; *director of a teacher-training college or institute*—1,000; *department chairman*—300. (In 1965, the official exchange rate was 11.74 forints to the U.S. dollar. See footnote 54, chapter III.)

Members of the teaching faculty are covered by a general law concerning pensions, with retirement eligibility at age 60 for men and 55 for women. In most cases, however, they do not retire until the age of 65 or 70. They are entitled to an annual vacation of 48 days and in exceptional cases may be given a 3-month sabbatical leave to complete a book or accomplish something similar.

Members of the teaching faculty belong to the higher education section of the Teachers Union.[85]

Extra-Academic Activities

Under certain conditions, higher education institutions as institutions and individual members of the teaching staff (table 43) may engage in extra-academic activities of a scientific or technical nature. In such an activity, the institution or staff member might—

1. Test materials and equipment in a laboratory.
2. Test models.
3. Work to improve new technical processes; prepare new materials and chemicals.
4. Prepare and submit expert opinions and advice.
5. Prepare technical plans.
6. Prepare technical equipment, give technical supervision, or render a similar service.

Work of this type may be accepted for an institution by its head only, and only if the work falls within the framework of the institution's regular work, requires advanced scientific training, helps further the scientific and educational development of the young instructors, does not interfere with the institution's scientific-educational responsibilities, and will not require equipment or personnel beyond what the institution already has. These stipulations and the payment to be made to the institution for the services are spelled out in a contract.

Individual members of the teaching staff may assume extra-academic responsibilies only with the written consent of the head of the institution, and this consent depends upon the department chairman's recommendation. Payment for an individual's services is made to the institution. The general criteria for his acceptance of an extra-academic assign-

[85] *World Survey of Education*. IV. *Higher Education*, op. cit. p. 591 and 593. For the salary scales that were in effect in the late 1950's and early 1960's see Cabinet Decree No. 26/1956. (IX.2.)M.T. in *Magyar Közlöny*, No. 76, September 2. 1956. p. 465-67.

ment and the contract provisions are similar to those applying to an institution.[86]

The Hungarian Academy of Sciences

Scope and Functions

Hungary's highest scientific institution, entrusted with the advancement of science and the organization, direction, and synchronization of pure and applied research, is the Hungarian Academy of Sciences (*Magyar Tudományos Akadémia*). Under its auspices or that of its scientific institutions are conducted many of the extra-academic activities of the scientific and instructional staff of higher education institutions. Although many of these staff members are also members of the Academy and work for its various institutes, the Academy itself (unlike the USSR Academy of Sciences) does not conduct formal graduate studies. Such studies and programs leading to a higher degree are offered by the universities. The Academy, however, plays an important role in the operation of the Scientific Qualification Committee concerned with the awarding of degrees.[87]

The Academy is based on its pre-World War II organizational-scientific structure as modified in 1949 by Law XXVII and further regulated in 1960 by Law No. 24.[88]

The Academy's function is to—

1. Promote the development of individuals engaged in scientific work and help them in their scientific activities.
2. Expand conditions and opportunities for scientific research and publication of scientific books and periodicals.
3. Nurture and develop international relations for Hungarian science.

The Academy operates under the immediate supervision and direction of the Government. In this role, the Government—

1. Decides what tasks shall be entrusted to the Academy in its work of directing the country's scientific life.
2. Approves the Academy's organizational structure and the bylaws which its general assembly has adopted.
3. Supervises the Academy's activities that are related to its direction of the country's scientific life.

The Academy's scientific activities are conducted in the institutes operating under the Academy's various sections, in the scientific in-

---

[86] Until June 30, 1969, the extra-academic assignments of universities and colleges were regulated by the following decree: "A művelődésügyi miniszter 5/1958. (XI.7.)M.M. számú rendelete az egyetemek és főiskolák által végzett külső megbizások szabályozásáról" (Decree No. 5/1958. (XI.7.)M.M. of the Minister of Culture Concerning the Regulation of Extra-Mural Work Assumed by the Universities and Colleges). *Magyar Közlöny*, No. 102, November 7, 1958. p. 740-43 (this decree was abrogated by Decree No. 7/1968. (IX.10.)MM of the Minister of Culture; for text, see *Magyar Közlöny*, No. 74, September 18, 1968. p. 694.); "Az épitésügyi miniszter 7/1959. (V.6.)É.M. számú rendelete az egyetemek és főiskolák által végezhető műszaki tervezési tevékenységről" (Decree No. 7/1959. (V.6.)É.M. of the Minister of Constructions Concerning the Technical Planning Work that Can Be Assumed by Universities and Colleges). *Magyar Közlöny*, No. 50, May 6, 1959. op. cit. p. 352-53.

[87] See p. 127-28.

[88] "A Népköztársaság Elnöki Tanácsának 1960 évi 24. számú törvényerejű rendelete a Magyar Tudományos Akadémiáról" (Decree No. 24 of 1960 of the Presidential Council of the People's Republic Concerning the Hungarian Academy of Sciences). *Magyar Közlöny*, Budapest, No. 88, October 15, 1960. p. 615-16.

stitutes of various ministries, or in institutions of higher education (appendix D).

Besides organizing and conducting scientific activities as such, the Academy also engages in certain related activities. Among other things, it—

1. Supports individual, collective, and institutional scientific research and contracts for scientific projects.
2. Organizes scientific meetings, congresses, and symposia and publishes books and periodicals.
3. Arranges for representatives of Hungarian science to maintain contact with foreign scientists and participate in foreign scientific congresses and symposia; and (under certain circumstances) for foreign scientists to take part in Academy activities.
4. Cooperates with other scientific and technical associations and related institutions to improve the general cultural level of the Hungarian people.[89]

Membership

Academy members are divided into the following categories: honorary, external, regular, and corresponding. The number of regular and corresponding members is determined each year; they are elected by the general assembly on recommendation of the presidium board of directors or the directors of State and social organizations. Foreigners can be elected only as honorary or external members.

From 1961 to 1966 the total of regular and corresponding members each year was the following:[90]

Year	Members	Year	Members
1961	157	1964	159
1962	158	1965	165
1963	155	1966	161

Organization and Structure

The Academy is organized as follows: general assembly, board of directors, presidential council, divisions, committees; and subordinated enterprises, institutions, laboratories, libraries, and research groups. Each organizational entity has a chairman, a deputy chairman, and a number of secretaries as required by its size.

The highest organ of the Academy is the general assembly (*közgyülés*). Its duties are to—

1. Set up guidelines for the Academy's activities and determine its scientific-political objectives.
2. Evaluate and approve the directors' report concerning the Academy's work.
3. Approve and amend the Academy's statutes.
4. Establish, reorganize, or consolidate divisions.
5. Elect the president, vice presidents, secretary general, deputy secretaries general, and members of the board of directors.
6. Elect new members.

[89] Aurél Hencz. *A müvelődési intézmények és a müvelődésigazgatás fejlődése*, op. cit. p. 226.
[90] *Statisztikai évkönyv 1966* (Statistical Yearbook 1966). Budapest: Központi Statisztikai Hivatal, 1967. p. 361.

7. Settle appeals against the board of directors' decisions regarding ousters.
8. Make decisions on all matters when requested by the board of directors.

The president of the Academy is appointed with the concurrence of the Presidential Council of the Hungarian People's Republic and the other officers on the board of directors are appointed with the Government's approval.

The board of directors *(elnökség)* consists of the president, vice-presidents, the secretary general, deputy secretaries general, division secretaries, and elected members. The president, vice-president, secretary general, and deputy secretaries general constitute the presidential council of the Academy *(elnökségi tanács)*.

The Academy's scientific tasks are carried out under the auspices of its divisions *(osztályok)* and the institutes subordinated to them.[91] Each division includes a number of specialized scientific committees *(bizottságok)* in charge of a specific resarch area. In the late 1960's the Academy had the following nine divisions:[92]

Agricultural sciences
Biological sciences
Chemical sciences
Linguistics and literature
Mathematical and physical sciences
Medical sciences
Psychology
Social-historical sciences
Technical sciences

The social-historical division, for example, includes the following committees:

Archeology
Art history
Economics
Education
Geography
History
Philosophy
Political science and law
Sociology

In the early 1960's the Academy's library consisted of 636,000 books, 136,000 periodicals, 246,000 manuscripts, and 6,000 microfilms. The library was built up from 30,000 volumes donated by Count József (Joseph) Teleki in 1826.

The Publishing House of the Hungarian Academy of Sciences (*Akadémiai Kiadó*) was founded in the 1830's and recognized in its present form in 1950. It publishes, both in Hungarian and foreign languages, books approved by the board of directors. Each year it produces approximately 200 books and 80 periodicals in Hungarian and other languages.[93]

[91] For details on the Academy's research institutes, see Zoltán Halász, ed. *Cultural Life in Hungary*. Budapest: Pannonia Press, 1966. p. 76-81. For a list of major Hungarian research institutes, see appendix D of the present publication. For details on the Psychological Institute, see p. 163-64 of the present publication.

[92] Ibid. p. 73. For details on the Pedagogical Committee, see p. 164-65 of the present publication.

[93] Among the foreign-language periodicals of the Academy are: *Acta Agronomica; Acta Antiqua; Acta Archeologica; Acta Biologica; Acta Botanica; Acta Chimica; Acta Chirurgica; Acta Ethnographica; Acta Geologica; Acta Historiae Artum; Acta Historica; Acta Juridica; Acta Linguistica; Acta Litteraria; Acta Mathematica; Acta Medica; Acta Microbiologica; Acta Morphologica; Acta Orientalia; Acta Paediatrica; Acta Physica; Acta Physiologica; Acta Technica; Acta Veterinaria; Acta Zoologica; Studia Archaeologica; Studia Historica; Studia Musicologica; and Studia Slavica*. Ibid. p. 75.

Table 43.—Total number of staff members in the five higher education departments and in selected fields of those departments; and number of instructors and researchers: 1966[1]

Department and field	Staff			
	Department and field	Total	Instructors[2]	Researchers
Grand Total	708	11,359	6,946	601
Agronomic Sciences				
Total	*103*	*1,367*	*574*	*128*
Selected Fields:				
Animal husbandry and veterinary medicine	26	326	140	31
Legumiculture and gardening	31	572	190	65
Mechanization of agriculture	10	151	82	3
Medical Sciences				
Total	*122*	*2,790*	*1,947*	*90*
Natural Sciences				
Total	*163*	*3,053*	*1,571*	*231*
Selected Fields:				
Biology	43	749	332	78
Chemistry	44	1,177	522	100
Geology	18	204	101	6
Mathematics	34	405	336	16
Physics	20	485	264	30
Social Sciences				
Total	*218*	*1,892*	*1,584*	*58*
Selected Fields:				
Arts	10	102	83	13
Economics	28	342	277	10
Education	16	161	131	10
Geography	13	86	64	0
History	21	115	102	3
Languages and literature	59	467	397	16
Philosophy	30	439	381	1
Political science and law	37	152	129	2
Technical Sciences				
Total	*102*	*2,257*	*1,270*	*94*
Selected Fields:				
Chemical industry	11	392	177	25
Construction	11	210	150	7
Food industry	2	37	18	4
Light industry	1	26	12	0
Machines, tools, and telecommunications	42	1,039	623	27
Metallurgy	5	72	28	9
Mining	4	71	29	6
Power economy	5	90	47	3
Transportation	9	103	66	3

[1] January through December.

[2] Instructors are expected to spend about 20 percent of their work time on research.

SOURCE OF DATA: *Statisztikai évkönyv 1966* (Statistical Yearbook 1966). Budapest: Központi Statisztikai Hivatal, 1967. p. 360.

VIII. Teachers and Teacher Education

Postwar Problems and Objectives

Soon after Hungary's liberation on April 4, 1945, it became increasingly apparent that the country's planned democratic reorganization required, as a first priority, reorganization of the antiquated educational system. This in turn demanded not only that the anti-democratic characteristics of the old system be eliminated but that the existing teacher corps be retrained and a new corps trained from the ground up.

These objectives became the subject of nationwide, often passionate, debates that involved the emerging governmental and political leaders and the leading educators, many of whom had suffered under the previous regimes.[1] The issues acquired a momentum of their own, when, with the return of relative stability, stock was taken of the losses in school buildings[2] and of the available teaching force. Though the losses in physical facilities of education were staggering, they seemed to be overshadowed by the chronic teacher shortage. This problem was further aggravated by the qualitative shortcomings of many of the available teachers.

The qualitative weaknesses of these teachers could be traced partly to their inadequate preparation in the subjects they had to teach in the upper elementary and general secondary schools and to the antiquated, if not reactionary, educational philosophy of the normally church-oriented teacher-training institutes from which they graduated.[3]

Retraining

Responding to public clamor for reorganization and revitalization of the educational system, the then Ministry of Religion and Education (*Vallás és Közoktatásügyi Minisztérium*) adopted a series of measures calculated to assure democratization of the educational process.

---

[1] The most important contributions to the debate were collected and published in the following volume: *Demokrácia és Köznevelés* (Democracy and Public Education). Budapest: Országos Köznevelési Tanács, 1945.

[2] According to former Minister of Culture Tibor Erdey-Grúz, in Hungary as a whole about 30 percent of all the classrooms were destroyed and 50 percent were damaged. The destruction was even more extensive in Budapest where as a result of the long siege of December 1944-February 1945 not a single school remained intact. Gyula Simon *and* József Szarka. *A magyar népi demokrácia nevelésügyének története* (History of the Educational System of the Hungarian People's Republic). Budapest: Tankönyvkiadó, 1965. p. 10.

[3] Until the 1948 reorganization of the educational system 79 percent of the teacher-training institutes for boys and 90 percent of such institutes for girls were under church control. Gyula Bizó. "Az általános-iskolai nevelőképzés alakulása 1945-től" (The Evolution of Teacher Training for the General Schools Since 1945). *In: Tanulmányok a magyar népi demokrácia neveléstörténetéből* (Studies in the History of Education in the Hungarian People's Republic.) Budapest: Vol. I. Pedagógiai Tudományos Intézet, 1961. p. 259.

One of the most important of such measures was the organization of a series of lectures offered by recognized authorities in their respective fields. To the dismay of the four major political parties dominating the Provisional Government and the local governmental units, however, these lectures tended to emphasize artistic and literary subjects at the expense of the then more pertinent historical and political subjects. The four parties further criticized the retraining program under which the directors of provincial school districts (*vidéki tankerületi főigazgatok*), many of them diehard reactionaries, were empowered to select teachers for the program.[4]

In light of the political criticisms against the program and of the Government's immediate postwar-months experience, the Ministry reorganized the content of the retraining courses for academic year 1946-47.[5] Although those courses now placed greater emphasis on socioeconomic and political subjects,[6] nevertheless, along with gradual changes in the political-governmental structure of the Soviet-dominated East European countries, demands became ever more vocal for retraining and further training of teachers along "progressive, Marxist lines."[7]

A new 3-year retraining program was launched at the beginning of academic year 1947-48. Although techniques and training methods remained unchanged (continuing to emphasize the lecture-discussion method), subject matter increasingly acquired a political coloration. Lectures gradually tended to question the fundamental assumptions of bourgeois democracy and then, with increasing conviction, to emphasize the virtues of "socialism." Teachers were subjected to intensive 4-month courses offered by "progressive" lecturers.

With the country transformed into a "people's democracy" in 1949, the role of the Communist Party in educational matters became decisive. The March 1950 Party decisions served as an impetus for training propagandists to take over teacher retraining in the spirit of Marxism-Leninism.

A new decree of the Ministry of Culture stipulated that 2-year teacher retraining courses be introduced. These courses were to have a prescribed curriculum aiming at the "advancement of scientific socialism . . . and at raising the professional qualification of the teachers through the application of Marxism-Leninism."[8]

In summer 1950, an intensive 4-week program was launched to train propagandists for the teacher-retraining courses. During the 1950-51 academic year the number of participants in these retraining courses reached about 10,000, mostly elementary and secondary school teachers; with the beginning of 1951, kindergarten teachers were also included.

The retraining program was built on a system of collective work

---

[4] *Tanulmányok a neveléstudomány köréből, 1965* (Studies in Education, 1965). Budapest: Akadémiai Kiadó, 1966. p. 412-15.

[5] Order No. 91291/1946. III. Pál Bakonyi. "A pedagógusok átképzése és továbbképzése" (The Re- and Further Training of Teachers). *In: Nevelésügyünk húsz éve, 1945-1964* (Twenty Years of Our Educational System, 1945-1964). Budapest: Tankönyvkiadó, 1965. p. 564.

[6] The courses included such topics as "The Place of the Hungarian Nation Among the Nations of the World" and "The Relation of Teachers to Workers and Peasants." Ibid.

[7] The most important articles and speeches reflecting this new spirit were collected in *Továbbképzés és demokrácia* (Further Training and Democracy). Budapest: Egyetemi Nyomda, 1947.

[8] Decree No. 1030-5T-15/1950. Pál Bakonyi, op. cit. p. 570.

(*munkaközösségi rendszer*). The work collectives operated under the auspices of the educational sections of the district councils.

With teacher retraining well under way, the regime began to concentrate its attention on the top school administrators. On November 30, 1950, it opened the first 3-month course for principals, especially those serving in the provinces. These so-called "principals' schools" aimed at both ideological and professional reorientation.

By 1951, the Party and Government were ready to establish a permanent framework for further teacher training. Looking back to Soviet experience they first established the Budapest Institute for Further Teacher Training (*Budapesti Pedagógus Továbbképző Intézet*) in 1951 to serve the needs of Budapest's educational system, and then in 1952 formed the Central Institute for Further Teacher Training (*Központi Pedagógus Továbbképző Intézet*) to serve national educational needs.[9]

Organization and Functions

General guidelines concerning the organization and functions of teacher-education institutions were outlined in Article 20 of Law No. III of 1961.[10] Thus, according to paragraphs 2-4 of the Article, kindergarten teachers and teachers for the lower elementary grades are to be trained in institutes (*felsőfokú intézetek*),[11] subject teachers for the upper elementary grades in colleges (*főiskolák*), and secondary school teachers in universities or university-type institutions of higher education (*egyetemek és egyetemi jellegű főiskolák*).

In accordance with these general guidelines, teacher education in Hungary is offered under the auspices of the following institutions:

1. Institutes for kindergarten teachers
   (*Óvónóképző intézetek*)
2. Teacher-training institutes
   (*Tanárképzö intézetek*)
3. Teachers colleges
   (*Tanárképző főiskolák*)
4. Departments of education in universities
   (*Egyetemi tanári szakok*)
5. A teachers college for teachers of handicapped children
   (*Gyógypedagógiai tanárképző főiskola*)

A few other specialized schools are concerned with the education of music and art teachers and of instructors for sports and physical education.

Although these institutions are all considered a part of Hungary's system of higher education, their admission requirements, training period, and curriculums vary considerably.

---

[9] For details on further training of teachers, see p. 161-62.

[10] "1961. évi III. törvény a Magyar Népköztársaság oktatási rendszeréről" (Law No. III of 1961 Concerning the Educational System of the Hungarian People's Republic). *Magyar Közlöny* (Hungarian Gazette), Budapest No. 74, Oct. 17, 1961. p. 568.

[11] Although *felsőfokú intézet* can be literally translated as "higher institute" it is here rendered simply as "institute."

Historical Background

Kindergarten teacher education in Hungary can be traced back to 1837, when under the initiative of István Wargha an institution of this type was first established.[12] Admitting only male students at least 21 years old, this institution offered an intensive 1-year course. Theoretically, the training was increased to 2 years in 1874 and to 4 years in 1926. After 1926, the 4th year was devoted primarily to practice teaching. Under an 1891 law, kindergarten teacher training was entrusted to institutions which were similar to upper secondary schools and which admitted 14-year old graduates (by 1926, mostly girls) of the 8-year elementary or 4-year secondary schools. Kindergarten teacher training tended to keep pace with enrollment increases. By 1938, 23.6 percent of kindergarten-age children were enrolled in such institutions, whose teachers numbered 1,593.[13]

After World War II, kindergarten education experienced a remarkable development spurred by the complete emancipation of women, the regime's intention to attract women into productive fields, and its increased concern for education in general. Like the other levels of education, however, kindergartens suffered from an acute teacher shortage[14] and from what the regime considered the ideological and political "backwardness" of the available corps.

Although the political retraining of kindergarten teachers was postponed to 1951,[15] the shortage was being solved through special 1-year education courses that admitted elementary school graduates. These courses were normally organized under the auspices of the existing kindergarten teacher-training schools. Some, however, were launched under the initiative of a number of mass organizations, especially the Democratic Association of Hungarian Women (*Magyar Nők Demokratikus Szövetsége*).

With the general reorganization of teacher-training institutions in 1949, kindergarten teacher-training schools were transformed into 4-year pedagogical gymnasiums (*pedagógiai gimnáziumok*). Lasting only for the 1949-50 academic year, these 4-year institutions for training kindergarten teachers gave way to 3-year institutes, and once again training such teachers was entrusted to a 3-year program.

Pressed by immediate necessities and by postwar shortages, the institutes continued to produce half-educated and half-trained 17-year-old kindergarten teachers.

The qualitative problem came to the fore in 1956, when the quantitative one was already partially solved. The Ministry of Culture [16] began its plan for reorganizing kindergarten teacher education through institutes that would admit only graduates of secondary schools. Interrupted

[12] For a detailed historical review of the kindergarten teacher education system see Alice Hermann. "Az óvoda és az óvónőképzés" (The Kindergarten and the Education of Kindegarten Teachers). *In: Nevelésügyünk húsz éve*, op. cit. p. 365-418.

[13] Ibid. p. 368 and 409.

[14] In 1947, there were 1,670 kindergarten teachers in Hungary, only 77 more than in 1938. Ibid. p. 409.

[15] See p. 141.

[16] By this time the Ministry was known as Ministry of Culture *(Oktatásügyi Minisztérium)*. See footnote 37 of chapter III.

by the military events of October-November 1956, this plan was implemented in 1957-58 through the initiative of the Department of Teacher and Kindergarten Teacher Training (*Tanító- és Óvónőképző Szakosztály*) of the Ministry. On the basis of the plan, the three kindergarten teacher-training institutes (*óvónőképző intézetek*) began their operation on September 8, 1959, with 260 students.[17]

Organization and Functions

The kindergarten teacher-training institutes operate under the auspices of the Ministry of Culture in accordance with general principles outlined in Decree No. 26 of 1958.[18] Their number and location are determined jointly by the Minister of Culture, the Minister of Finance, and the President of the National Planning Office (*Országos Tervhivatal*). They are organized like Hungary's other higher education institutions.[19]

Each institute is headed by a director, who is assisted by an institute staff consisting of an assistant director, instructors, and the head and teachers of the kindergartens attached to the institute for experimental purposes.

The main function of the kindergarten teacher-training institutes is to train educators who "love and know their profession and reflect the Communist conception of the world and morality."[20]

Offering a 2-year course, these institutes admit secondary school graduates who possess the secondary school certificate or its equivalent and who have successfully passed an admission examination covering three subjects: Hungarian history, Hungarian language, and Hungarian literature. The age limit for the day sessions is 30 and for the correspondence courses 40.

In 1968, three kindergarten teacher-training institutes were in operation, one each in Kecskemét, Sopron, and Szarvas. The one in Sopron also specializes in training German kindergarten teachers; those in Szarvas, Romanian, Slovak, and Yugoslav.

Curriculum and Examinations

After many years of experimentation, the curriculum of these institutes was finalized in summer 1964 and went into effect during academic year 1964-65 (table 44).

Although such professionally important courses as methodology, psychology, and theory of education now receive greater prominence than in the earlier curriculum, Russian and Marxism-Leninism continue to be emphasized.

At the end of each semester, students are expected to take a *colloquium* examination in most subjects. During the 2d year, they are further expected to spend 6 weeks in practical training at pre-selected

---

[17] Alice Hermann, op. cit. p. 414.
[18] *Magyar Közlöny*, Budapest, No. 80, Sept. 6, 1958. p. 592-93.
[19] See p. 103-06.
[20] Article 2 of Decree No. 26 of 1958.

Table 44.—Number of hours per week, per subject, in the 2-year training institutes for kindergarten teachers, by semester: 1964–65

Subject	Semester			
	1	2	3	4
Total	32	32	28	23
Anatomy—Physiology	2	0	0	0
Drawing and handwork	2	2	2	1
History of education and organization of kindergartens	0	0	0	3
Kindergarten hygiene	0	0	2	0
Logic	2	0	0	0
Marxism—Leninism	4	3	3	3
Methodology	4	6	0	0
Music and singing	3	3	4	4
Native tongue and literature	4	2	0	3
Physical education	2	2	2	2
Practical work	0	5	10	5
Psychology	2	3	3	2
Puppetry *(bábozás)*	1	0	0	0
Russian	2	2	2	0
Theory of education	4	4	0	0

SOURCE OF DATA: *Nevelésügyünk húsz éve, 1945-1964* (Twenty Years of Our Educational System, 1945-1964). Budapest: Tankönyvkiadó, 1965. p. 415.

kindergartens[21] and prepare a thesis (*záródolgozat*) that until 1966-67 had to be defended during the State examination.[22] When the student has successfully fulfilled these requirements, he receives a kindergarten teaching certificate. His final graduation grade appearing on that certificate is the average of the grades in his dissertation defense, in his practical work during the second year, and in his courses on Marxism-Leninism, psychology, and theory of education.[23]

Enrollment

The number of students in the day session and correspondence courses[24] tended to increase until 1964-65, when it reached a total of 1,185; the next year it declined to 1,124 and in 1966-67 to 884. These figures represent about 1 percent of the enrollment in all higher education.

A breakdown of these total figures reveals the following:[25]

Year	*Day session*		*Correspondence courses*	
	1st year	*2nd year*	*1st year*	*2nd year*
1964–65	292	276	353	264
1965–66	275	280	270	299
1966–67	324	265	61	234

[21] *Nevelésügyünk húsz éve,* op. cit. p. 416.

[22] Beginning with the 1966-67 academic year, the thesis defense as an integral part of the State examination was replaced by an examination in practical education and methodology and in philosophy and theory of education. Ministry of Culture. *Report on Educational Progress in the 1966-67 Academic Year Presented at the XXXth Session of the International Conference on Public Education, Geneva, July 1967.* p. 32.

[23] *Nevelésügyünk húsz éve,* op. cit. p. 416.

[24] Evening sessions are not used for training kindergarten teachers.

[25] *Statisztikai évkönyv 1966* (Statistical Yearbook 1966). Budapest: Központi Statisztikai Hivatal, 1967. p. 348-51.

Evolution

The present system of teacher training for the lower and upper grades of the 8-year elementary schools has been the result of a series of changes adopted since 1945. The teacher shortage that characterized the entire educational system in the immediate postwar period was particularly acute in the elementary schools. The lack of adequately trained teachers was felt especially after the 8-year free and compusory school had been introduced. For lack of subject teachers, general class teachers had to be employed in the upper grades.[26]

The first proposals for revamping teacher education came from the National Council of Education (*Országos Köznevelési Tanács*) and the Teachers Union (*Pedagógus Szakszervezet*). These proposals were later supplemented by others stemming from officials and educators all over the country. On the basis of the latter proposals, the first pedagogical college (*pedagógiai főiskola*) was established at Budapest in November 1947. This one was soon followed by others at Eger, Pécs, and Szeged. (The one at Eger originally started operating at Debrecen.)

These colleges, replacing the old intermediate teacher-training institutes,[27] offered a 3-year course to train both class teachers for the lower elementary grades and subject teachers for the upper elementary grades. At the end of the first year, the colleges graduated 127 students and at the end of the 2d and 3d years, 348 and around 800, respectively.[28]

The colleges' low productvity, coupled with an ever-increasing demand for teachers, induced the Government to reorganize them and to reduce the period to 2 years by revising the curriculum. The colleges henceforth were to train subject teachers for the upper elementary grades; training class teachers for the lower elementary grades was first entrusted (1949-50) to pedagogical gymnasiums (*pedagógiai gimnázium*) and then, under Decree No. 43 of the Presidential Council of 1950, to the re-established teacher-training institutes.

Admitting graduates of the 8-year elementary schools, these teacher-training institutes offered a 5-year program in which the last year was devoted to practical teaching. Beginning in 1954, the pedagogical colleges again increased their period to 3 years.

In spite of these changes, however, both the institutes and the colleges were subjected to increasing criticism for their failure to train sufficient numbers of adequately educated teachers and for their outdated and overburdened curriculum. The debates that followed in the wake of this criticism laid the foundation for the present system under which teacher-training institutes train class teachers for the lower elementary grades

[26] According to Zoltán Rozsondai, in 1948 Hungary had 2,622 public 4-year elementary schools *(népiskolák)* with 3,443 teachers and 4,760 8-year elementary schools with 23,580 teachers and 3,805 professors. If all the 7,382 schools had been transformed into full-fledged 8-year schools the country would have needed 44,292 subject and 29,528 general teachers; if only the 8-year elementary schools had been transformed into full-fledged institutions the need would have been reduced to 28,560 professors; i.e. there was a need for 24,755 additional professors. *Nevelésügyünk húsz éve*, op. cit. p. 428.

[27] The intermediate teacher-training institutes were first dissolved by Order No. 160.950 of May 2, 1948, of the Ministry of Culture. Gyula Bizó. "Az általános-iskolai nevelőképzés alakulása 1945-től," op. cit. p. 260.

[28] Ibid. p. 252.

and teachers colleges (*tanárképző főiskolák*) train subject teachers for the upper elementary grades.

Teacher-Training Institutes

Structure and Functions.—Like the kindergarten teacher-training institutes, the institutes for training classroom teachers for the lower elementary grades are organized in accordance with the principles of Decree No. 26 of 1958. These are exclusively State institutions operating under the auspices of the Ministry of Culture, which has primary responsibility for curriculums and syllabuses, examinations, and regulations. Employment conditions, professional level, and teaching load are determined by the Ministers of Culture, Finance, and Labor, and by the President of the Teachers Union.

Each institute has one or several practice elementary schools attached to it. The institute's head is a director assisted by a staff composed of the assistant director, the instructors, and the principal and teachers of the attached elementary school.

Admission.—The teacher-training institutes are 3-year institutions that admit high school graduates who hold the secondary school certificate and who have passed the admission examination in Hungarian history, Hungarian language, and Hungarian literature. Non-resident students may also apply for admission to the institute's collegium.[29]

Objectives.—Like all other institutes of this type, the teacher-training institutes aim to produce competent educators who love their profession and are imbued with the Communist spirit and morality. Toward this aim, the institutes are expected to:

1. Acquaint students with education's contemporary achievements.
2. Expand secondary school training.
3. Inform students as to the characteristics of childhood and the factors responsible for child development.
4. Stimulate their creativity; encourage them to practice independent thinking.
5. Develop their esthetic appreciation and their love for the arts.
6. Acquaint students with the requirements for a healthy life and good physical development.
7. Broaden their Marxist conceptions through application of dialectical materialism.
8. Help develop in students the traits of socialist morality, including those of patriotism, proletarian internationalism, etc.
9. Acquaint students with the problems confronting the various youth movements, especially the Pioneers and KISZ (Communist Youth League).[30]
10. Prepare students for their role as advisers to their elders on various aspects of economic and cultural life.
11. Arouse in them the desire for further learning.
12. Encourage them to do research in their field, especially in the problems of teaching 6-to-10-year-old children.

[29] See p. 189-92.
[30] See p. 182-89.

13. Induce them to contribute to the advancement of the cultural life of the community.[31]

Curriculum and Examination Requirements.—Broadly speaking, the curriculum covers three subject areas: art, education, and social sciences (table 45). In addition to their theoretical training, the students have periodic practice teaching in the elementary schools assigned to the particular institute. During their 3rd year, they devote one full semester to it.

Table 45.—Number of hours per week, per subject, in the 3-year teacher-training institutes, by semester: 1964–65

Subject	Semester				
	1	2	3	4	5–6
Total	27	30	31	28	29
Agriculture	0	0	2	2	0
Drawing and its methodology	3	3	2	2	4
Extracurricular activities	0	0	0	5	4
Geography	0	0	2	0	0
Handwork and its methodology	3	0	0	0	2
History of education	0	0	0	2	3
Logic	2	0	0	0	0
Marxism-Leninism	3	3	3	3	3
Mathematics	2	2	0	0	0
Methodology:					
Arithmetic	0	2	2	0	0
Native tongue	0	2	2	2	0
Native tongue	2	2	0	0	0
Pedagogy:					
Education	0	2	2	0	0
Teaching	0	4	0	0	0
Physical education and its methodology	2	2	3	2	4
Practical work	0	0	6	6	6
Psychology	3	2	3	0	0
Russian	2	2	2	2	0
Singing and its methodology	3	2	2	2	3
Youth literature	2	2	0	0	0

SOURCE OF DATA: *Nevelésügyünk húsz éve, 1945-1964* (Twenty Years of Our Educational System, 1945-1964). Budapest. Tankönyvkiadó, 1965. p. 446.

The curriculum of some teacher-training institutes includes training for students who will become teachers in elementary schools for the national minorities: The institute at Baja trains German and Serbo-Croatian mother-tongue teachers; the one at Budapest, Slovakian; and the one at Debrecen, Romanian. (Students who will become language teachers, whether in Hungarian or national minority elementary schools, receive their specialized training at teacher-training *colleges:* at Pécs for German and Serbo-Croatian and at Szeged for Romanian and Slovakian.)

The curriculum at Debrecen and at Szombathely also provides training for cultural workers and librarians to serve the needs of "people's culture homes" and libraries (especially those in villages and factories).

Examination requirements are relatively simple. There is a *colloquium* at the end of each semester and during the third year students are expected to complete a thesis or dissertation which until 1966-67 they had to defend in the so-called State examination.[32] When they complete their

[31] Gyula Bizó, op. cit. p. 267-69.
[32] See footnote 22.

studies students must also pass State examinations in Marxism-Leninism, methodology, and pedagogy. If successful in those examinations, they then receive their teaching licenses.

Enrollment.—After teacher-training institutes were established in 1959, their enrollment increased at an encouraging rate until 1964-65, when it reached an all-time high of 3,899.[33] From that year on, it declined to 3,422 in 1965-66 and 2,838 in 1966-67, representing in the latter year a decrease of 27 percent.

A breakdown of the 1966-67 total of 2,838 (3.1 percent of the enrollment in all higher education) reveals the following: [34]

Year of study	*Day session*	*Correspondence courses*
Total	[1] *2,018*	[2] *820*
1st	719	145
2d	621	309
3d	678	366

[1] 1,763 were women.
[2] 640 were women.

Teachers Colleges

Scope.—The primary function of the teachers colleges is to train subject teachers for the elementary schools, especially the upper grades. The admission requirements of these colleges are similar to those of the teacher-training institutes. They offer a 4-year program which includes recitation courses, practice teaching, and practical work in shops, factories, or governmental institutions, depending upon the students' areas of specialization.

Program.—In a program for further training of elementary school teachers, the colleges offer both a day-session program and correspondence courses. Beginning with the 1959-60 academic year,[35] every student has been required to major in three subjects. He must choose two of his majors from a list of paired subjects prepared by the Ministry of Culture, but he may elect his third major.

The specialized areas in which a student may major were specified by the Ministry on August 25, 1959 in Decree No. 6/1959. (VIII.25.)M.M. as follows: [36]

- Agriculture
- Biology
- Chemistry
- Drawing
- Geography
- German and German literature
- History
- Hungarian language and literature
- Mathematics
- Music
- Physical education
- Physics
- Russian and Russian literature
- Serbo-Croatian and Serbo-Croatian literature
- Slovakian and Slovakian literature
- Technology

[33] Originally 11 such institutes were established. The one in Szeged was transformed into a teachers college on June 2, 1963, under Government Decree No. 14/1963. (VI.2.). *Magyar Közlöny*, Budapest, No. 38, June 2, 1963. p. 251. The 10 institutes operating in 1968 were located at Baja, Budapest, Debrecen, Esztergom, Győr, Jászberény, Kaposvár, Nyiregyháza, Sárospatak, and Szombathely.

[34] Based on tables 19-22 of section XX of *Statisztikai évkönyv 1966*, op. cit. p. 348-52.

[35] The teachers colleges were reorganized under Resoulution No. 1,023/1959. (VIII.19.) of the Government. *Magyar Közlöny*, Budapest, No. 77, July 19, 1959. p. 640.

[36] *Magyar Közlöny*, Budapest, No. 87, August 25, 1959. p. 767-68.

The paired subjects in which students may specialize vary from college to college. The one in Eger, for example, offered the following paired subjects in 1965-66: [37]

- Biology–agriculture
- Biology–drawing
- Biology–physical education
- Geography–drawing
- Geography–physical education
- Hungarian–drawing
- Hungarian–drawing and music
- Hungarian–history
- Hungarian–Russian
- Mathematics–chemistry
- Mathematics–music
- Mathematics–physics
- Mathematics–technology
- Russian–drawing and music
- Russian–physical education

The applicant takes his admission examination in the paired subjects which he has selected for two of his three majors.

Enrollment.—In 1968, four teachers colleges were operating in Hungary: [38] one each in Eger, Nyiregyháza, Pécs (with a branch at Zalaegerszeg), and Szeged (with a branch at Békéscsaba and another branch at Szolnok).

As with the teacher-training institutes, enrollment in the teachers colleges at first tended to increase dramatically and then gradually to decrease. Their 1961 total enrollment of 4,561 increased in 1964-65 to 11,414, but decreased in 1966-67 to 9,556.

A breakdown of the 1966-67 total of 9,556 (10.7 percent of the enrollment in all higher education) reveals the following:

Year of study	*Day session*	*Correspondence courses*
Total	[1] *3,586*	[2] *5,970*
1st	990	500
2d & 3d	1,671	2,942
4th	925	2,528

[1] 2,772 were women.
[2] 3,956 were women.

In 1966, the teachers colleges graduated 2,774 students—563 in the day session and 2,211 in the correspondence courses.[39]

III. EDUCATION OF TEACHERS FOR THE HANDICAPPED

Scope, Requirements, and Curriculum

Hungary has one teachers college for teachers of handicapped children (*Gyógypedagógiai tanárképző főiskola*) located in Budapest. Originally founded in 1924, it offers a 4-year program including both general courses in education and specialized training for teaching the handicapped. It admits graduates who hold the secondary school certificate and who have successfully passed the admittance examinations in biology and Hungarian.

Every student must major in three areas, two of them required: (1) therapeutic education of mentally deficient children; (2) therapeutic

[37] *Tájékoztató a magyar felsőoktatási intézményekről, 1965* (Guide to the Hungarian Institutions of Higher Learning, 1965). Budapest: A Művelődésügyi Minisztérium Kiadványa, 1965. p. 77.

[38] The college of Eger was founded in 1949; that of Nyiregyháza in 1962 by Decree No. 11 of 1962 *(Magyar Közlöny*, Budapest, No. 38 May 28, 1962. p. 363.

[39] Based on tables 19-22 of section XX of *Statisztikai évkönyv 1966*, op. cit. p. 348-52.

education of children suffering from speech disorders. Beginning with the fourth semester, he may choose one of two electives: therapeutic education of children suffering from hearing deficiencies or therapeutic education of children suffering from vision deficiencies.

The curriculum includes standard courses in education such as developmental psychology, methodology, theory and practice of education, and some specialized courses dealing with the particular problems of teaching the handicapped. These courses include functional anatomy, functions of the healthy child's nervous system, and physical and psychological characteristics of the handicapped.[40]

Enrollment

In contrast to its 1960-61 enrollment of 330, the college had a 1966-67 enrollment of 668, the latter representing 0.7 percent of all students in higher education. Of these, 245 were in the day session and 423 in correspondence courses.

The overwhelming majority of the 668 students are women: they total 547 (200 in the day session; 347 in the correspondence courses).

The 1966-67 graduates numbered 64 in the day session and 49 in the correspondence courses.[41]

Hungary also has an Institute for Training Instructors of Motor-Disorder Victims (*Mozgássérültek Nevelőképző és Nevelőintézete*) also located in Budapest. It was established on December 21, 1963, under Government Decree No. 36/1963. (XII.21.), which converted the National Therapeutic Institute for Victims of Motion Disorders *(Országos Mozgástherápiai Intézet)* into the new institute. Offering a 4-year program for instructors,[42] this institute trains preschool and school-age children to overcome their motor disorders to an extent that they can attend school, and trains adults to carry on some trade compatible with their disorders. It also conducts research.[43]

The institute's director is appointed by the Minister of Culture.

IV. EDUCATION OF PHYSICAL EDUCATION TEACHERS

Scope, Requirements, and Curriculum

Physical education instructors for both secondary and higher education are trained at the Hungarian College of Physical Education (*Magyar Testnevelési Főiskola*) located in Budapest. It offers a 4-year program leading to specialization either in classroom teaching or physical training. Admission is restricted to unmarried males and females holding the secondary school certificate or its equivalent. The admittance examination, which normally lasts for 3 days, consists of a thorough medical check-up, oral examinations, and practical examinations.

The curriculum is composed of subjects in general education, physical

---

[40] *Tájékoztató a magyar felsőoktatási intézményekről, 1965*, op. cit. p. 81-82.
[41] Based on tables 19-22 of section XX of *Statisztikai évkönyv 1966*, op. cit. p. 348-52.
[42] *Magyar Közlöny*, Budapest, No. 89, December 21, 1963. p. 682.
[43] In 1965-66, the institute had 23 evening-session students. *Statisztikai évkönyv 1966*, op. cit. p. 350.

education, and the social sciences. While enrolled in the college, students must practice and engage in sport activities only within the framework of the Sport Association of the College of Physical Education (*Testnevelési Főiskola Sportegyesülete*).[44]

Enrollment

During the 1966-67 academic year, the college had an enrollment of 821 (0.9 percent of all students in higher education) as against only 486 in 1960-61 and 904 in 1964-65. Of these, 377 were in the day session and 444 in the correspondence courses.

Of the total 821 students in 1966-67, 299 were women (175 in the day session; 124 in the correspondence courses). The 1966-67 graduates numbered 70 in the day session and 107 in the correspondence courses.[45]

V. EDUCATION OF ART AND MUSIC TEACHERS

Normally, the colleges of industrial and fine arts, music, and theater and cinematography train art and music teachers (chapter VII for specific programs and requirements).[46]

VI. EDUCATION OF SECONDARY SCHOOL TEACHERS

Evolution

The problems that confronted Hungary's system of education for secondary school teachers in the pre-World War II period continued for many years thereafter.[47] Some of these problems persist today despite solutions offered by the regime.

The major problems of the prewar period—the system of electives that prevailed in the departments of education, the shortcomings of the various theoretical and practical courses in education and psychology, and the unsystematic manner in which practice teaching was organized and implemented [48]—were further aggravated immediately after the liberation by many others caused by the war: the destruction of physical facilities, the low number of applicants, and the absence of university professors, many of whom had fled the country with the withdrawing fascist forces.[49]

The first steps toward reorganizing secondary school teacher training

[44] *Tájékoztató a magyar felsőoktatási intézményekről*, 1965, op. cit. p. 83.

[45] See tables 10 and 12 of chapter VII.

[46] See p. 123-25.

[47] In the prewar period, the sytem for educating secondary school teachers was based on Law No. XXVII of 1924. For details on the historical evolution of secondary school teacher-training, see Andor Ladányi. "A középiskolai tanárképzés" (The Education of Secondary School Teachers). *In: Nevelésügyünk húsz éve*, op. cit. p. 451-557.

[48] The system of practice teaching was first regulated in 1929 and then in a more detailed manner in 1933. Its basic weaknesses included the overcrowding of schools assigned to practice teaching, the non-availability in some areas of such schools, practice teaching only during the fifth year, and reduction of the practice period to half for students subject to military service. Andor Ladányi. "A középiskolai tanárképzés," op. cit. p. 456.

[49] The situation was especially difficult in Debrecen and Szeged, the two eastern university cities first liberated by Soviet troops. In Debrecen, for example, only 9 of the 50 full-time professors remained behind; of these, only 2 were affiliated with the school of philosophy. In Szeged, the two schools—philosophy and natural sciences—were left with only two professors each. Ibid. p. 458.

were taken on September 1, 1945, when the National Council of Education appealed to the four university schools (faculties) in charge of such training and to the leadership of the three secondary schools used for practice teaching to submit their proposals for reform. Although the Council's report—The Reorganization of Teacher Training in Hungary (*A nevelőképzés újjászervezése Magyarországon*)—was completed by February 1946 and although it incorporated many of the submitted suggestions, reform did not become effective until 1948, when the entire educational system of Hungary was revamped.[50]

The 1948-49 academic year was launched on the basis of the reform, which featured, among other things, required programs, compulsory attendance, majoring in two areas, and revised curriculums and syllabuses.

On the basis of the new regulations, students training to teach in secondary schools were required to follow a prescribed yearly program and to take semester-end and year-end examinations. They could fulfill their requirements for specialization by majoring in one of the following paired subject areas:

Biology
and
Chemistry

Biology
and
Geography

History
and
Geography

History
and
Modern language and literature

Hungarian and Hungarian literature
and
History

Hungarian and Hungarian literature
and
Modern language and literature

Hungarian language and literature
and
Latin and Latin literature

Latin and Latin literature
and
Modern language and literature

Mathematics
and
Physics

Mathematics
and
Physics and descriptive geometry

Modern foreign language and literature
and
Another modern language and literature

Philosophy
and
Psychology and social sciences

Physics
and
Chemistry

The revised curriculums and syllabuses entailed primarily placing greater emphasis on the education subjects proper and on the "democratization" of the social sciences. Although Marxism-Leninism was not yet introduced as an independent subject, its influence was increasingly felt in the revised teaching of esthetics, history, logic, philosophy, and related subjects.

The demanding pressures for secondary school teachers, the overburdened curriculum (exceeding 40 hours per week in the School of Natural Sciences), and the breakdown of practice teaching (through the 1949 severance of ties with the secondary schools affiliated with the de-

[50] The schools of philosophy and natural sciences (the ones primarily engaged in training secondary school teachers) were reorganized under Government Decree No. 260 of January 1949. Ibid. p. 484.

Table 46.—Number of hours per week, per subject, in each year of the 5-year university program to train secondary school teachers specializing in physics, by semester: 1965–66

Subject	Theoretical		Practical	
	First Semester	Second Semester	First Semester	Second Semester
First Year				
Total	*13*	*19*	*19*	*17*
Algebra and geometry	4	3	2	1
Chemistry	3	3	4	4
Descriptive geometry and industrial design	0	2	0	2
Experimental physics	0	4	4	2
Mathematical analysis	4	4	3	2
Philosophy	2	3	0	0
Physical education	0	0	1	1
Russian	0	0	2	2
Workshop practice	0	0	3	3
Second Year				
Total	*17*	*18*	*19*	*13*
Experimental physics [1]	7	7	3	2
Mathematical analysis	4	5	2	2
Mechanics	3	3	1	1
Philosophy	3	0	2	0
Physical education	0	0	1	1
Physics, laboratory	0	0	5	5
Russian	0	0	2	0
Second foreign language	0	0	0	2
Vector analysis	0	3	0	0
Workshop practice	0	0	3	0
Third Year				
Total	*21*	*21*	*14*	*13*
Calculus of probabilities	2	0	1	0
Electrodynamics	5	0	1	0
Experimental atomic physics	3	3	0	0
Major subject	2	2	0	0
Mathematical analysis	3	2	0	0
Numerical methods and graphics	0	2	0	1
Optics	0	2	0	0
Physics, laboratory	0	0	8	8
Political economy	4	4	0	0
Practical electricity	2	2	1	1
Practical work in physics	0	0	1	1
Second foreign language	0	0	2	2
Theory of relativity	0	2	0	0
Thermodynamics	0	2	0	0
Fourth Year				
Total	*19*	*19*	*13*	*9*
Experimental nuclear physics	0	3	0	0
Major subject	4	4	0	0
Molecular physics	0	4	0	0
Nuclear physics	0	3	0	0
Physics, laboratory	0	0	8	8
Practical work in physics	0	0	1	1
Quantum electrodynamics	0	2	0	0
Quantum theory	4	0	1	0
Scientific socialism	2	3	0	0
Second foreign language	0	0	2	0
Solid state physics	2	0	0	0
Statistical mechanics	3	0	1	0
Technology of materials	4	0	0	0
Fifth Year				
Total	*11*	*8*	*23*	*23*
History of physics [2]	0	0	1	1
Major subject	8	8	0	0
Practical work in physics	0	0	2	2
Scientific socialism	3	0	0	0
Special laboratory	0	0	20	20

[1] Experimental physics is listed twice under the 'Second year" heading in the original source.

[2] The original source lists the hours in "History of physics" under "Practical."

SOURCE OF DATA: *World Survey of Education.* IV: Higher Education. New York: UNESCO, 1966. p. 588.

partments of education) led to a series of new reforms. In January 1950, the teacher-training program was reduced from 5 to 4 years, Marxism-Leninism and Russian became required subjects, and (beginning with 1951) the requirements for majoring were reduced from two to one, and in some cases to one-and-a-half subject areas. (The "half-specialization" simply denoted a de-emphasis on the second, or minor subject.)

Concurrently with these reforms, measures were taken to improve the composition of the student body by adopting a system favoring students of peasant-worker origin at the expense of students of "bourgeois origin" —a criterion which was often determined by loyalty to the regime rather than actual social origin. In the early 1950's, around 50 percent of all students in higher education were of peasant-worker origin.[51]

These latter reforms also seem to have failed within a few years after their enactment. The system of double specialization was reintroduced in 1954 and in 1957 the program was re-extended to 5 years. In 1958, a few secondary schools were again placed under the jurisdiction of the departments of education for purposes of practice teaching.[52] Also in 1958, so-called "teacher-training councils" (*Tanárképző tanácsok*) were established to help formulate, implement, and supervise the teacher-training programs.[53] In the fall of 1959, the Division of Higher Education (*Felsőoktatási Főosztály*) in the Ministry of Culture established a special Teacher-Training Committee (*Tanárképzési Bizottság*) in order to effectuate central administration of training for secondary school teachers.

Enrollment in the departments of education tended to fluctuate during the years from 1949-50 to 1964-65, as shown by the figures for first-year students in the university teacher-training programs: [54]

Year	Students	Year	Students
1949–50	1,229	1957–58	605
1950–51	1,819	1958–59	794
1951–52	1,934	1959–60	982
1952–53	1,520	1960–61	1,071
1953–54	1,320	1961–62	1,204
1954–55	439	1962–63	1,551
1955–56	437	1963–64	1,633
1956–57	493	1964–65	1,572

The Department of Education in Universities

Organization and Structure

Secondary school teachers are trained primarily under the auspices of the education departments *(tanári szakok)* in the Schools of Philosophy

[51] Ibid. p. 492.

[52] The shortcomings of the 1949 decision to dissolve the ties between the universities and the secondary schools selected for practice teaching were already recognized in 1952. In that year, the "Apáczai Cs. János," "Varga Katalin," and "Szilágyi Erzsébet" gymnasiums of Budapest were reorganized into practice schools cooperating with the Eötvös Loránd University; the "Fazekas Mihály" gymnasium and the one on Kossuth Lajos Street in Debrecen were made to cooperate with the Kossuth Lajos University; and the "Radnóti Miklós" and "Tömörkény István" gymnasiums were transformed into practice institutions cooperating with the József Attila University. Gyula Simon *and* József Szarka. *A magyar népi demokrácia nevelésügyének története* (History of the Educational System of the Hungarian People's Republic). Budapest: Tankönyvkiadó, 1965. p. 139.

[53] The councils were dissolved in 1963 and their responsibilities assumed by the departments of education. Andor Ladányi. "A középiskolai tanárképzés," op. cit. p. 547-48.

[54] Ibid. p. 492, 511, and 527.

(*Bölcsészettudományi Kar*) and Natural Sciences (*Természettudományi Kar*) at József Attila University (in Szeged), Kossuth Lajos University (in Debrecen), and Eötvös Loránd University (in Budapest).[55]

Regulations for admission, attendance, examinations, grading, scholarships, and tuition are the same as those for the other departments and schools of the three universities.

The departments offer a 5-year program under which a student must specialize in one of the paired subject areas specified by the particular school. To get into the program he must take the admittance examination for the two subjects constituting the paired specialization area he has selected. For example, in 1965-66 the School of Philosophy at Eötvös Loránd University offered the following paired specializations:

Foreign language and literature
and
Another foreign language and literature (Bulgarian, Czech, Romanian, Serbo-Croatian, and Slovakian may not be paired here.)

History
and
Foreign language and literature

Hungarian language and literature
and
Foreign language and literature (Bulgarian, Czech, English, French, German, Italian, Latin, Romanian, Russian, Serbo-Croatian, Slovakian, and Spanish)

Hungarian language and literature
and
History

The School of Natural Sciences of the same university offered only three paired specialization areas during 1965-66: biology-chemistry, chemistry-physics, and mathematics-physics.

The university departments of education are not normally engaged in education research, although individual faculty members may be involved in such projects within the framework of the National Pedagogical Institute or the related institutes of the Hungarian Academy of Sciences (*Magyar Tudományos Akadémia*).[56]

Curriculum

Throughout the postwar period, the departments of education in the higher education institutions tended to adjust the curriculum to periodic changes in the structure and scope of the teacher-training programs.

Following the structural reorganization of the late 1950's, both theoretical and practical subjects were subjected to careful re-examination and revised in accordance with the regime's changing objectives and the secondary schools' needs. The new programs were first tested in 1960-61, and on the basis of the experience accumulated during that and

[55] Specialists are also trained by other institutions. For example, teachers of technical subjects are trained at the Polytechnical University of Budapest *(Budapesti Müszaki Egyetem)*; of agriculture, at the University of Agronomic Sciences *(Agrártudomanyi Egyetem)*; of economics at the Karl Marx University of Economics *(Marx Károly Közgazdaságtudományi Egyetem)*; of music, at the Liszt Ferenc College of Music *(Liszt Ferenc Zenemüvészeti Föiskola)*; of drawing, at the College of Fine Arts *(Képzömüvészeti Föiskola)*; etc.

[56] See p. 136-38.

the next two academic years, those programs took effect with some minor changes during the 1963-64 academic year.

Some of the program's farthest reaching effects appeared in the core curriculum. For example:

1. The Marxism-Leninism syllabus was expanded to include elements of ethics and elements of the Marxist critique of religion.
2. Continuity was assured in education courses and those of related subjects by requiring students to take the following in sequence—general psychology *(2d semester)*, developmental and educational psychology *(3d semester)*, history of education *(4th semester)*, and specialized education courses *(5th and 6th semesters)*.
3. By the time students reach the 10th semester they are ready to take the special education seminar, which is devoted entirely to problems that have arisen during their practice teaching; and to discussions on contemporary educational developments.

Although the education departments give education and related courses, the appropriate schools and departments (for example, see table 46) give the specialized courses composing the student's major(s).

The changes in the practical aspects of teacher training required that basic principles be reformulated and that the system for implementing these principles be restructured.

Currently emphasized principles assert that the practical aspects ought to:

1. Form an integral part of the education process.
2. Be implemented on a continuing basis rather than concentrated in any particular semester.
3. Involve the active participation of all education students.
4. Serve as a basis to formulate new theories—not merely as a vehicle to test educational ideas.
5. Take into consideration the latest developments in practice teaching techniques.
6. Provide an opportunity to prepare students thoroughly for their role in education.
7. Serve as a source for multilateral practical experience.[57]

In accordance with these principles, the practical part of the teacher education program was also revised. During their 2d, 3d, and 4th years, education students fulfill their practical work requirements by attending demonstration classes, especially those related to their study of education, methodology, and psychology; and by devoting a number of hours a week (and a few weeks in the summer) to the Pioneers Movement program in the elementary schools or to that of the Communist Youth League in the secondary schools.[58]

During their 5th year, education students are expected to fulfill their practical work requirements by devoting from 18 to 22 hours to practice teaching for each of the subjects they specialize in. Also, they must spend about 3 weeks in a school other than the one associated for experimental purposes—normally a provincial school. They must teach at least 20

[57] Andor Ladányi. "A középiskolai tanárképzés," op. cit. p. 540.
[58] See p. 180-89.

hours. Emphasis is placed on independent work, the students preparing their own lessons in accordance with the syllabuses of the school where they do their practice teaching.

Employment and Conditions of Service

Placement of Graduates

The system of teacher placement is basically similar to the one prevailing in any Western country. The top graduates of the teacher-training institutes and colleges are normally recommended to prospective employers by their teachers and school officials. Others may be assigned to teaching positions in accordance with the provisions of scholarship contracts. Still others apply for teaching provisions by responding to competitive bids published in the educational journals, especially the *Köznevelés* (Public Education), an organ of the Ministry of Culture. The system of teacher placement by competitive bidding is regulated by the Ministry.[59]

Many graduates of the secondary teacher-education program are disappointed, for secondary schools cannot absorb them at the rate the universities train them.[60] This has been especially true during the 1960's, when a teacher shortage that characterized the school system during the first 15 years was solved, at least quantitatively, at the secondary level. Any shortage would be felt primarily in the outlying provincial communities. Since the number of applicants for the secondary teacher-training program tends to be two to four times the capacity of the institutions of higher learning, admission to that program has become more selective.

Owing to a lack of vacancies in the secondary schools, more and more graduates are placed in the elementary schools, where they are employed as subject teachers in the upper grades, supplementing the functions of the teacher-training colleges. Thus, for example, in 1954, 21 percent of the graduates found employment in elementary schools. By 1955, their percentage increased to 60 and by 1965 to 77.[61]

Another disappointment for many of these graduates is that they are unable to find jobs in either the elementary or the secondary schools of Budapest, the center of the country's cultural and educational life; they tend to feel that having to teach in the provinces is like having to serve a jail sentence.

In conjunction with the Teachers Union and other interested governmental organizations, the Ministry of Culture sets general employment

---

[59] Order No. 17.275/1967. III. For an evaluation of the system see, Ferenc Rehák. "A pedagógus állások pályázati rendszere" (The Competitive System of Teaching Positions). *Köznevelés*, XXIII:5:161. March 10, 1967. Advertisements for available teacher positions gathered momentum in 1968. See for example "Pályázatok pedagógus állásokhoz" (Competitions for Teaching Positions). *Köznevelés*, XXIV:7-8:271-320. April 12, 1968, listing about 3,000 teacher vacancies arranged by counties and districts. Subsequent issues of the journal publish similar but shorter lists of vacancies.

[60] In 1967, for example, only 614 secondary school teaching positions were advertised by the Government agencies as available throughout the country, but the institutions of higher learning nevertheless graduated 1,268 secondary school teachers. Jenő Lugossy. "Közoktatáspolitikánk néhány időszerű kérdéséről" (Concerning a Few Timely Questions About Our Educational Policy). *Köznevelés*, XXIII:17:644. September 8, 1967.

[61] Andor Ladányi, op. cit. p. 516. See also "A tanárképző főiskolák végzett hallgatóinak elhelyezkedéséről" (Concerning the Placement of the Graduates of the Teachers' Colleges). *Köznevelés*, XX:1:22-23. January 10, 1964.

conditions for elementary and secondary teachers. At work, they are under the immediate jurisdiction of the education authorities of the local people's councils in accordance with general guidelines issued by the Ministry of Culture.

Responsibilities and Functions

Like all State employees, elementary and secondary school teachers have functions and responsibilities that are clearly delineated in a special regulation.[62] Article 8 of the regulations promulgated under Order No. 123/1964(MK 11.) MM of the Ministry of Culture, stipulates that elementary and secondary teachers must:

1. Perform their tasks in accordance with established curriculums and programs and with methodological and other instructions given by the principal or higher authorities.
2. Cooperate in developing a socialist-type school community and in advancing the school's ideological-educational goals.
3. Be fully informed about the Ministry's regulations.
4. Keep on trying to perfect their general, special, and ideological training.
5. Prepare a detailed syllabus for the course(s) or the year's work and a suitable outline for each lesson.
6. Use Ministry-supplied maps, programs, and textbooks exclusively.
7. Correct all written examinations within 10 days.
8. Pay special attention to the work of the Pioneer and Communist Youth League organizations in the school.
9. Take part in parent-teacher meetings; keep weekly office hours.
10. Appear in the classroom at least 15 minutes before class begins.
11. Keep the school informed about their address during both school and vacation periods.
12. Inform school authorities at least 1 day in advance (at least 15 minutes before school begins, in an emergency) about any intention to cut a class or to be absent for a day.
13. Refrain from tutoring any child for pay if the child is enrolled in the school where they teach.

    (Localities having only one school are an exception. In such localities teachers may tutor a child not in their own classes.)
14. Refrain from accepting gifts, gratuities, or loans from students or their families.[63]

Article 8 is binding also on part-time and substitute teachers.

Awards and Honors

Resolution No. 1,036/1951. (XIII.5.) Mt.h. instituted an award and honor system for teachers. This resolution stipulated that outstanding

---

[62] *Rendtartás az általános iskolák és a gimnáziumok számára* (Regulations for the General and Secondary Schools). Budapest: Tankönyvkiadó, 1964, p. 128. For an evaluation of the regulation see, Emil Gábor *and* Lajos Vékony. "Az új, egységes általános iskolai és gimnáziumi Rendtartásról" (Concerning the New Unified Regulations for General and Secondary Schools). *Köznevelés*, XX:24:921-23, December 18, 1964.

[63] Ibid. p. 17-19.

teachers would be decorated and it designated a Teachers Day (*Pedagógus Nap*), to be celebrated toward the end of the academic year.

The decorations "Outstanding Teacher" (*Kiváló tanár*), and "Outstanding Kindergarten Teacher" (*Kiváló óvónő*), coupled with monetary rewards, are awarded by the Minister of Culture [64] on the basis of recommendations from local educational organs cooperating with the central governmental organs to which the schools are subordinated.

Teachers Day celebrations also offer an occasion for rewarding elementary and kindergarten teachers who received their diplomas 50 or 60 years earlier and who have spent at least 30 years in the educational system, either as teachers or administrators, under "exemplary" conditions. Such educators may apply to the educational sections of their respective local governmental organs for a "gold or diamond certificate." If the request is supported by the district office of the Teachers Union and approved by the chief of the appropriate educational section and the director of the local teacher-training institute or college, the certificate will be issued by the director of the institute or college.[65]

The regime has also provided so-called "homes for educators" (*Pedagógus otthonok*) to serve the needs of retired or aged teachers and school administrators.[66]

Salary

Although kindergarten, elementary, and secondary school teachers have considerable prestige and influence, especially in small communities, their pay rate is relatively low. The Central Statistical Office (*Központi Statisztikai Hivatal*) publishes no data in its annual *Statistical Yearbook (Statisztikai évkönyv)* on the income of professionals. Nevertheless, it is possible to determine from various secondary sources and personal information that the 1965 average monthly salary of elementary school teachers in Budapest [67] ranged from approximately 1,000 to over 2,000 forints.[68] For Budapest high school teachers the range was higher. In rural areas, the 1965 average monthly salary for all teachers was somewhat lower than the average for industrial workers (1,766 forints) and for construction workers (1,810 forints).[69]

To a certain degree counterbalancing their low salaries, certain privileges accrue to teachers in cultural events, housing, and transportation.

---

[64] Until September 1964, the decorations were awarded by the Council of Ministers. On that date this function was assumed by the Minister of Culture under Resolution No. 1025/1964 (IX.13.) of the Government. *Magyar Közlöny*, Budapest, No. 57, September 13, 1964. p. 495-96.

On May 25, 1969, the Hungarian Government passed a Resolution providing for a maximum of 72 teacher awards per year. To be made on Teachers Day (the last Sunday in June), the awards are 6,000 forints each (for the value of the forint, see footnote 54 of chapter III). Resolution No. 1022/1969. (V.25.) of the Hungarian Revolutionary Worker-Peasant Government Concerning the Decoration of Outstanding Teachers and the Teachers Day. *Magyar Közlöny*, No. 39, May 25, 1969. p. 374-75.

[65] Decree No. 1/1960. (III.27.) MM of the Minister of Culture. *Magyar Közlöny*, No. 25, March 27, 1960. p. 137-38. Rewarding teachers and administrators was stipulated also in Article 28 of Law III of 1961 on the educational system of the People's Republic of Hungary. *Magyar Közlöny*, No. 74, October 17, 1961. p. 569.

[66] Aurél Hencz. *A művelődési intézmények és a művelődésigazgatás fejlődése, 1945-1961* (The Evolution of Educational Institutions and Administration, 1945-1961). Budapest: Közgazdasági és Jogi Könyvkiadó, 1962. p. 119, 381.

[67] Mrs. Gyula Xantus. "Tantestületünk 1965 szeptemberében" (Our Teaching Staff in September 1965). *Köznevelés*, Budapest, XXII:2:56-58, January 21, 1966.

[68] The official rate of exchange in 1966 was 11.74 forints to the U.S. dollar. See footnote 54 in chapter III.

[69] *Statisztikai évkönyv 1966* (Statistical Yearbook 1966). Budapest: Központi Statisztikai Hivatal, 1967, p. 57.

For example, if they teach in rural areas they are assured very favorable construction loans.[70] But in Budapest, on the other hand, they encounter great difficulty in finding suitable housing. Nevertheless, many graduates of teacher-training colleges and institutes prefer to teach in Budapest because it is the country's center of culture and entertainment.

In January 1966, attempting to improve the relative salary position of teachers and offset the impact of inflation, the Government increased its education budget by 350 million forints and raised the basic salaries of elementary and secondary school teachers by 13 to 14 percent. Of the gross increase, 260 million forints were assigned to increase basic salaries, 20 million to increase supplementary salaries of school administrators, and 70 million to raise overtime and part-time rates.

Like basic salary rates, increases were also determined from certain criteria: level of training, length of service, and type of work performed. Accordingly, the average monthly increase for teachers with university degrees was 240 forints; for subject and class teachers, 200 forints; and kindergarten teachers, 190 forints. The supplementary monthly allowance of secondary school principals increased from 250-850 forints to 350-1,000 forints, and of general school principals from 250-700 forints to 300-900 forints.[71]

Faculty members of colleges, polytechnical institutes, and universities earn a monthly salary ranging from 2,750 to 4,050 forints; of teacher-training institutes, 1,900 to 3,450 forints. Tenured professors, heads of departments, and directors, rectors, and other top administrative officers receive a supplementary monthly allowance, normally about 1,000 forints.[72]

Further Education of Teachers

Background

When it had finished one phase of reorganizing Hungary's educational system and had completed the teacher-retraining program, the regime focused its attention on setting up a systematic program for continuous further education of the teaching and administrative staff. The first phase began in 1951 and 1952, with the new Budapest Institute for Further Teacher Training and the new Central Institute for Further Teacher Training.[73] This phase ended in August 1962 when the latter institute was consolidated with the National Pedagogical Institute.[74]

Scope and Administration

At first compulsory for all teachers and administrators in the pre-university school system, the program of further education is now volun-

[70] "A pénzügyminiszter és a művelődésügyi miniszter 1/1965. (XII.30.)PM-MM számú eggyüttes rendelete a pedagógusok kedvezményes lakásépitéséről" (Joint Decree No. 1/1965. (XII.30.)PM-MM of the Minister of Finance and Minister of Culture Concerning the Favorable Construction of Homes by Teachers). *Magyar Közlöny*, Budapest, No. 75, December 30, 1965. p. 645-48.

[71] "A pedagógusok fizetésemeléséről" (Concerning the Pay Increases of Teachers). *Köznevelés*, Budapest, XII: 2:41-42. January 21, 1966.

[72] *World Survey of Education. IV. Higher Education*. New York: UNESCO, 1966. p. 593.

[73] See p. 142.

[74] See p. 163.

tary. The educational authorities, however, retain the right to compel certain teachers or administrators to pursue refresher courses organized by the education sections of local governmental organs. Theoretically, the program aims to help its participants keep abreast of educational developments in their particular fields and to improve their professional performance. The program also aims to assure that educational or cultural policy directives of the regime are implemented.

Teachers and administrators interested in improving their professional performance and in enriching their intellectual and educational background may choose either formal or informal ways of doing so.

Normally, those interested in pursuing their formal studies toward a degree or higher degree enroll in correspondence courses of the teacher-training colleges. The State pays full cost for travel to the place where examinations are held for teachers in grades 1-4, and travel costs and full maintenance for subject teachers in grades 5 to 8.[75]

Those interested in undertaking informal further education may do so through self-education faculty meetings, joint faculty-administration meetings, and locally or centrally organized courses or conferences. The National Pedagogical Institute normally provides literature and sets up the program for each on a 1- or 2-year basis. For example, the 1964-65 and 1965-66 further education program for kindergarten, elementary, and secondary school teachers focused on implementing the general reform directives outlined in Law III of 1961 concerning reorganization of Hungary's educational system.[76]

Specifically, the 2-year 1964-66 program called for the teachers to:

1. Analyze and evaluate the methodological questions and the educational-psychological interrelationships pertaining to school reforms introduced after 1961.
2. Develop further unity between the teachers' ideological-political and educational objectives in order to implement the reforms effectively.
3. Investigate how the faculty's educational and political-ideological integration affects students' development.
4. Investigate how the reformed teaching system affects socialist relations between teachers and students and how it affects the school's general socialist atmosphere.
5. Evaluate the new teaching methods which aim to develop student independence in learning.

The program's authors provided the participants (and persons generally interested in the informal system of further education) with specific syllabuses outlining the topics and the literature.[77]

The aims of the further education system, like those of education in general, are advanced also through the specialized and professional services rendered by educational and related institutes and teacher organizations.

---

[75] Article 4 of Government Resolution No. 1,023/1959. (VII.19) of July 19, 1959. *Magyar Közlöny*, Budapest, No. 77, July 19, 1959. p. 640.

[76] "Az óvodai, általános- és középiskolai nevelők pedagógiai továbbképzésének 1964-65. és 1965-66. évi terve" (The 1964-65 and 1965-66 Plan for the Further Education of Kindergarten, General, and Secondary School Teachers). *Pedagógiai Szemle* (Review of Education), Budapest, XXIV:9:822-33. 1964.

[77] Ibid.

Education Research

National Pedagogical Institute

Evolution.—The National Pedagogical Institute (*Országos Pedagógiai Intézet*) was established in August 1962 by Decision No. 1021 of the Government.[78] In accordance with the Decision, the National Pedagogical Institute absorbed the Central Institute for Further Teacher Training (*Központi Pedagógus Továbbképző Intézet*) (an agency concerned with the further training and specialization of elementary and secondary school teachers) and the Scientific Pedagogical Institute (*Pedagógiai Tudományos Intézet*), an institute primarily engaged in pedagogical-methodological research.

Like its predecessors, the National Pedagogical Institute operates under the jurisdiction of the Ministry of Culture.

Structure and Functions.—In 1965, the Institute had 17 specialized departments (*tanszék*) employing 76 scholars, researchers, and auxiliary personnel.[79] Although most of the departments are concerned with specific academic subjects, some of them are general in scope; for example, departments dealing with adult education, general pedagogy, lower elementary education, Marxism-Leninism, and polytechnical education.

The National Pedagogical Institute is entrusted with a wide range of well-differentiated functions: further education of teachers, preparation of educational reform programs and of curriculums, issuance of pedagogical plans and handbooks, and publication of educational-methodological journals. It provides a framework for a variety of educational research projects and controlled experiments in methods of personality development, use of modern techniques in foreign language teaching, pedagogical-methodological problems in adult education, and communal self-government. Since the Institute has no experimental schools of its own, it usually conducts experiments with the cooperation of selected schools throughout the country.

The Institute's research and scientific activities are greatly facilitated by its library of 40,000 volumes, which, together with the holdings of the National Pedagogical Library (*Országos Pedagógiai Könyvtár*),[80] constitutes an invaluable source of classical and modern educational materials published both at home and abroad.

The Institute maintains close contacts with related institutions in a number of countries, especially the socialist ones. These contacts involve not only exchange of information and publications, but also cooperative research.

The basic means by which Hungarian educators are kept abreast of educational developments is the Institute's official monthly organ, the *Pedagógiai Szemle* (Review of Education).

Psychological Institute of the Academy

Established on January 1, 1965, the Psychological Institute of the Hun-

---

[78] *Magyar Közlöny*, No. 61, August 12, 1962. p. 520.

[79] László Gáspár. "A pedagógia műhelyei. 1. Országos Pedagógiai Intézet" (The Shops of Pedagogy. 1. The National Pedagogical Institute). *Köznevelés* (Public Education), Budapest. XXVII:1:37-38. Jan. 15, 1965.

[80] See p. 165-66.

garian Academy of Sciences (*A Magyar Tudományos Akadémia Pedagógiai Bizottsága*) is one of Hungary's most important institutions for educational research and pedagogical-psychological studies. It came into existence through absorbing and expanding the Institute of Child Psychology (*Gyermeklélektani Intézet*).

In 1965, the Institute had eight departments: Clinical-Medical Psychology, Criminal Psychology, Developmental Psychology, Educational Psychology, General Psychology, Psychology of Art and Philosophy, Psychology of the Handicapped, and Psychology of Labor.

The departments are engaged in a great deal of pure and applied research that interests both teachers and parents. The Department of Educational Psychology (*Pedagógiai Pszichológiai Osztály*), for example, has launched a number of projects on such topics as — [81]

1. Effect of manual work on personality development.
2. Processes of differentiated instruction in the lower elementary grades with special emphasis on the development of the pupils' capacities.
3. Psychological problems arising in the course of teaching.
4. Psychological problems of transition from kindergarten to elementary school.

The Institute keeps track of psychological developments through foreign specialized journals.

Pedagogical Committee of the Hungarian Academy of Sciences

Cooperating with the Ministry of Culture, the Pedagogical Committee of the Hungarian Academy of Sciences (*A Magyar Tudományos Akadémia Pedagógiai Bizottsága*) is a most important agency entrusted with coordinating, guiding, and supervising educational research in Hungary. It is the only Committee of the Academy having subcommittees. With three such subcommittees, the Pedagogical Committee is able to operate with special efficiency.

Tabulated below are a few details concerning the three subcommittees:

Name	*Year established*	*Primary Functions*
Subcommittee on the History of Education *(Neveléstörténeti Albizottság)*	1953	Preserve education's valuable traditions. Organize activities to honor past and present educators of note. Publish memorial volumes for these activities.[82]
Subcommittee on Educational Theory *(Neveléselméleti Albizottság)*	1962	Supervise and coordinate research on educational theories.

[81] László Gáspár. "A pedagógia műhelyei. 2. A Magyar Tudományos Akadémia Pszichológiai Intézete" (The Shops of Pedagogy. 2. The Psychological Institute of the Hungarian Academy of Sciences). *Köznevelés*, Budapest, XXI:2:77-78. January 29, 1965.

[82] For a review of the Subcommittee's activities since its establishment in 1953, see Éva Földes. "A magyar neveléstörténeti kutatás húsz estendeje" (Twenty Years of Hungarian Research in the History of Education). *In: Tanulmányok a nevelėstudomány köréből, 1965* (Studies in Education, 1965). Budapest: Akadémiai Kiadó, 1966. p. 237-58.

Name	*Year established*	*Primary Functions*
Subcommittee on Didactics and Methodology *(Didaktikai-Metodikai Albizottság)*	1962	Organize scientific sessions on the fundamental aspects and problems of didactics, the mutual relationships between didactics and methodology, and the educational problems of textbooks and syllabuses.

The papers read at the subcommittees' scientific sessions and those prepared under their auspices or supervision are occasionally published in the Committee's two official publications:

1. *Tanulmányok a neveléstudomány köréből* (Studies in Education), an annual collection of articles on methodological, practical, and theoretical aspects of education published since 1958 by the *Akadémiai Kiadó* (Publishing House of the Academy).
2. *Magyar Pedagógia* (Hungarian Pedagogy), a quarterly containing basically the same type of material as the annual.[83]

National Pedagogical Library

Education research and the educational process in general are greatly facilitated by the holdings and services of the National Pedagogical Library (*Országos Pedagógiai Könyvtár*). Established on September 1, 1958, through consolidation of the Pedagogical Library of the Ministry of Culture *(A Művelődésügyi Minisztérium Pedagógiai Kőnyvtára)* and the Pedagogical Library of the Szabó Ervin Library of Budapest *(A Fővarosi Szabó Ervin Kőnyvtár Pedagógiai Könyvtára)*, it fulfills many important functions in the educational life of the country. The library is first of all a national scientific institution for the collection of pedagogical literature; it is further a national documentation center and a methodological center serving the network of school libraries.

The library's accessions have increased from year to year. By the end of 1964, it had 195,925 items, especially books and journals; together with documentary materials and translations from foreign literature, a total of 231,876 items. Library users have at their disposal about 500 domestic and foreign journals and a few special holdings, such as 19,800 Hungarian textbooks, 16,400 children's books, and 13,000 reference volumes and reports. The library's acquisition section maintains close contact with such sections of similar libraries throughout the world, especially those in socialist countries. With them, it is engaged in an extensive exchange program.

A 40-seat reading room is provided with about 1,000 reference volumes. Persons outside Budapest may receive books through an interlibrary exchange system with local libraries.

The library's reference department provides an invaluable service for teachers and scholars engaged in education research by making available to them a series of bibliographies and reference studies. In 1959, for

[83] László Gáspár. "A pedagógia műhelyei. 3. A Magyar Tudományos Akadémia Pedagógiai Bizottsága" (The Shops of Pedagogy. 3. The Pedagogical Committee of the Hungarian Academy of Sciences). *Köznevelés*, Budapest. XXI:3:116-17, February 12, 1965.

example, it began publication of the Hungarian Pedagogical Literature (*Magyar Pedagógiai Irodalom*), an annual bibliography listing books and articles published in Hungary. This is complemented by the Bulletin of Education *(Neveléstudományi Tájékoztató)* (a quarterly since about 1950), which keeps Hungarian researchers and educators abreast of developments abroad by featuring abstracts or full translations of the most important foreign articles in education. Some of these translations are made available to the *Köznevelés* (Public Education),[84] a monthly which features them in its "Translations From Foreign Specialized Literature" (*Forditások a külföldi szakirodalomból*).

The professional and methodological instruction of librarians in elementary and secondary schools and in teacher-training institutions is the responsibility of the Methodological Section of the Library (*Módszertani Osztály*). It carries out this function by visiting provincial school libraries periodically, by organizing seminars, and by distributing its monthly publication, the Bulletin of School Librarians *(Iskolai Könyvtárosok Tájékoztatója).*[85]

Hungarian Pedagogical Association

Established on April 21-22, 1967, on the initiative of the Central Directorate of the Teachers Union (*Pedagógusok Szakszervezetének Központi Vezetősége*),[86] the Hungarian Pedagogical Association (*Magyar Pedagógiai Társaság*) aims to—

1. Assure that social organizations cooperate to popularize scientific achievements.
2. Establish cooperative unity among all teachers at all levels and grades of education for joint solution of mutual problems.
3. Help synchronize theoretical research and practical education.
4. Keep abreast of educational developments abroad.
5. Advance management and planning techniques in education through exhibitions, lectures, and meetings.[87]

Primarily, the Associations's members are persons engaged in various aspects of educational research, lecturers in education and related subjects at institutions of higher learning, and education-oriented scholars and teachers in related fields. The original plan called for setting up a number of provincial branch offices and 17 national departments: [88]

1. Adult Education
2. Child Protection
3. Education of the Handicapped
4. Educational Sociology
5. Further Education of Teachers
6. General Education

---

[84] See p. 225.

[85] László Gáspár. "A pedagógia műhelyei: 4. Országos Pedagógiai Könyvtár" (The Shops of Pedagogy: 4. The National Pedagogical Library). *Köznevelés*, Budapest, XXI:4:157-58. Feb. 26, 1965. For details concerning the library's history, holdings, and structure, see Eszter Waldapfel. "Az Országos Pedagógiai Könyvtár a neveléstudományi kutatás szolgálatában" (The National Pedagogical Library in the Service of Educational Research). *In: Tanulmányok a neveléstudomány köréből, 1962* (Studies in Education, 1962). Budapest: Akadémiai Kiadó, 1963. p. 179-213.

[86] See p. 167-68.

[87] "A Magyar Pedagógiai Társaság megalakulásáról" (Concerning the Establishment of the Hungarian Pedagogical Association). *Köznevelés*, Budapest. XXIII:2:46. January 27, 1967.

[88] *Köznevelés*, Budapest. XXIII:9:324, May 12, 1967.

7. Higher Education
8. History of Education
9. Kindergarten
10. Methodology and Didactics
11. Organization, Leadership, and Management
12. Pedagogical Information and Propaganda
13. Secondary Education
14. School-Family Relations
15. Theory of Education
16. Vocational Education
17. Youth Movements

The Teachers Union

Organization and Functions

During the 25 years preceding Hungary's liberation in 1945, teachers had no meaningful trade union organization of their own. Their status and conditions of service depended to a large extent on the attitudes of the governmental, church, or private organization under which they served.

The postwar Teachers Union (*Pedagógusok Szakszervezete*) can be traced to February 2, 1945, when Ernő Béki formed a committee to organize workers in education and culture. The Union's membership increased phenomenally: The original number of 547 in March 1945 rose to around 25,000 in 1946 and 130,000 in 1965.[89]

The membership increase was paralleled by a commensurate expansion in the Union's influence. It tended to consolidate the small union organizations at various levels and types of education and assert itself as the sole union of all workers in education and culture. In January 1947, it absorbed the National Association of Teachers of Teacher-Training Institutes (*A Tanitóképző Intézeti Tanárok Országos Egyesülete*).

Shortly after its organization, the Union launched its official organ, the *Pedagógus Értesitö* (Teachers Bulletin), which served as the primary vehicle to propagate the Union's objectives. At first these objectives included rehabilitation of teachers persecuted during the Horthy and Szálasi eras, reorganization of Hungary's educational system, and introduction of the 8-year free and compulsory elementary schools.

With the gradual change in the country's political climate and the ascendancy of the Communist Party, however, the Teachers Union, like all other Hungarian mass organizations, was transformed into a tool of the Party, serving as a transmission belt for implementing the regime's directives in education and culture. Beginning with 1947-48, when its leadership was changed, the Union emerged as the champion for school nationalization and ideological retraining of teachers. After the "people's democratic" regime was established in 1949, the Union's policies became indistinguishable from those of the Party and Government.

The close collaboration between the Union and the Ministry of

[89] Ernő Péter: "20 éves a Pedagógusok Szakszervezete" (The Teachers Union Is Twenty Years Old). *Köznevelés*, Budapest, XXI:13-14:497. July 9, 1965. Concerning the union's general activities. consult *A Pedagógusok Szakszervezetének VII. kongresszusa. 1963. február 15-16* (The Seventh Congress of the Teachers' Union. February 15-16, 1963). Budapest: A Pedagógusok Szakszervezete, 1963. 131 p.

Culture was formalized on December 7, 1966.[90] They agreed to undertake joint action for solving all problems affecting education and culture at both the national and local levels. The Union's loyalty and effective action in the Party-State system are assured by the care with which Union leaders are selected and by the presence of about 10,000 dedicated activities within the Union.

---

[90] "Megállapodás a Művelődésügyi Minisztérium és a Pedagógusok Szakszervezete között" (Agreement Between the Ministry of Culture and the Teachers Union). *Köznevelés*, Budapest. XXII:24:934. December 24, 1966.

IX. Special Types of Education

In addition to the standard educational levels, Hungary has a relatively well developed network of special education, including adult, art, remedial (for the physically handicapped), military, and Party education.

Adult Education

Articles 24 and 25 of the Basic Education Law of 1961 [1] outlines the principles for adult education. It is offered in the evening session and the correspondence courses of elementary, secondary, and higher education institutions. If a student fulfills the requirements for admission and successfully passes the examinations, he receives a diploma on the particular educational level equivalent to the one awarded by the day session. Instruction takes place within the special divisions of the schools or in institutions established within the framework of enterprises and plants.

The bases of adult education were laid in the fall of 1945 by Decree No. 11130/1945.M.E.,[2] which provided special courses for the accelerated education of gainfully employed adults who, for reasons beyond their control, had been unable to complete their schooling. Emphasis at first was placed on short courses leading to completion of secondary and vocational and other intermediate schooling.

During school year 1945-46, the Ministry of Culture permitted adult education courses to be established for grades 1-8 of secondary school, grades 1-4 of upper elementary school, grades 1-5 of the teacher-training colleges, and grades 1-4 of the kindergarten teacher-training institutes. Beginning in 1946-47, adult education was extended to industrial and commercial secondary schools. During the first 6 years after the 1945 liberation, adult education was offered only in the evening session. Correspondence courses were added in 1951 in agricultural technical education; by 1953 they had been extended gradually to cover the entire elementary and secondary school program.

During its first phase, adult education aimed primarily at filling the educational gaps in the lives of persons who had been educationally disadvantaged during the prewar regime. Beginning in 1948, however, it

[1] "1961. évi III. törvény a Magyar Népköztársaság oktatási rendszeréről" (Law No. III of 1961 Concerning the Educational System of the Hungarian People's Republic). *Magyar Közlöny* (Hungarian Gazette), Budapest, No. 74, October 17, 1961. p. 568.

[2] Gyula Simon *and* József Szarka. *A magyar népi demokrácia nevelésügyének története* (History of the Educational System of the Hungarian People's Republic). Budapest: Tankönyvkiadó, 1965. p. 164.

attempted to assure further training and cultural uplifting for any workers and peasants who desired them. Following the radical 1947-48 political changes and the subsequent reorganization of higher education, the new regime, in its attempt to create a new intelligentsia from the working class, established courses to prepare workers for so-called "special" secondary school certificate examinations (*szakérettségi*).

Theoretically, these preparatory courses were open to all gainfully employed workers of both sexes between the ages of 17 and 32. In point of fact, however, an applicant could get in only if his plant committee and trade union organization recommended him and if he won the approval of a committee composed of the director of the Budapest school district, delegates of the trade union council, and delegates of the United Organization of Hungarian University and College Students (*Magyar Egyetemisták és Főiskolások Egységes Szervezete*).

With a 40-hour weekly program and a 1-year duration, the courses prepared students for the following higher education fields: economics, education, law and public administration, medicine, philosophy, and polytechnics.

A considerable proportion of the curriculum was devoted to composition and spelling and to Hungarian language and literature. For example, a student preparing to specialize in history and Hungarian language and literature, had 40 weekly hours of classes as shown below:[3]

Total	*40*
Geography	2
Geography exercises	2
History	8
History exercises	5
Hungarian language and literature	10
Latin exercises	4
Orthography and style exercises	5
Social studies	4

Adult education enrollment consisted mostly of urban industrial workers. Following are selected enrollment figures for selected years:[4]

Year	*Number of students*	*Place*
1945-46	4,355	90 schools
1948-49	20,000	Evening session
1953-54	25,000	Correspondence courses
1963-64	291,406	All schools

The year 1963-64 was adult education's peak year for enrollment. That year's total of 291,406 was distributed as follows:[5]

[1] 116,670 elementary school
[2] 174,736 secondary school

[1] This total was divided as follows: 5,452 in grades 1-4; 98,685 in grades 5-8 (evening session); and 12,533 in correspondence courses.

[2] This total was divided as follows: 52,661 in the evening session and 122,075 in correspondence courses.

Since 1962-63, adult education has experienced sharply declining school enrollments, especially in the elementary schools (table 47).

[3] Ibid. p. 168.

[4] Ibid. p. 165, 168-69.

[5] Ibid. p. 169. Also see table 47 in present publication.

Table 47.—Number of students in the 8-year elementary education program for adults and number graduating from that program: 1960–61—1966–67

[—Indicates that source did not show any figures]

School year	Grades 1–4	Grades 5–8		8th-grade graduates of—	
		Evening session	Corre-spondence courses	Evening session	Corre-spondence courses
1960–61	1,852	80,744	16,719	24,049	4,810
1961–62	2,608	75,192	13,332	26,418	4,551
1962–63	5,603	92,338	14,023	26,364	4,296
1963–64	5,452	98,685	12,533	36,469	4,506
1964–65	4,343	78,914	9,434	32,235	3,693
1965–66	3,181	51,453	6,805	20,200	2,808
1966–67	2,877	36,263	5,577	—	—

SOURCE OF DATA: *Statisztikai évkönyv 1966* (Statistical Yearbook 1966). Budapest: Központi Statisztikai Hivatal, 1967. p. 345.

The courses preparing students for the "special" secondary school certificate examinations experienced rising and then falling enrollment, as shown below:[6]

1948-49	520
1951-52	6,558
1954-55	1,131

The year 1954-55 was the final one for the "special" preparatory course. By then, higher education institutions had begun to de-emphasize worker-class social origin as a criterion for admission and to restore standard admission requirements.

Adult education's quantitative expansion caused a significant change in the cultural structure of Hungarian society. It also gave rise, however, to a series of educational-methodological problems as to how to adapt curriculums, programs, and textbooks to particular requirements of this form of education. Convened in December 1963, Hungary's first adult education conference concerned itself with discussions of adult education's initial 15 years in that country and adopted a series of measures to solve the problems revealed by those discussions.[7] The conference delegates numbered 350 from Hungary and foreign countries.

The problems of adult education have been the subject also of numerous summer meetings and individual studies: how to apply programed teaching, how to integrate professional further training with cultural further training, and how to develop methodological tools specifically related to adult education.[8]

As an additional means for advancing the adult worker's educational background, the regime has established cultural homes (*művelődési otthonok*) to raise his general, ideological, and political level. Established by cooperatives, enterprises, institutions, and local people's coun-

[6] Ibid. p. 167-68.

[7] *Első Országos Felnöttoktatási Konferencia* (The First National Conference on Adult Education). Budapest: Táncsics, 1965.

[8] Marianne Sz. Várnagy, Gyula Csoma, László Gellért, *and* Rezső Gere. "Az iskolarendszerű felnöttnevelés helyzete és perspektivái" (The Status and Prospects of Adult Education as a System of Education). *In: Tanulmányok a nevelėstudomány köréböl 1965* (Studies in Education 1965). Budapest: Akadémiai Kiadó, 1966, p. 339-79. See also "A programozott tanitás és a felnöttnevelés problemái a Szegedi Nyári Egyetemen" (The Problems of Programed Teaching and Adult Education at the Summer University of Szeged). *Köznevelés* (Public Educaion), Budapest. XXI:16:621-25, August 20, 1965.

cils, these homes operate under the general supervision of the Ministry of Culture.[9] The Scientific Association for the Propagation of Knowledge (*Tudományos Ismeretterjesztő Társulat*), an organization dedicated to the educational uplifting of workers and youths through lectures in the natural and the social sciences, also plays an important role in advancing the Government's purposes for cultural homes.[10]

Music and Art Education

Before World War II, music and general art education was the prerogative of a relatively small proportion of the Hungarian people. No basic difference existed between group and individual training, and many institutions at various levels offered identical instruction. In 1951, the Presidential Council established secondary schools for music and for fine and industrial arts, and in 1952 a Government decree differentiated among lower, intermediate, and higher types of musical education.

In 1949 the School of Dance Arts *(Táncművészeti Iskola)* was started, benefiting ballet instruction; in 1951 it was converted into the State Ballet Institute *(Állami Balett Intézet)*.[11] Like most music[12] and art schools, the institute also provides elementary and secondary school education.[13]

Students wishing to have private individual or group instruction in dance or music outside the schools may engage their own instructors. These instructors, however, are required to work within the framework of so-called "voluntary" work collectives *(munkaközösségek)*. Dance instructors are members of the Hungarian Association of Dance Artists *(Magyar Táncművészek Szövetsége)* and music instructors of the Hungarian Association of Musical Artists *(Magyar Zeneművészek Szövetsége)*. Also, both are members of the Association of Art Trade Unions *(Művészeti Szakszervezetek Szövetsége)*.

Responsibility for operating the music and art institutions was retained in 1956 by the new and greatly expanded Ministry of Culture.

Education of the Handicapped

Article 4 of Law No. III of 1961 concerning Hungary's educational system outlines basic provisions for educating the handicapped. The article stipulates that mentally and physically deficient children of school age are to be taught in institutions for the handicapped, and that children who are not trainable are to be exempt from compulsory school attendance.

---

[9] "A Magyar Forradalmi Munkás-Paraszt Kormány 2/1960. (I.6.) számú rendelete a művelődési otthonokról" (Decree No. 2/1960. (I.6.) of the Hungarian Revolutionary Worker-Peasant Government Concerning the Cultural Homes). *Magyar Közlöny*, No. 2, January 6, 1960. p. 5-6.

[10] Aurél Hencz. *A művelődési intézmények és a művelődésigazgatás fejlődése, 1945-1961* (The Evolution of Educational Institutions and Administration, 1945-1961). Budapest: Közgazdasági és Jogi Könyvkiadó, 1962, p. 155. See also Vera Biró. "Adult Education." *In*: *Cultural Life in Hungary*. Edited by Zoltán Halász. Budapest: Pannonia Press, 1966. p. 291-300.

[11] Aurél Hencz. *A művelődési intézmények és a művelődésigazgatás fejlődése*, op. cit. p. 72.

[12] For a list of the music schools in operation in 1956, see *Magyar Közlöny*, No. 40, May 16, 1956. p. 237-38.

[13] For information on the formal secondary and higher educational institutions of art, see p. 77, 123-24.

Committees for screening handicapped children began to operate in every county in 1946. Composed of representatives from the education section of the people's council, a general school teacher, a neurologist, and a specialist in education of the handicapped, these committees classify children for placement in special classes.

In 1952, several institutions were established for vocational training of the handicapped. These institutions aim to further the children's education and to provide them with a trade skill. Normally, these institutions enroll handicapped children between 12 and 18 years of age.

The people's councils are responsible for educating the handicapped and maintaining proper schools[14] (table 48). Instructors for these schools are trained at special teacher-training colleges.[15]

Table 48.—Number of institutions, classrooms, teachers, and pupils in schools for the handicapped: 1952–53—1966–67

School year	Institutions [1]	Classrooms	Teachers	Pupils					
				Total	Boys	Girls	Supported by the State	Per teacher	Per classroom
1952–53	64	534	795	10,168	6,209	3,959	1,362	12.8	19.0
1953–54	64	533	771	9,946	5,791	4,155	1,736	12.9	18.7
1954–55	64	541	885	9,972	5,718	4,254	1,326	11.3	18.4
1955–56	77	630	939	10,818	6,308	4,510	1,191	11.5	17.2
1956–57	80	655	987	11,491	6,689	4,802	1,226	11.6	17.5
1957–58	81	680	1,038	12,470	7,266	5,204	1,221	12.0	18.3
1958–59	85	745	1,160	13,984	8,214	5,770	1,486	12.1	18.8
1959–60	87	813	1,267	15,512	9,133	6,379	1,550	12.2	19.1
1960–61	88	878	1,382	17,278	10,289	6,989	1,988	12.5	19.7
1961–62	94	953	1,521	19,123	11,357	7,766	2,415	12.6	20.1
1962–63	96	1,025	1,630	20,298	12,108	8,190	2,726	12.5	19.8
1963–64	101	1,089	1,779	21,683	13,035	8,648	2,943	12.2	19.9
1964–65	107	1,164	1,901	22,685	13,716	8,969	3,161	11.9	19.5
1965–66	109	1,229	2,003	23,429	14,101	9,328	3,367	11.7	19.1
1966–67	108	1,276	2,090	24,481	14,596	9,885	3,343	11.7	19.2

[1] Does not include schools with special classes for the handicapped.

SOURCE OF DATA: *Statisztikai évkönyv 1966* (Statistical Yearbook 1966). Budapest: Központi Statisztikai Hivatal, 1967. p. 358.

Military Education

To insure the loyalty of its armed forces, the Hungarian people's democratic regime places considerable emphasis on training a professionally competent and politically reliable officers corps. Guided by this policy, the Government has established and developed a military education system for a carefully selected and indoctrinated student body.[16]

The military education system and network changed periodically. Immediately before the revolutionary events of October-November 1956, Hungarian officers were trained mostly in the six military educational institutions then in existence—two military academies and four cadet

[14] Articles 10-14 of Decree No. 14 of 1962 of the Presidential Council concerning elementary schools. *Magyar Közlöny*, No. 43, June 16, 1962. p. 391. The articles also discuss the compulsory character of education for the handicapped.

[15] See p. 150-51.

[16] The expectations of the regime were not corroborated in the fall of 1956, when many students and former graduates of the military schools either remained passive or openly joined the insurgents.

schools.[17] Some of the officers have been, and continue to be, trained in the Soviet Union, especially at the prestigious Frunze and Voroshilov academies.[18]

In the post-1956 era, officer training took place primarily at the United Officers School for the People's Army (*A Néphadsereg Egyesitett Tiszti Iskolája*) and its various affiliated branch schools.

Beginning September 1, 1967, the Hungarian officers schools were transformed into military colleges and made part of the higher education system. The change affected specifically the Kossuth Lajos Military College (*Kossuth Lajos Katonai Főiskola*)—the former prestigious "Ludovica" of the Horthy era—the Zalka Máté Military Technical College (*Zalka Máté Katonai Műszaki Főiskola*)—both in Budapest—and the Kilián György Air Force Technical College (*Kilián György Repülő Műszaki Főiskola*) in Szolnok.[19]

Operating under the immediate jurisdiction of the Minister of Defense (*Honvédelmi Miniszter*), the military colleges are guided by the Ministry of Culture as to general academic curriculum, examination procedure, and degree requirements. The diplomas earned at these military colleges qualify the holders not only for military commissions, but also for jobs in their technical specialties or for jobs as elementary school teachers.[20]

Applications for admission to military institutions may be filed by Hungarian citizens under 21 years of age during their last year of secondary school or later, if they possess the secondary school certificate. Applicants must be unmarried and in good physical health. The application documents consist of a handwritten autobiography, a birth certificate copy, school records, and the application itself. All are carefully screened in order to assure that potentially capable, professionally competent, and politically reliable candidates are selected.[21]

Determined by a point system (maximum score of 20), the order of admission, theoretically at least, is based on secondary school achievement level and that of the admission examinations. The maximum composite score is established by allocating 5 points each to excellent achievement in secondary school, to the examinations for the secondary school certificate, and to the written and oral admission examinations. The point system is not applied to children of war heroes, "martyrs of

---

[17] These were the Zrinyi Military Academy, the Petöfi Military Academy, the Dózsa School for Infantry and Tank Officers, the Zalka School for Communications and Engineering Officers, the Kossuth Lajos Military School, and the Áron Gábor Military School. General Béla Király. Hungary's Army: Its Part in the Revolt. *East Europe*, New York, 7:6:11 June 1958.

[18] Ibid. p. 9. According to General Béla Király, advanced training of Hungarian officers began in 1948. The officer-training candidates, normally Party members, were selected by their service commanders and the heads of the political departments after careful screening by security police. Before departure to the Soviet Union, the Hungarian officers were put through an intensive preparatory course for learning the Russian language.

[19] "A Népköztársaság Elnöki Tanácsának 1967. évi 13. számú törvényerejű rendelete a Magyar Néphadsereg tiszti iskoláinak katonai főiskolává nyilvánitásáról" (Decree No. 13 of 1967 of the Presidential Council of the People's Republic Concerning the Identification of the Officers Schools of the Hungarian People's Army as Military Colleges). *Magyar Közlöny*, No. 37, June 11, 1967. p. 318.

[20] The upgrading of some of the technical degrees at the officers schools to equivalency with those at higher education institutions had already been effected in 1961 and 1962 under Decrees No. 1/1961. (VI.24.)HM-MM and 1/1962. (VIII.19.)HM-MM. *Magyar Közlöny*, No. 48, June 24, 1961. p. 363 and No. 63, August 19, 1963, p. 528. Both of these decrees, however, were subsequently abrogated by Joint Decree No. 1/1963. (VI.9.)HM-MM of the Minister of Defense and the Minister of Culture, which regulated anew the system of technical training and degrees offered by military schools. *Magyar Közlöny*, No. 39, June 9, 1963. p. 257-58.

[21] *Tájékoztató a magyar felsőoktatási intézményekről 1965* (Guide to the Hungarian Institutions of Higher Learning 1965). Budapest: A Művelődésügyi Minisztérium Kiadványa, 1965, p. 18-19, 90.

the workers' movement," or recipients of the "For Worker-Peasant Power Medal" *(Munkás-Paraszt Hatalomért Emlékérem),* who have received at least a passing grade in the admission examinations.

Military college students receive no scholarships as such, but the State assumes the cost of their schooling and maintenance. In addition, they receive a modest amount of cash for pocket money (ranging from 100 to 200 forints per academic year in 1965), which is supplemented by a small bonus varying with achievement in studies.

When he has successfully completed the 4-year course, the student receives a diploma deemed equivalent to diplomas from higher *technikums* or teacher-training colleges. Because of the military colleges' dual objectives (training men to become competent both in the military and the technical or educational spheres), the curriculum is highly diversified. Students preparing for a military-teaching career study not only military subjects but also such education-related subjects as chemistry, geology, German language and literature, mathematics, physical education, physics, and Russian language and literature. Those preparing for a technical career study subjects like accounting, engineering technology, machine building technology, motor vehicle technology, radio chemistry, railroad and road construction, and telecommunication microwaves.[22]

Party Education

Scope

The objectives of Party education are manifold: to give political indoctrination in accordance with a specific line, to advance general understanding regarding political and social-economic factors underlying societal phenomena, and to train Party cadres and activists.

These objectives are achieved through informal periodic lectures offered by both Party and social organizations and through formal lectures in Party educational institutions. Although both Party and non-Party individuals attend the informal lectures, usually only Party members attend the formal ones in Party educational institutions.

Administration

The general plans for Party education are determined yearly by the Politburo *(Politikai Bizottság)* or the Secretariat of the Central Committee *(Központi Bizottság Titkársága).* The lecture series are organized by the Agitation and Propaganda Section *(Agitációs és Propaganda Osztály),* which also works out the methodological techniques to be used, checks the propaganda materials, and supervises the training of Party propagandists. Beginning with the 1966-67 Party school year, the organization and supervision of mass propaganda at the local level have been entrusted to the Party committees in the city of Budapest and in the counties. These Party committees have been authorized to modify

[22] MTI [*Magyar Távirati Iroda*; Hungarian Telegraph Office] September 18, 1967.

the program and lecture content to fit local conditions and needs within the framework of general instructions issued by the Agitation and Propaganda Section.

Informal Education

So-called informal lectures based on timely topics of interest to the Party are organized by the Party committees of the municipalities and counties on the basis of materials received from the higher Party organs. Some of these lectures are televised under the direction of the Agitation and Propaganda Section, while others are offered under the auspices of the trade unions or other non-Party mass organizations.

Formal Party Education

Formal Party educational institutions are of three types operating at three different levels. Highest is the Party College (*Pártfőiskola*), which operates under the immediate jurisdiction of the Party Central Committee. Another high-level one is the Political Academy *(Politikai Akadémia)*. A forum for major Party pronouncements, it normally operates without a definite schedule or formal requirements. Beginning with the 1968-69 academic year, a new Party institution of higher learning —the Political College of the Hungarian Socialist Workers Party (*A Magyar Szociálista Munkáspárt Politikai Főikoslája*)—began to provide necessary political background on a university level for persons in leading positions in public life. Placed under the jurisdiction of the Central Committee of the Party, the Political College offers not only general theoretical and political training in economic, political, and propaganda work, but also supplementary and refresher courses for persons already employed in leading positions throughout the country "in accordance with the demands of practical tasks and problems." [23]

Somewhat lower in the Party school system than the institutions just described are the Evening Universities of Marxism-Leninism (*Marxizmus-Leninizmus Esti Egyetemek*) which offer 2 or 3 years of training and which devote themselves mainly to training Party cadres.

Higher Party institutions have stringent admission requirements; their diplomas are equivalent to those granted by regular colleges. Some evening universities operate under the auspices of the Ministry of Defense.[24]

At the intermediate level are the 1-year Evening Secondary Schools of Marxism-Leninism *(Esti Középfokú Iskolák)*, also devoted mainly to training Party cadres, but for the Party's and Government's lower echelons.

---

[23] "A Népköztársaság Elnöki Tanácsának 1968. évi 15. számú törvényerejű rendelete Politikai Főiskola létesitéséről" (Decree No. 15 of 1968 of the Presidential Council of the People's Republic Concerning the Establishment of the Political College). *Magyar Közlöny*, No. 46, June 4, 1968. p. 504.

[24] Graduates of the Evening Universities of Marxism-Leninism transferring to evening sessions or correspondence courses of regular universitites or colleges are exempt from taking courses or examinations in Marxism-Leninism. See Government Resolution No. 1,088/1957. (XI.21.) in *Magyar Közlöny*, No. 123, November 21, 1957. p. 850. Concerning the equivalency of degrees awarded by the higher Party schools with those of regular colleges see Government Decree No. 17/1963. (VII.2.) in *Magyar Közlöny*, No. 45, July 2, 1963. p. 293.

At the lowest level are the so-called Theoretical Conferences *(Elméleti Konferenciák)*. Conferences of this type are organized in communities—usually small ones—which have no evening universities or schools.

In recent years lectures and courses have been oriented towards the economic problems confronting Hungary since the reforms of the late 1960's. Among the new 1967-68 courses were Basic Economic Knowledge, Political Economy, and Problems of World Economy and International Politics. The political-ideological indoctrination program emphasizes a new course, History of the Hungarian Revolutionary Workers Movement, based on a three-volume text of the same title.[25]

Enrollment

Attendance at formal and informal Party schools is large, the number of students reaching 840,000 (more than ten percent of the total adult population) in the fall of 1966. About 250,000 of these were non-Party members. For 1967-68 Party schools were to be concerned primarily with the more demanding and higher-level training of Party members; and of Party, State, and mass organization cadres and propagandists. Lectures for non-Party members were to be organized mostly by the trade unions and other mass organizations.[26]

[25] "A Politikai Bizottság 1967. április 6-i határozata a pártoktatás 1967/68. évi feladataira" (The Resolution of the Politburo of April 6, 1967 Concerning the Tasks of Party Education in 1967-68). *Pártélet* (Party Life,) Budapest, May 1967.

[26] *Népszabadság*, Budapest, June 13, 1967.

X. Youth and Sport Organizations

Scope

A nation's educational system, it is generally agreed, forms a part of its political and ideological framework. Authoritarian States of the past exhibited this characteristic and those of today likewise do.

Although the so-called socialist and people's democracies during recent years have considerably modified the socioeconomic structures and policies which they earlier established, they nevertheless continue to adhere to the traditional orthodox Marxist concept of the role of education in societal transformation. The Marxist world assumes that education, like all other social and political institutions, is a part of the "relations of production," the superstructure reflecting the underlying economic base. As such, education becomes primarily an instrument in service to the dominant or ruling class.

The pseudo-scientific theory of historical materialism (with its emphasis on economic determinism), views education as an important element in the class struggle—a struggle which that theory contends is bound to end in ultimate victory for the working class. Theoretically, workers (practically, upper echelons of the Communist Party) acquire power and gradually obtain a monopoly over it. At that point, then, education comes into its heritage as an instrument for building a superior, classless society and for creating the new man—totally socialist and ultra-competent.

To achieve these complex but interrelated tasks requires, among other things, that the content and orientation of education be radically revised, especially in the ideological and political realm. This idea is to be viewed in its dynamic rather than in its static connotation, for revision must be continuous in order to reflect the regime's changing interests and emphasis.

Preservation of the regime, expansion of its influence, and effective exercise of its power depend to a large extent on how successfully it mobilizes the masses. In this context the political-ideological campaign assumes paramount importance in a Comunist society. Although the Communist blueprint for remolding society places great emphasis on re-educating all segments of the people, it considers that indoctrinating the school population is vital for the success of Communism.

Conscious of the role that education must play in societal transformation, the Hungarian Communists, after openly assuming power in 1948, proceeded to reorganize the schools radically along socialist lines.

The process gathered momentum when the Hungarian schools were nationalized and Soviet schools were adopted as a model.

The primary objective of the Hungarian Soviet-type school is to produce professionally competent and politically reliable individuals. Article 1 of the fundamental education act of 1961 [1] reflects this same concept, namely, that the primary goal of the educational system of the Hungarian People's Republic to provide—

> . . . general and professional knowledge . . . to satisfy the requirements of the economy for skilled labor . . . and to develop and strengthen in the students a Marxist-Leninist conception of life . . . and raise conscious, educated, patriotic, upright and law-abiding citizens who are faithful to the people, who cooperate in the building of socialism with useful work, who build and protect the people's State . . .

Education's primary function is therefore interconnected with the "building of socialism" and the protection of the "people's State." The content, techniques, and methods of education must be subordinated to the requirements of the ultimate goal—Communism, which also presupposes a constant and relentless struggle against bourgeois influences.[2]

The tasks of Communist education were spelled out in greater detail in the guidelines of the Central Committee of the Communist Youth League [3] of April 1963.[4] According to these guidelines, the primary function of education in the Communist upbringing of Hungarian youths is to propagate Marxist-Leninist ideas and continuously upgrade their political-ideological level. Hungarian youths must be made to believe that Marxist ideas are valid and that Communism will inevitably and ultimately triumph. They must be made acquainted with Party views and policies and with the political-ideological problems associated with building socialism—problems which the Party solves with the "creative application" of the principles of Marxism-Leninism. The new generation must be further educated to love and trust the Party and live in the spirit of socialist patriotism and proletarian internationalism, that is, in accordance with the requirements of Communist morality.

Political-ideological education in the Hungarian People's Republic, as in all other socialist and people's democracies, is a complex and multilateral process. It involves permeating intensively, though not always effectively, all subjects—in all grades and at all educational levels—with Marxist-Leninist views. The process also involves systematically indoctrinating students with these views even during organized extracurricular activities. These activities are planned and implemented

---

[1] "1961. évi III. törvény a Magyar Népköztársaság oktatási rendszeréről" (Law No. III of 1971 Concerning the Educational System of the Hungarian People's Republic). *Magyar Közlöny* (Hungarian Gazette), Budapest, No. 74, October 17, 1961. p. 566.

[2] Sándor Nagy *and* Lajos Horváth, eds. *Neveléselmélet* (Theory of Education). Budapest: Tankönyvkiadó, 1965. p. 130-31.

[3] For details on the structure and functions of the Communist Youth League, see p. 182-89.

[4] *KISZ Központi Bizottságának irányelvei a magyar ifjúság kommunista nevelésének néhány kérdéséről* (Guidelines of the Central Committee of the Communist Youth League Concerning Some Questions of Communist Education of Hungarian Youth). Budapest, April 18, 1963, as described in the following article: Vera Méhes Balázs. "Az osztályfönök feladatai osztálya KISZ-alapszervezetének munkájában" (The Tasks of the Home-Room [or Class-Master] Teacher in His Class' Work in the Basic Organization of the Communist Youth League). *In: Az iskolai közösségi nevelés* (Communal Education in the School). Edited by Jenő Bársony. Budapest: Tankönyvkiadó, 1964. p. 120-60. See especially p. 121-23.

under the auspices of the Pioneer movement, the Communist Youth League, the so-called "collegiums," and the sport organizations.

The Pioneer Movement

Evolution

Hungarian Communist historiography traces the evolution of the Pioneer movement (*úttörőmozgalom*) to spring 1945, when representatives of the Social Democratic Party and the Communist Party decided to organize a mass youth movement within the National Association of the Friends of Children *(Gyermekbarátok Országos Egyesülete)*.[5] The association's bylaws were revised in 1946, when members of the youth movement came to be identified as "pioneers" (*úttörő*), using the word "Forward" (*Előre*) as their official greeting.

The increasingly political coloration of the movement placed it in conflict with the older youth organizations, notably the Association of Hungarian Boy Scouts *(Magyar Cserkészfiúk Szövetsége)*, the *Diákkaptár* (Student Hive), and the Red Cross and sport groups, as well as the newer, principally Catholic youth organizations, like the Szívgárda (Heart Guard) and the *Mária-kongregáció* (Maria Congregation).

In addition to the Catholic-sponsored youth organizations, a variety of Party-affiliated youth groups were established. Most of them cooperated with each other under the auspices of the Hungarian Democratic Youth Association *(Magyar Demokratikus Ifjusági Szövetség*—MADISZ). The latter, increasingly under "progressive" leadership, took a more "positive" attitude toward the political orientation of the Pioneer movement.

Reflecting the political changes then taking place in the country, the Minister of Culture permitted the Pioneer movement to be organized in the school system beginning with the 1947-48 school year.[6] The attempt to keep the organization non-political failed by the following year, when, with the Communists' open assumption of power, the Pioneer movement was separated from the National Association of the Friends of Children and integrated into the new, Communist-controlled Popular Association of Hungarian Youth *(Magyar Ifjuság Népi Szövetsége)*. Concurrently, the older and the newer children's organizations, by now under new leadership, were consolidated into the Pioneer movement.

The tasks of the expanded movement were redefined at its first national conference in May 1948 as follows:

1. Pioneer groups must be organized in every elementary school.
2. The Pioneer adult and youth leaders must acquire adequate organizational and educational training in leader-training schools to be organized in large cities and modeled after the National Leader-Training School (*Országos Vezetőképző Iskola)*.

---

[5] Mrs. György Szirmai. "A magyar úttörőszervezet" (The Hungarian Pioneer Organization). *In: Nevelésügyünk húsz éve, 1945-1964* (Twenty Years of Our Educational System, 1945-1964). Budapest: Tankönyvkiadó, 1965. p. 181. (Referred to hereafter as Mrs. György Szirmai.)

[6] By the 1947-48 school year, the Pioneer movement had about 50,000 members; by May 1948, 100,000; and by July 1949, 600,000. Mrs. György Szirmai, op. cit. p. 191, 197, and 200.

3. Every elementary school must provide a well-equipped Pioneer home.
4. Pioneer work must become multilateral through establishing ethnic, scientific, sport, and technical circles.
5. Every Pioneer group must develop its own self-governing body.
6. Special attention must be devoted to summer activities.[7]

The ultimate scope of the Pioneer movement—Communist education of youth—became crystallized in June 1950, when (after dissolution of the Popular Association of Hungarian Youth) the Association of Working Youth *(Dolgozó Ifjúság Szövetsége*—DISZ) was established on the Soviet *Komsomol* model. An arm of the Communist Party, DISZ was made responsible for education and leadership in the Pioneer movement: its job was to train Pioneers to "love the Soviet Union . . . and live and work according to the teachings of the Party." [8]

These objectives (or illusions) were shattered during the October-November 1956 Revolution. Soviet-tank crushing of the uprising on November 4 signaled not only the end of the aspirations of the "freedom fighters" but also the end of the DISZ. During October-November, the Association of Sentry Guards *(Örszemcsapatok Szövetsége)* replaced the Pioneer movement and the DISZ. But this association was short-lived: when the new Soviet-supported Hungarian Revolutionary Worker-Peasant Government *(Magyar Forradalmi Munkás-Paraszt Kormány)* consolidated its powers, it dissolved the association on February 18, 1957 and concurrently established the Association of Hungarian Pioneers (*Magyar Úttörők Szövetsége*).

Structure and Functions

Identified as a voluntary mass organization for children ages 8 to 14, the Association of Hungarian Pioneers operates under the auspices of the Communist Youth League *(Kommunista Ifjusági Szövetség*—KISZ), which succeeded DISZ in March 1957.

The organization has three types of members:

1. "Little Drummer" (*Kisdobos*) for children ages 8 to 10.
2. "Probationary Pioneer" for children applying for admission to a Pioneer group.
3. "Pioneer" for children ages 11 to 14 who have served as Probationary Pioneers for at least 6 months.[9]

An applicant is admitted after passing certain age-differentiated tests. For a leadership assignment to any of the Pioneer levels, an applicant must pass special tests.

The Pioneer structure follows the pyramidal form charateristic of Communist mass organizations.

Guided by the central association in accordance with general guide-

[7] Ibid. p. 198.
[8] Ibid. p. 205.
[9] For details see Ferenc Szabó. "A kisdobos és úttörő probarendszer" (The System of Tests for the Little Drummers and Pioneers). *Köznevelés* (Public Education), Budapest, XXIV:17:653-54. September 6, 1968.

lines of the Communist Youth League,[10] the Pioneers of a given elementary school constitute the "Pioneer group" (*úttörőcsapat*). The groups are divided into "troops" *(rajok),* which in turn are subdivided into "patrols" (*őrsök*), the smallest units. Each patrol consists of from 6 to 12 Pioneers, and each troop includes from 2 to 4 patrols. The Little Drummers are first assigned to "novice troops" (*újoncőrsök*); Probationary Pioneers to "novice patrols" *(újoncrajok).*[11]

The most important Pioneer entity in the school is the "Pioneer group leadership" (*csapatvezetőség*), composed of the "group leader" (*csapatvezető*), his deputy, the troop leaders, and the group secretary, treasurer, and equipment custodian. The group leader is appointed jointly by the school principal and the particular KISZ organization that exercises direct control over the Pioneer group in that school. The leader is expected to work closely with the principal in implementing the organization's goals, especially those for extracurricular activities. Such activities normally revolve around physical education and sport circles *(sportkörök),* academic or technical-subject circles *(szakkörök),* and youth Red Cross groups.[12] The group leader, like other group leadership members, is responsible to the Party organization for all his activities in the school.[13]

Pioneers are expected to wear their uniforms of white shirt and red scarf especially while in school.

Since the Pioneer organization is the only mass organization which elementary school pupils may belong to, its membership has increased steadily. By 1956, it reached 900,000. During and immediately after the October-November Revolution, however, it fell drastically, if it did not disintegrate. When the movement was reorganized in 1957, its membership again rose, gradually reaching 600,000 by 1964.[14]

During the late 1960's, the overwhelming majority of elementary school pupils are Pioneers. In the upper grades, especially those of urban schools, the Pioneer ratio is much higher than it is in the lower grades. That higher ratio may be attributed to pragmatism rather than to enthusiasm, since admission to a secondary school (even to a good vocational school) depends on (among other things) proof of Pioneer membership.

The Communist Youth League

Evolution

Modeled after the Soviet *Komsomol* movement, the Communist Youth League—KISZ—is the successor of the Association of Working Youth—

[10] The general guidelines were adopted on May 25, 1961. See *A KISZ Központi Bizottságának irányelvei a Magyar Úttörők Szövetsége munkájára és a KISZ feladataira* (Guidelines of the Central Committee of KISZ Concerning the Work of the Association of Hungarian Pioneers and KISZ's Tasks). Budapest: KISZ, 1962.

[11] Ferenc Abent. "A Magyar Népköztársaság közoktatásügye" (The Educational System of the Hungarian People's Republic). *In: A közoktatásügy Eurspa Szociálista országaiban* (Public Education in the Socialist Countries of Europe). Budapest: Tankönyvkiadó, 1965. p. 291.

[12] For further details on the specific functions of the pioneer organizations, see Mrs. György Szirmai, op. cit. p. 225-32, and "Az úttörőszervezet nevelőmunkája az általános iskolában és a pedagógusok feladatai a KISZ VI. Kongresszusa után" (The Educational Work of the Pioneer Organization in the General School and the Tasks of Teachers Following the Sixth KISZ Congress). *Köznevelés,* Budapest. XXI:20:764-67. October 22, 1965.

[13] *Rendtartás az általános iskolák és a gimnáziumok számára* (Regulations for the General Schools and Gymnasiums). Budapest: Tankönyvkiadó, 1964. p. 19-21.

[14] Ferenc Ábent. "A Magyar Népköztársaság közoktatásügye," op. cit. p. 290.

DISZ—which disintegrated during the October-November 1956 Revolution.

DISZ itself came into being in June 1950, when the Communists solidifying their power, decided to dissolve all youth organizations and consolidate their members into one new association directly subordinated to the Party. This put an end to the many youth organizations and secondary school and university student associations that sprang up in the immediate post-World War II period.

The associations thus extinguished included the following:

1. Hungarian Democratic Youth Organization (MADISZ)[15]—of the Socialist Youth Movement (*Szociálista Ifjúsági Mozgalom*—SZIM) affiliated with the Social Democratic Party.
2. Independent Youth Association (*Független Ifjúsági Szövetség*—FISZ)—of the Independent Smallholders' Party (*Független Kisgazdapárt*).
3. National Association of Hungarian Students (*Magyar Diákok Nemzeti Szövetsége*)—of the secondary school group.
4. National Association of Hungarian University and College Students (*Magyar Egyetemisták és Főiskolások Egységes Szövetsége*—MEFESZ).

As a result of consolidating the youth organizations and campaigning relentlessly for new members, the DISZ grew tremendously, to a total of 620,000 by 1951. Of these, 170,000 were in Budapest.[16] Following the Party's March 1, 1952 decision to transfer all Party members under age 24 into DISZ, the membership further increased by an additional 110,000 to 120,000. Nevertheless, the Party considered the membership drive a failure. According to Mihály Farkas, then Minister of Defense *(Honvédelmi Miniszter)*, only 35 percent of the 1,812,000 DISZ-age youths (ages 14-24; later 14-26) were members. In the countryside only 1,038 of the 4,930 producer cooperatives had DISZ organizations.[17]

When the so-called "New Course" program was introduced in Soviet bloc nations after Stalin's death in 1953, the DISZ membership began to fall and student interest in Communist-sponsored political affairs gradually declined. Commensurate with the decline in that interest, came an interest in Western styles of art, clothing, and music. A partial return to Stalinist techniques in the latter half of 1955 (characterized by the policies of the re-emerged Moscow-oriented hardliners), however, signaled the beginning of a tougher line toward youth in general and university students in particular. Almost daily, the Party press began to feature ever-sharper attacks against youth's "apolitical tendencies," "chauvinism," "clericalism," and "nationalism," and against their readiness to denigrate socialism's achievements and to praise those of the West.

At first, the young people themselves and their teachers were blamed. But after the Twentieth Congress of the Communist Party of the Soviet Union denigrated Stalin, and Khrushchev attacked the so-called "per-

---

[15] By August 1945, MADISZ had 238,500 members. László Dobos. "Nevelőmunka középiskolás ifjúsági szervezeteinkben" (Educational Work in Our Secondary School Youth Organizations). *In: Nevelésügyünk húsz éve, 1945-1964*, op. cit. p. 241.

[16] *Szabad Nép* (Free People), Budapest, June 17, 1951.

[17] The Minister of Defense gave vent to his disappointment in a speech of June 28, 1952. For a more recent evaluation of the political situation of the farm youth see György Molnár. "A termelőszövetkezeti ifjúság helyzetéről és jövőjéről" (The Situation and Future of the Agricultural Cooperative Youth). *Társadalmi Szemle* (Social Review), Budapest. XXII:4:79-86. April 1967, p. 79-86.

sonality cult" in February 1956, the blame was extended to the Party and KISZ leaders.

The ensuing "liberalization" drive at home and the new "peaceful coexistence" policy abroad gave impetus to "democratization" experiments within the youth movement. An intellectually oriented group composed mostly of university students managed to bring to life the so-called Petőfi Circle *(Petőfi Kör)* to serve as a DISZ discussion forum. Embracing an ever-larger number of artists and writers, and crystallizing the requirements for building socialism in Hungary in accordance with conditions there, the Petőfi Circle played an important role in October 1956, when it became independent.

Youth Movements During the Revolution

The democratization drive in Hungary, like a concurrent one in Poland, was spearheaded by students. It reached a climax on October 16, 1956, when at a meeting in Szeged the local university students declared they were withdrawing from DISZ and were reestablishing MEFESZ. Students at other universities and colleges followed. On October 23, students organized a mass demonstration in support of the Poles, who were demanding greater freedoms from the Russians, and issued their own 16-point demands for the democratization of Hungarian socialism. Referred to by the regime as a counterrevolution and sparked by the shots fired at protesters on that October 23, the Revolution brought a virtual end to the Communist youth organizations. In their place new organizations, both independent and Party-affiliated, came into existence.

Re-emerging during the Revolution were the SZIM and FISZ, the Association of Christian Youth (*Keresztény Ifjúság Szövetsége*—KISZ), a Catholic organization, and the Organization of Christian Youth (*Keresztény Ifjúsági Egyesület*—KIE), a Protestant youth group. Attempts were made to unify the non-party youth organizations under the auspices of the short-lived United Association of Hungarian Youth *(Magyar Egységes Ifjúsági Szövetség)* and even to establish a special youth party, the Hungarian Revolutionary Youth Party (*Magyar Forradalmi Ifjúsági Párt*).

The suppression of the Revolution that followed the Soviet Army's intervention on November 4, 1956, brought an immediate end to all the non-Communist youth movements with the exception of MEFESZ, which continued to function until January 12, 1957, when its leadership was arrested. Two months later, on March 17, the Central Committee of the Communist Party decided to reestablish the unitary character of the youth movement through organizing the Communist Youth League as the successor of DISZ.

Organization and Structure

Operating directly under the guidance and control of the Communist Party, the Communist Youth League has the same vertical structure as its parent organization.[18] Like the latter, it theoretically operates on

[18] See p. 6-8.

highly democratic principles: all power emanating from the membership and the executive KISZ organs elected by and responsible to the assemblies composed of "freely" elected delegates. In reality, however, power flows from the top down with ultimate decision-making power concentrated in the Party Politburo or Central Committee.

Theoretically, the highest organ of power in the League is the KISZ Congress *(KISZ Kongresszus)*, entrusted with evaluating past policy, formulating new programs, and electing the organ to act in its behalf during the time between meetings—the Central Committee *(Központi Bizottság)*. The lowest KISZ units are the so-called "basic organizations" *(alapszervezetek)*, each guided by a "general meeting" *(taggyülés)* and its executive organ, the "leadership" *(vezetőség)*.[19]

Functions

As the only legally recognized political mass organization for both school and working youths, KISZ carries out, in its activities, the important function of implementing the Party's policies and directives.

Perhaps the most important function of KISZ is to help implement general objectives that relate to Communist education of the new generations of youth.[20] Details of the KISZ organizations' specific tasks in schools and enterprises appear in the guidelines *(irányelvek)* periodically issued by the central KISZ organizations.[21]

In October 1961 KISZ's Central Committee adopted guidelines for carrying out its secondary school responsibilities. Those responsibilities entailed specific tasks under each of the following categories:[22]

1. Solidifying socialist outlook and morality.
2. Strengthening, developing, and enriching KISZ organizations.
3. Strengthening the Party's leading role.
4. Studying diligently to build up socialism.

At the same time, the Central Committee adopted guidelines for carrying out its vocational school responsibilities.[23]

Important as KISZ activities are in secondary and vocational schools, they are perhaps overshadowed by its activities in higher education institutions. The Party daily press and the Party's ideological-political organs are full of articles dealing with political education for the student body. Most of these articles tend to emphasize that it would be

---

[19] Sándor Nagy *and* Lajos Horváth, *eds. Neveléselmélet*, op. cit. p. 355-57. KISZ's new organizational statutes were adopted at the 7th KISZ Congress in June-July 1967. *Népszabadság* (People's Freedom), Budapest, July 2, 1967.

[20] See p. 179-80.

[21] "A Magyar Forradalmi Munkás-Paraszt Kormány 1016/1967. (VI.26.) számú határozata az ifjúság körében végzendő munkáról" (Resolution No. 1016/1967. (VI.26.) of the Hungarian Revolutionary Worker-Peasant Government Concerning the Work To Be Carried Out Among the Youth). *Magyar Közlöny*, No. 42, June 26, 1967. p. 339-42. A similar resolution was already adopted in 1957 (Resolution No. 1.087/1957 of November 21, 1957). See *Magyar Közlöny*, No. 123, November 21, 1967. p. 848-49.

[22] *Magyar Ifjúság* (Hungarian Youth), Budapest, January 6, 1962. See also "A KISZ nevelőmunkája a középiskolákban és a pedagógusok feladatai a KISZ VI. Kongresszusa után" (KISZ's Educational Work in the Secondary Schools and the Responsibilities of Teachers After the Sixth KISZ Congress). *Köznevelés*, XXII:20: 768-70. October 22, 1965; *Rendtartás az általános iskolák és a gimnáziumok számára*, op. cit.

[23] *Magyar Ifjúság*, op. cit. See also "A közép- és szakmunkásképző iskolák és KISZ-szervezeteik együttműködése" (Collaboration Between the Secondary and Vocational Schools and Between Their KISZ Organizations). *Köznevelés*, XXIII:11:401-04. June 9, 1967.

desirable to "improve" political education, either by intensifying the teaching of Marxism-Leninism or by invigorating the role of KISZ.

The persistent weaknesses in political-ideological training at the higher education level were revealed by the Minister of Culture in a detailed report to the National Assembly on November 11, 1965. He admitted that here much remained to be done, for although many students "learn" about Marxism-Leninism they do not necessarily "accept" it as their world outlook; and he criticized students for continuing to harbor bourgeois and petty bourgeois views.[24]

In some higher education institutions, these "asocial" views seemed "to contaminate the atmosphere . . . in a harmful manner" with some students "turning against the socialist order . . . and even the State order."[25]

The Government's campaign to improve the indoctrination process at the higher education level is centered around KISZ. Besides raising course and examination requirements in Marxism-Leninism,[26] KISZ in recent years has adopted certain organizational changes to improve the quality of teaching for this subject.

Since the beginning of academic year 1960-61, KISZ has assumed responsibility for guiding the so-called "scientific student circles," originally created in 1952 under a Ministry of Culture directive.[27] Organized around curriculum subjects, these circles operate in the appropriate academic departments under the immediate supervision of a faculty member recommended by KISZ. Overall supervision and direction is entrusted to the Student Circle Council *(Diákköri Tanács)* composed of circle secretaries, institutional representatives, and KISZ delegates. One of the KISZ delegates is the KISZ member in charge of academic affairs for his organization. He is automatically head of the Student Circle Council.

This same council plays an important role in organizing periodic Student Circle Conferences *(Országos Diákköri Konferencia)* and in awarding the University and College Scholarships of the People's Republic *(Népköztársasági Egyetemi és Főiskolai Ösztöndíj)*.[28]

To further strengthen KISZ's grip over university and college students, a National University and College Council *(Országos Egyetemi és Főiskolai Tanács)* was established on September 17, 1966, to serve as an "advisory body." With 45 members composed of students and KISZ and Government leaders, the council is designed to advise KISZ on questions of youth policy.[29]

---

[24] Pál Ilku. "Népünk általános és szakmai műveltségének emeléséért" (For Raising the General and Professional Cultural Level of Our People). *Köznevelés*, XXI:23:886. December 3, 1965.

[25] *Hajdú-Bihari Napló* (Diary of Hadju-Bihar), [Debrecen] December 5, 1965. Here are a few samples of this type of critical articles: István Sztankó. "A világnézeti politikai nevelés helyzete felsőfokú technikumainkban" (The Status of Political-Ideological Education in Our Higher *Technikums*). *Felsőoktatási Szemle* (Review of Higher Education), Budapest. XV:1:16-19. January 1966. Péter Vajó. "Merre tart az egyetemi ifjúsag?" (Which Way Are the University Students Going?). *Társadalmi Szemle*, Budapest. XXII:1:45-56. January 1967; and L. Toth. (We Must Improve Ideological Education). *Népszabadság*, August 25, 1967.

[26] The failure to suitably stress Marxism was revealed in the following article published by the organ of the Hungarian Academy of Sciences: (Enforcement of Stress on Marxist Ideology in Ph.D. Theses on Social Science Subjects). *Magyar Tudomány* (Hungarian Science), Budapest, February 1966.

[27] Aurél Hencz. *A művelődési intézmények és a művelődésigazgatás fejlődése, 1945-1961* (The Evolution of Educational Institutions and Administration, 1945-1961). Budapest: Közgazdasági és Jogi Könyvkiadó, 1962. p. 115.

[28] *Ibid.* p. 115-16. See also Rudolf Rajnai. "A tudományos diákkörökről" (Concerning the Scientific Student Circles). *Felsőoktatási Szemle*. XX:3:121-24. March 1953.

[29] *Népszabadság*, September 18, 1966.

The authority of KISZ in student affairs was further expanded in fall 1968. According to certain Ministry of Culture directives, the KISZ organizations were henceforth to be represented in academic committees and councils.[30] KISZ's apparent transformation into a fullfledged partner in higher educational matters reflects the regime's continued endeavors to strengthen the influence of this youth organization and thus weaken that of the faculty in selecting and training the new elite class.

KISZ's new power over higher education faculty supplements its earlier power over the teacher-training system as a whole. In March 1960, the KISZ Central Committee acquired protectorate powers over the training of elementary and secondary school teachers in order to assure that "the future teachers are prepared for the tasks of the future not only by their teaching, but also by their support of the youth movement."[31] One immediate result of these new powers has been that education majors must fulfill part of their practice teaching by working in either the KISZ or the Pioneer organizations.

Formulating policy and supervising the implementation of Party directives for higher education are the primary responsibility of the University and College Division of the Central Committee of KISZ (*KISZ Központi Bizottságának Egyetemi és Főiskolai Osztálya*).

The KISZ organizations are also engaged in mass campaigns to protect or help develop the people's democratic system. One such campaign is the action by the Young Guard *(Ifjú Gárda)*, a vigilante group dedicated to eradicating "hooliganism" and combating "rotten Western bourgeois spirit."[32]

Again, KISZ organizations are very much in the forefront of the movement to have cooperatives, factories, individuals, or shops compete to achieve and over-fulfill economic targets; to mobilize youth for participation in "voluntary" projects; and to organize summer work camps through which hundreds of thousands of students offer their "free services" for approximately 2 weeks to "the construction of socialism."

To stimulate youthful interest in communal work and Communist education, the regime launched the "Youth For Socialism" (*Ifjúság a Szocializmusért*) movement. A participant in that movement receives a medal if he successfully—

1. Contributes at least 20 hours of communal labor.
2. Participates in Party- or KISZ-organized political education courses.
3. Participates in cultural or sport activities (many of which are organized by collegiums and sport associations).

In recent years the Government has devoted increasing attention to the patriotic and paramilitary training of youth. Such training is rationalized by three major arguments:

1. The defense of socialism and the fatherland requires that youth be drawn closely into that defense.

[30] *Ifjú Kommunista* (Young Communist), Budapest, September 1968.
[31] Aurél Hencz. *A művelődési intézmények és a művelődésigazgatás fejlődése*, op. cit. p. 114.
[32] *Népszabadság*, June 30, 1961. Immediately after its founding, KISZ was especially active in combating the "counterrevolution." Those who distinguished themselves in the campaign received the "KISZ Ságvári Endre Medal" *(KISZ Ságvári Endre Emlékérem)*.

2. Aggressions of war and tensions are working against the forces of socialism.
3. Since youths are drafted at age 18 (when they normally finish secondary education), military service is the natural next step in education after that of the secondary level.

According to a study by the National Pedagogical Institute, to develop socialist patriotism and proletarian internationalism, the education system must—

1. Nurture in students a love for the native land, the socialist homeland, and the working people.
2. Lead students to appreciate the working people's material and cultural achievements and to dedicate themselves to the further advancement and protection of these achievements.
3. Foster use of the native tongue.
4. Help youths understand and appreciate the nation's cultural heritage and its progressive and revolutionary traditions.
5. Develop in students a love and appreciation for the Soviet Union, the socialist world order, and progressive mankind.
6. Nurture in students a feeling of faithfulness and solidarity with all who fight to aid human progress and to establish conditions for a more just society.[33]

To complement this intensified indoctrination of youth in socialist patriotism, the regime has adopted the Soviet pattern of national defense instruction. Certain Ministry of Culture directives spelled out just what that instrucion was to consist of.[34] Introduced in school year 1968-69, national defense instruction is compulsory for all students beginning with the seventh grade of the elementary school.

The Ministry of Defense (*Honvédelmi Minisztérium*), the Hungarian National Defense Association (*Magyar Országos Honvédelmi Szövetség*), armed forces units, and KISZ units all cooperated in setting up the national defense courses. Conducted for about 20 hours a year, the theoretical training takes place during periods assigned to physical education and home-room activities. Physical training takes places on school-free work days. No examinations are given and performance in national defense training is not graded.

Membership

The Communist Youth League admits to membership all young men and women between the ages of 14 and 26 who accept the organization's statutes and programs, symbolized by its motto: "Together with the masses of youth, for the socialist Hungary!" (*Együtt az ifjúság tömegeivel, a szociálista Magyarországért!*).

To become a member of the Communist Youth League an applicant must successfully fulfill three requirements which the League introduced in 1959: [35]

[33] Országos Pedagógiai Intézet. "Ifjúságunk szociálista hazafiságra nevelése és a honvédelmi nevelés" (The Education of Youth in Socialist Patriotism and Instruction in National Defense). *Köznevelés*, XXII:21:801-12. November 4, 1966. See especially, p. 803.

[34] *Népszabadság*, August 8, 1968.

[35] Ferenc Ábent. "*A Magyar Népköztársaság közoktatásügye*," op. cit. p. 292; László Dobos. "Nevelőmunka középiskolás ifjúsági szervezeteinkben," op. cit. p. 263.

1. Become informed about the League's principles and goals and create opportunities for KISZ members to become acquainted with him.
(The György Kilián Test—*Kilián György Próba*)

2. Achieve greater knowledge and understanding of the League's history and accomplishments, of the Soviet *Komsomol,* and of other progressive youth movements.
(The Young Communist Test—*Ifjú Kommunista Próba*)

3. Demonstrate skill in a specific field.
(The Professional Test—*Szakpróba*)

In March 1957, when KISZ began, it had only 30,000 members (approximately 2 percent of the KISZ-age youth).[36] Theoretically, 26 was the upper age limit. Following are a few statistics (released during the Seventh KISZ Congress of June 29–July 1, 1967) concerning its steady growth: [37]

Year and month	*Members* *Number*	*Members* *Percent of KISZ-age population*	*Organizational units*
1960 (Dec.)	525,424	29	14,423
1967 (June)	743,769	(1)	(1)

[1] Source did not give any figures.

The KISZ Congress further reported that of the 743,769 members of June 1967:

1. A total of 300,000 joined KISZ in 1964.[38]

2. The percents in various age groups were as follows:

Below 18 years old	48.2
18-20	18.3
21-26	27.4
Above 26	6.1

3. 55 percent had part-time jobs.

4. Nearly 600,000 had already fulfilled the three requirements for joining the "Youth for Socialism" movement.[39]

One of the principal requirements for joining the "Youth for Socialism" movement is active participation in communal, cultural, and sport activities, many of which are organized under the auspices of collegiums.

The Collegiums

The collegiums *(kollégiumok)* basically hostels and dormitories for secondary school and university and college students, are operated in close cooperation with the educational institutions and in accordance with the basic objectives and principles of the Communist Youth League. They are self-governing institutions pursuing the same educational goals

[36] *Magyar Ifjúság,* June 29, 1957.
[37] The 1960 figures in the tabulation are from *Magyar Ifjúság,* December 17, 1960.
[38] High as this figure is, it is only one-third the approximately 900,000 members DISZ had immediately before the October-November, 1956, Revolution.
[39] *East Europe,* New York. XVI:8:45. August 1967.

as formal academic institutions, namely, education of the new socialist man. Giving preference to students of working-class and peasant background, they serve primarily the needs of out-of-town students.

Collegium at the Polytechnical University of Heavy Industry

Evolution

Official historiography traces collegiums to activities associated with the "Győrffy István Kollégium" established in 1942, which included a number of "progressive students" in its midst.[40] After the 1945 liberation, this collegium took the initiative in launching the Movement for Building People's Collegiums (*Népi Kollégiumokat Építő Mozgalom*) dedi-

[40] Ferenc Juhász. "Pedagógiai törekvések a népi kollégiumi mozgalomban" (Pedagogical Aspirations in the People's Collegium Movement). *In: Nevelésügyünk húsz éve*, op. cit. p. 319-64.

cated to supporting and housing students of peasant and working-class background. The movement succeeded in establishing a number of such collegiums under the auspices of secondary and higher educational institutions. At that point the "Győrffy István Kollégium" organized the National Association of Peoples' Collegiums (*Népi Kollégiumok Országos Szövetsége—NEKOSZ*), which strove during the pre-Communist era to pursue a relatively moderate democratic program publicized in its organ, "People's Collegiumist" (*Népi Kollégista*).

After the Communists had openly assumed power in 1948, they severely criticized the NEKOSZ leadership for failing to understand the Association's place and role in the development of the people's democracy. The Party Politburo decision of September 19, 1948, acknowledged some of NEKOSZ's achievements,[41] but declared the following as its basic shortcomings:

1. NEKOSZ failed to recognize that the Party and the working class played a determining role in establishing and strengthening it.
2. NEKOSZ's Communist leaders were too patient and too liberal toward the peasant-worshipping ideology that was the antithesis of Marxism-Leninism.
3. NEKOSZ was isolated from Party-directed youth movements and students associations.
4. NEKOSZ neglected the needs of vocational-professional training.
5. NEKOSZ gravely violated Communist morality.[42]

These shortcomings, however, were subsequently overcome when new "reliable" leaders were appointed and a new NEKOSZ organ was launched—the "People's Collegium Educator" (*Népi Kollégiumi Nevelő*).

The management of student welfare programs and the direction of educational tasks within the by now nationalized collegiums were entrusted to the National Office of Collegiums and Student Welfare (*Országos Diákjóléti és Kollégiumi Hivatal*).[43] On January 15, 1950, this national office was dissolved and its responsibilities transferred to the "Collegium Center" (*Kollégiumi Központ*), a newly established division of the Ministry of Culture.[44]

Also during 1950, the higher education collegiums (basically student hostels) were placed under the School-Supply Enterprise (*Tanfolyamellátó Vállalat*) of the Ministry of Internal Trade (*Belkereskedelmi Minisztérium*). That ministry naturally was concerned more with supply than with educational matters.[45]

In 1952, these collegiums were reassigned to the Ministry of Culture. At first, they were identified primarily as *social* rather than *educational;* in 1956, however, they were identified as university collegiums. In 1959 KISZ took the initiative in having them transformed into "socialist" collegiums.[46]

---

[41] By 1948, NEKOSZ had 160 collegiums with about 10,000 students. Ferenc Juhász. "Pedagógiai törekvések a népi kollégiumi mozgalomban," op. cit. p. 344.
[42] Ibid. p. 345.
[43] The national office was established under Government Decision No. 9990/1948. (215) Korm. Ibid. p. 362.
[44] Ibid.
[45] Aurél Hencz. *A művelődési intézmények és a művelődésigazgatás fejlődése*, op. cit. p. 106.
[46] Ibid. p. 107-08.

Organization and Structure

According to the 1959 KISZ guidelines, a collegium may be established at a higher education institution by the joint approval of the KISZ Central Committee and the Minister exercising jurisdiction over the particular institution. The collegium operates under the immediate supervision of the local educational section of the people's councils.

Emulating the one-man management principle employed in all socialist enterprises, each collegium is headed by a director or principal. In discharging his duties, he relies on the support of the Collegium Advisory Body (*Kollégiumi Tanácsadó Testület*), whose members are appointed with the concurrence of the local educational section of the people's council and the KISZ committee. The membership includes the director of the collegium (who is also head of the Advisory Body), the collegium's KISZ leader, the educational institution's representative, the student council's delegate, and the higher KISZ organization's representative.[47]

The main decision making body of a collegium is the general assembly (*közgyülés*), theortically organized as a democratic self-governing unit. Each assembly elects its own student council (*diáktanács*) of 7 to 13 members—the number depending on the collegium's size. These members are formally appointed with the consent of the local KISZ organization.

In carrying out its responsibilities, the council works closely with KISZ. The council's decisions cannot go against the school's resolutions, the collegium's statutes, or the higher KISZ organizations' decisions.[48] The council's functions are carried out under the leadership of a secretary who is appointed from among its members, with KISZ consent.

Collegium members are divided into primary units such as brigades, cooperatives, and study groups. The collegium determines the size and character of the units.

During academic year 1966-67, 31,409 secondary school and 24,523 higher education students were living in collegiums (table 6).[49] No data are available concerning the social or economic backgrounds of these students.[50]

Sport Organizations

Physical education and sports constitute an integral part of the educational process calculated to bring about the new socialist man. According to Karl Marx, Communist education of youth requires physical education combined with practical labor and instruction "not only as a means for increasing social production but as the only way of producing fully

[47] Ibid.

[48] Sándor Daroczy. "A középiskolai kollégiumi nevelés helye, szerepe, sajátos feladata köznevelésünk rendszerében" (The Place, Role, and Tasks of Secondary Collegium Education in Our System of Public Education). *In: Középiskolai kollégiumi nevelés* (Secondary School Collegium Education). Edited by Miklós Habuda. Budapest: Tankönyvkiadó, 1965. p. 35-36.

[49] Sándor Daroczy. "Kollégiumok a hátrányos helyzetükért" (Concerning the Disadvantageous Position of the Collegiums). *Köznevelés*, XXII:10:381-82. May 20, 1966.

[50] For further details on the collegiums see Sándor Szvetek. "A kollégiumi nevelés" (Collegium Education). *In: Neveléselmélet*, op. cit. p. 333-46. See also Julia Mészáros. "A II. országos kollégiumi konferencia" (The Second National Collegium Conference). *Köznevelés*, XXII:10:379:80. May 20, 1966.

developed beings."[51] The idea of *mens sana in corpore sano* is taken very seriously in Hungary, as in all other people's democratic and socialist states. Policies for physical education and sports are formulated and implemented under the auspices of a central governmental agency whose scope and competence have varied as time has passed.

Evolution

The first major administrative decision concerning physical education and sports during the post-World War II era was taken in 1946, when ultimate responsibility was entrusted to the Ministry of Culture.[52] The technical aspects of sports continued to remain the prerogative of the National Sport Committee (*Nemzeti Sport Bizottság*). Failure to develop harmonious relations between the Ministry and the Committee led to an administrative reorganization in 1948 establishing a National Sport Office (*Országos Sporthivatal*).[53]

The Office absorbed the Ministry's responsibilities and the Committee's administrative functions. The members of the Committee's board of directors were appointed to head the then newly established National Council of Sports and Physical Education (*Országos Sport és Testnevelési Tanács*). The president of the Office also served as secretary general of the Council, thus assuring the desired harmonious collaboration between the two bodies.

The National Sport Office supervised the physical education of youth, organized lower units to administer sport activities, controlled sport organizations and associations, and developed foreign contacts in the field of sports.

The central organizational system was again revised in 1951, when a National Committee on Physical Education and Sports (*Országos Testnevelési és Sport Bizottság*) was established under the immediate jurisdiction of the Council of Ministers. This agency operated until 1958, when the Presidential Council of the People's Republic replaced it with the Hungarian Council of Physical Education and Sport (*Magyar Testnevelési és Sport Tanács*) as the main policy-determining body and the Hungarian Office of Physical Education and Sport (*Magyar Testnevelési és Sport Hivatal*) as its administrative organ.[54]

Physical education and sport, like the entire curriculum, were again subjected to scrutiny after the fundamental education act of 1961 was adopted.[55]

In November 1963 the educational system was revised and the central governmental organs, entrusted with administering physical education and sports, were reorganized. As a result of the reorganization, the Council was replaced by the Hungarian Association of Physical Education and

---

[51] Maurice J. Shore. *Soviet Education. Its Psychology and Philosophy*. New York: Philosophical Library, 1947. p. 52.
[52] See footnote 37 of chapter III.
[53] Aurél Hencz. *A művelődési intézmények és a művelődésigazgatás fejlődése*, op. cit. p. 264.
[54] Decree No. 4 of 1958. *Magyar Közlöny*, No. 5, January 12, 1958. p. 34. See also Government Decree No. 4/1958. (I.12.) implementing it. Ibid. p. 34-36.
[55] See p. 27.

Sports (*Magyar Testnevelési és Sportszövetség*)[56] whose competence and scope were considerably expanded in 1968.[57]

Organization, Structure, and Functions

The organizational structure and the functions of the Association are theoretically determined by the Association's Congress. Its specific plans in physical education and sports are determined and implemented with the cooperation of the interested State and social organs.

In addition to its main function—the central guidance, synchronization, and supervision of all aspects of physical education and sports—the Association:

1. Exercises inspection rights over the Hungarian College of Physical Education (*Magyar Testnevelési Főiskola*),[58] the Scientific Research Institute of Physical Education (*Testnevelési Tudományos Kutató Intézet*), and enterprises concerned with sports and tourism.
2. Exercises jurisdiction in all matters concerning the use and management of sport establishments.
3. Is an advisor for the schools' compulsory physical education programs.
4. Decides where to distribute State-allocated funds for sports and supervises their expenditure.
5. Makes recommendations concerning the physical education portion of the national economic plan.
6. Awards the two medals, "Outstanding Physical Education and Sport Worker" (*Testnevelés és Sport Kiváló Dolgozója*) and "Meritorious Physical Education and Sport Worker" (*Testnevelés és Sport Érdemes Dolgozója*); makes recommendations for awarding other State medals.
7. Determines rates and prices in areas within its competence.

Within educational establishments, sport activities are organized according to general directives and guidelines issued by the National Youth Sport Committee (*Orzágos Ifjúsági Sportbizottság*), which operates within the Communist Youth League. Cooperating with the Hungarian Association of Physical Education and Sports, the Ministry of Culture and the other ministries engaged in educational affairs, the Committee carries out its responsibilities through a number of central units, including the General School Sport Council (*Altalános Iskolai Sport Tanács*), the Student Sport Center (*Diák Sport Központ*), the University and College Sport Center (*Egyetemi és Főiskolai Sport Központ*), the Vocational Industrial Sport Center (*Iparitanuló Sport Központ*), and the Village Sport Center (*Falusi Sport Központ*).[59]

The physical education and sports program, both inside and outside the schools, is determined on the basis of advice and recommendations

---

[56] Decree No. 29 of 1963 of the Presidential Council of the People's Republic. *Magyar Közlöny*, No. 80, November 11, 1963. p. 622-23. See also Government Decree No. 29/1963. (XI.11.) implementing it. Ibid. p. 623.

[57] "A Népköztársaság Elnöki Tanácsának 1968. évi 4. számú törvényerejű rendelete a testnevelési és sportmozgalom társadalmi irányitásáról" (Decree No. 4 of 1968 of the Presidential Council of the People's Republic Concerning the Social Management of the Physical Education and Sports Movement). *Magyar Közlöny*, No. 16, February 25, 1968, p. 210-11. This was implemented by Government Decree No. 9/1968. (II.25.). Ibid. p. 212-13.

[58] See p. 124-25.

[59] Aurél Hencz. *A művelődési intézmények és a művelődésigazgatás fejlődése*, op. cit. p. 270.

from the Scientific Council of Physical Education (*Testnevelési Tudományos Tanács*).

In carrying out its functions, the Council relies on research and recommendations from the Scientific Research Institute of Physical Education. This institute operates within the framework of the Hungarian College of Physical Education and under the general direction of the Hungarian Association of Physical Education and Sports.[60]

Undoubtedly, among the Hungarian Government's highest satisfactions are those resulting from the great strides apparent in its physical education program. These great strides are reflected for all to see in national and international competitions in fencing, soccer, and swimming, for example. On their own merits, sports are tremendously popular throughout all Hungary. Their popularity and their successes in competition can be attributed not only to the intentions of the Government to build the new socialist man but also to the Hungarian people's traditional love for sports.

[60] "A Magyar Forradalmi Munkás-Paraszt Kormány 1.004/1959. (I.25.) számú határozata Testnevelési Tudományos Kutató Intézet létesitéséről" (Resolution No. 1,004/1959. (1.25.) of the Hungarian Revolutionary Worker-Peasant Government Concerning the Establishment of the Scientific Research Institute of Physical Education). *Magyar Közlöny*, No. 12, January 25, 1959. p. 64-65.

Appendixes

Appendix A. Glossary

Hungarian	English
A	
Agitációs és Propaganda Osztály	Agitation and propaganda section
Agrártudományi egyetem	Agronomic university
Alapszervezet	Basic organization
Alföld	Great Hungarian Plain
Állam- és Jogtudományi Kar	School *or* Faculty of Political Science and Law
Állami Egyházügyi Hivatal	State Office for Denominational Affiairs
Állatorvostudományi egyetem	University of veterinary medicine
Általános gimnázium	General gymnasium
——— *iskola*	"General" school (i.e., elementary school)
B	
Belkereskedelmi Minisztérium	Ministry of Internal Trade
Bizottság	Committee
Bölcsészettudományi Kar	School *or* Faculty of Philosophy
Bölcsőde	Nursery
Budapesti Műszaki Egyetem	Polytechnical University of Budapest
——— *Pedagógus Továbbképző Intézet*	Budapest Institute for Further Teacher Training
C	
Cimzetes egyetemi tanár	Tenured university professor
Csapatvezető	Group leader
D	
Dékán	Dean
Dékánhelyettes	Assistant *or* deputy dean
Diákkör	Student circle
Diáktanács	Student council
Dolgozó Ifjuság Szövetsége-DISZ	Association of Working Youth
Dunántul	Transdanubia

E

Egészségügyi Minisztérium	Ministry of Health
Egyetem	University
Egyetemi Számitóközpont	University Computation Center
——— *tanács*	University council
Elnök	Chairman
Elnöki Tanács	Presidential council
Elnökség	Board of directors
Első Titkár	First Secretary
Épitőipari és Közlekedési Műszaki Egyetem	Polytechnical University of Construction and Transportation
Érettségi	Baccalaureate (Matura; secondary school certificate) examination or certificate
Észak-Magyarország	Northern Hungary or Northern Uplands

F

Felsőfokú technikum	Higher *technikum* or technical school
Felsőoktatási Minisztérium	Ministry of Higher Education
——— *Tanács*	Council of Higher Education
——— *Tanulmányi Érdemrend*	Higher Education Studies medal
Feltételes felvétel; Előfelvétel	Conditional admission
Felvételi bizottság	Admissions committee
Főiskola	College
Földművelésügyi Minisztérium	Ministry of Agriculture
Független Ifjúsági Szövetség	Independent Youth Association
——— *Kisgazdapárt*	Independent Smallholders' party

G

Gimnázium	Gymnasium *or* secondary school
Gondnok	Building superintendent
Gyermekbarátok Országos Egyesülete	National Association of Friends of Children
Gyermeklélektani Intézet	Institute of Child Psychology
Gyermekotthon	Children's home
Gyogypedagógiai Tanárképző Főiskola	Teachers College for Teachers of Handicapped Children
Gyorsirókat és Gépirókat Vizsgáztató Országos Bizottság	National Committee for Examining Steno-Typists

H

Hazafias Népfront	Patriotic People's Front
Honvédelmi Minisztérium	Ministry of Defense

I

Idegen Nyelvi Továbbépző Központ	Center for Further Foreign Language Training
Ideiglenes Nemzeti Kormány	Provisional National Government
Időszaki napközi otthonos óvoda	Seasonal day home kindergarten
Ifjú Gárda	Young Guard
——— *Kommunista Próba*	Young Communist test

Ifjúság a Szociálizmusért	Youth for Socialism
Igazgató	Principal *or* director
Igazgatóhelyettes	Assistant principal *or* assistant director
Ipari technikum	Industrial *technikum or* technical school
Iparitanuló intézet	School for [industrial] apprentices
Iparügyi Minisztérium	Ministry of Industry
Irányelv	Guideline
Iskolatanács	School council
Iskolai körzet	School district
Ismétlő iskola	Continuation *or* supplementary school

J

Járás	District
Járási tanács	District people's council
Javitóvizsga	Repeat examination

K

Kar	School *or* faculty
Kari tanács	Faculty council
Kereskedelem- és Közlekedésügyi Minisztérium	Ministry of Trade and Transportation
Kereskedelmi Szakoktatási Tanács	Council of Trade Vocational Education
Kereskedőképző iskola	Training school for salespersons
Keresztény Ifjúság Szövetsége	Association of Christian Youth
——— *Ifjúsági Egyesület*	Organization of Christian Youth
Kisdobos	Little drummer
Kisgazdapart	Smallholders' party
Kitünő tanuló	Outstanding student
Kiváló óvónő	Outstanding kindergarten teacher
——— *tanár*	Outstanding professor
——— *tanitó*	Outstanding teacher
Kollégium	Collegium
Kollégiumi Tanácsadó Testület	Collegium Advisory Body
Kommunista Ifjúsági Szövetség-KISZ	Communist Youth League
Kommunisták Magyarországi Pártja	Communists Party of Hungary
Közgazdasági technikum	Economic *technikum or* technical school
Közoktatásügyi Minisztérium	Ministry of Public Education
Központi Bizottság	Central Committee
Központi Pedagógus Továbbképző Intézet	Central Institute for Further Teacher Training
——— *Statisztikai Hivatal*	Central Statistical Office
Községi tanács	Communal *or* village people's council
Különbözeti vizsga	Differential examination
Kulturális Kapcsolatok Intézete	Institute for Cultural Relations

L

Leánygimnázium	Girls' gymnasium *or* secondary school
Leckekönyv	Course book
Legfelsőbb Biróság	Supreme Court
Legfőbb Ügyész	Chief Public Prosecutor
Liceum	Lyceum *or* secondary school

M

Magyar Cserkészfiúk Szövetsége	Association of Hungarian Boy Scouts
——— *Demokratikus Ifjúsági Szövetség-MADISZ*	Hungarian Democratic Youth Association
——— *Diákok Nemzeti Szövetsége*	National Association of Hungarian Students
——— *Dolgozók Pártja*	Hungarian Workers' Party
——— *Egyetemisták és Főiskolások Egységes Szervezete*	United Organization of Hungarian University and College Students
——— *Egységes Ifjúsági Szövetség*	United Association of Hungarian Youth
——— *Forradalmi Ifjúsági Párt*	Hungarian Revolutionary Youth Party
——— ——— ——— *Munkás-Paraszt Kormány*	Hungarian Revolutionary Worker-Peasant Government
——— *Ifjúság Népi Szövetsége*	Popular Association of Hungarian Youth
——— *Kommunista Párt*	Hungarian Communist Party
——— *Nemzeti Függetlenségi Front*	Hungarian National Independence Front
——— *Nők Demokratikus Szövetsége*	Democratic Association of Hungarian Women
——— *Pedagógiai Társaság*	Hungarian Pedagogical Association
——— *Szociálista Munkáspárt*	Hungarian Socialist Workers' Party
——— *Táncművészek Szövetsége*	Hungarian Association of Dance Artists
——— *Testnevelési és Sportszövetség*	Hungarian Association of Physical Education and Sports
——— ——— ——— *Sport Tanács*	Hungarian Council of Physical Education and Sports
——— *Tudományos Akadémia*	Hungarian Academy of Sciences
——— *UNESCO Bizottság*	Hungarian National Commission for UNESCO
——— *Úttörők Szövetsége*	Association of Hungarian Pioneers
Magyarország	Hungary
Magyarországi Szociálista Párt	Socialist Party of Hungary
——— *Szociáldemokrata Párt*	Social Democratic Party of Hungary
Marxismus-Leninizmus Esti Egyetem	Evening University of Marxism-Leninism
Megye	County
Megyei oktatási tanács	County council of education
——— *tanács*	County people's council
Mérnök-közgazdász oklevél	Engineer-economist diploma
Mérnöki Továbbképző Intézet	Institute for the Further Training of Engineers
Mezőgazdasági és Élelmezésügyi Minisztérium	Ministry of Agriculture and Food
——— *szakmunkástanuló iskola*	Agricultural and vocational school
——— *technikum*	Agricultural *technikum* or technical school
——— *technikusi oklevél*	Agricultural technical diploma
Minisztertanács	Council of Ministers
Mozgássérültek Nevelőképző és Nevelőintézete	Institute for Training Instructors of Motor-Disorder Victims
Munkaerőtartalékok Hivatala	Office of Manpower Reserves
Munkaközösség	Work collective
Munkaközösségi rendszer	Collective work system
Munkaügyi Minisztérium	Ministry of Labor
Műszaki egyetem	Polytechnical university

——— *és Természettudományi Egyesületek Szövetsége*	Association of Technical and Scientific Societies
——— *középiskola*	Technical secondary school
——— *tanuló*	Technical student
Művelődési otthon	Cultural home
Művelődésügyi Minisztérium	Ministry of Cultural Affairs (rendered throughout this publication as Ministry of Culture
——— *osztály*	Section of education
Művészeti főiskola	Art college
——— *gimnázium*	Art secondary school
——— *Szakszervezetek Szövetsége*	Association of Art Trade Unions

N

Napközi otthon	Day home
——— *otthonos óvoda*	Day home kindergarten
Nehézipari Műszaki Egyetem	University of Heavy Industry
Nemzeti Sport Bizottság	National Sport Committee
Népi Kollégiumok Országos Szövetsége-NEKOSZ	National Association of Collegiums
——— *Kollégiumokat Építő Mozgalom* .	Movement for the Building of People's Collegiums
Népiskola	Public elementary school
Népjóléti Minisztérium	Ministry of Public Welfare
Népköztársaság	People's Republic
——— *Elnöki Tanácsa*	Presidential Council of the People's Republic
Népköztársasági Tanulmányi Ösztöndij ..	People's Republic Scholarship
Népművelési Intézet	Institute of Popular Culture
——— *Minisztérium*	Ministry of Public Culture
Nevelői közösség	Teachers' or educators' collective
Nyári napközi otthon	Summer day home

O

Oklevél	Diploma
Oktatásügyi Minisztérium	Ministry of Education
Őrs	Patrol
Országos Diákjóléti és Kollégiumi Hivatal	National Office for Collegiums and Student Welfare
——— *Diákköri Konferencia*	National Student Circle Conference
——— *Egyetemi és Főiskolai Tanács* ...	National University and College Council
——— *Gyermek- és Ifjúságvédelmi Tanács*	National Council for the Protection of Children and Youth
——— *Gyogyszerészeti Intézet*	National Pharmaceutical Institute
——— *Iparoktatási Tanács*	National Council for Industrial Education
——— *Középiskolai Tanulmányi Verseny*	National Secondary School Studies Competition
——— *Köznevelési Tanács*	National Council of Public Education
——— *Közoktatási Tanács*	National Council of Public Instruction
——— *Magyar Szinművészeti Akadémia*	National Academy of Dramatic Arts
——— *Munkaerőgazdálkodási Hivatal* ..	National Manpower Office
——— *Neveléstudományi Intézet*	National Scientific Institute of Education
——— *Oktatási Tanács*	National Council of Education
——— *Pedagógiai Intézet*	National Pedagogical Institute

——— ——— *Könyvtár*	National Pedagogical Library
——— *Politechnikai Kutató Munkaközösség*	National Work Collective for Polytechnical Research
——— *Rabbiképző Intézet*	National Jewish Theological Seminary
——— *Sporthivatal*	National Sport Office
——— *Szakorvosképesitő Vizsgabizottság*	National Examination Committee for the Qualification of Medical Specialists
——— *Szakmunkásképzési Jegyzék*	National Register for Training Skilled Workers
——— *Tervhivatal*	National Planning Office
——— *Testnevelési és Sport Bizottság* ..	National Committee for Physical Education and Sport
——— *Vezetőképző Iskola*	National Leader-Training School
——— *Országgyülés*	National Assembly
Őrszemcsapatok Szövetsége	Association of sentry guards
Osztály	Division, class, section
Osztályozó vizsga	Grade examination
Osztályvezető; Osztályfőnök	Class adviser *or* home-room teacher
Orvosdoktori oklevél	Diploma of Doctor of Medicine
Orvosi egyetem	Medical university
Orvostovábbképző Intézet	Institute for the Further Training of Physicians
Óvoda	Kindergarten
Óvónőképző intézet	Kindergarten teacher-training institute

P

Pályaválasztási Tanács	Career guidance council
Pártfőiskola	Party college
Pártkongresszus	Party congress
Pedagógiai gimnázium	Pedagogical gymnasium
——— *Tudományos Intézet*	Scientific Pedagogical Institute
Pedagógus Nap	Teachers Day
——— *otthon*	Teachers home
——— *Szakszervezet*	Teachers Union
Pénzügyminisztérium	Ministry of Finance
Polgári iskola	Upper elementary school
Politikai Bizottság	Political Committee (Politburo)

R

Raj	Troop
Reál gimnazium	*Réal* gymnasium (scientific secondary school)
Reáliskola	*Réal* school
Rektor	Rector *or* president *or* chancellor
Román Filológiai Intézet	Romanian Philological Institute

S

Szak	Specialty *or* department
Szakember Továbbképző Intézet	Institute for Further Training of Skilled Workers
Szakérettségi	Vocational secondary school certificate *or* examination
Szakigazgatási szerv	Administrative organ

Szakiskola	Vocational school; school for skilled workers
Szakiskolai oklevél	Technical school diploma
Szakkör	Academic or technical (hobby) circle
Szakközépiskola	Vocational secondary school
Szakmai minösitő vizsga	Trade-qualification examination
Szakmunkásbizonyitvány	Skilled-worker certificate
Szakmunkásvizsga	Skilled-worker examination
Szakorvos	Specialist physician
Szaktechnikusi oklevél	Skilled technician diploma
Szigorlat	*Rigorosum or* semester-end examination
Szláv Filológiai Intézet	Slavic Philological Institute
Szlovák Filológiai Intézet	Slovak Philological Institute
Szociáldemokrata Párt	Social Democratic Party
Szociálista Ifjúsági Mozgalom	Socialist Youth Movement
Szülői munkaközösség	Parental work collective

T

Taggyülés	General meeting
Tanács	Council *or* People's Council
Tanácsakadémia	People's Council Academy
Tanár	Professor
Tanárképzési bizottság	Teacher-training committee
Tanárképző tanács	Teacher-training council
Tanársegéd	Professorial assistant
Tanitóképző főiskola	Teacher-training college
——— *intézet*	Teacher-training institute
——— *Intézeti Tanőrök Országos Egyesülete*	National Association of Teachers in Teacher-Training Institutes
Tanonciskola	School for apprentices
Tanszék	Department *or* specialty
Tanszékvezető	Department chairman
Tanterv	Curriculum *or* school program
Társadalom- és Természettudományi Ismeretterjesztő Társulat	Association for the Propagation of the Social and Natural Sciences
Technikum	*Technikum or* technical school
Technikumi Tanács	*Technikum* Council
Természettudományi Kar	School *or* Faculty of Natural Science
Testnevelési főiskola	College of physical education
——— ——— *Sportegyesülete*	Sport Association of the College of Physical Education
Titkárság	Secretariat
Továbbképző iskola	Continuation school
Tudományegyetem	University
Tudományok doktora	Doctor of Science
——— *kandidátusa*	Candidate-in-Science
Tudományos és Felsőoktatási Tanács	Council of Science and Higher Education
——— *és Közoktatási Osztály*	Scientific and Public Education Section
——— *Ismeretterjesztő Társulat*	Scientific Association for the Propagation of Knowledge
——— *Minősitő Bizottság*	Scientific Qualification Committee

U

Úttörő	Pioneer
Úttörőcsapat	Pioneer group
Úttörőmozgalom	Pioneer Movement

V

Vallás- és Közoktatásügyi Minisztérium .. Ministry of Religion and Public Education
Végrehajtó bizottság .... Executive committee
Vidéki tankerület .... Provincial *or* village school district
Vizsgabizottság .... Examination committee

Z

Záródolgozat .... Thesis *or* dissertation

Appendix B. Hungarian Higher Education Institutions of University or College Caliber: 1968[1]

Institution, schools, city, and street	Years of study	Year founded[2]	Rector or director
I. UNIVERSITIES (*Tudományegyetemek*)			
Eötvös Loránd University (*Eötvös Loránd Tudományegyetem*), Budapest, 1-3 Egyetem Square	------	1635	Dr. Károly Nagy
School of Natural Science (*Természettudományi Kar*), 6-8 Múzeum Boulevard	5		
School of Philosophy (*Bölcsészettudományi Kar*), 1 Pesti Barnabás Street	5		
School of Political Science and Law (*Állam- és Jogtudományi Kar*), 1-3 Egyetem Square	4		
József Attila University (*József Attila Tudományegyetem*), Szeged	------	1921	Dr. Zoltán Szabó
School of Natural Science, 1 Aradi Vértanúk Square	5		
School of Philosophy, 2 Táncsics Mihály Street	5		
School of Political Science and Law, 54 Lenin Boulevard	4		
Karl Marx University of Economics (*Marx Károly Közgazdaságtudományi Egyetem*), Budapest, 8 Dimitrov Square	------	1948	Dr. Pál Pach Zsigmond
School of General Economics (*Általános Közgazdasági Kar*)	4		
School of Industry (*Ipari Kar*)	4		
School of Trade [Commerce] (*Kereskedelmi Kar*)	4		
Kossuth Lajos University (*Kossuth Lajos Tudományegyetem*), Debrecen	------	1912	Dr. András Rapcsák
School of Natural Science	5		
School of Philosophy	5		

See footnotes at end of table, p. 211.

Institution, schools, city, and street	Years of study	Year founded[2]	Rector or director
University of Pécs (*Pécsi Tudományegyetem*), Pécs	------	1923	Andor Csizmadia
School of Political Science and Law, 1 1848 Square	4		
II. MEDICAL UNIVERSITIES (*Orvostudományi Egyetemek*)			
Medical University of Budapest (*Budapesti Orvostudományi Egyetem*), Budapest, 26 Űllői Road	------	1769	Dr. József Sós
School of General Medicine (*Általános Orvostudományi Kar*)	6		
School of Pharmacy (*Gyogyszerésztudományi Kar*)	4½		
School of Stomatology (*Forgorvostudományi Kar*)	4½		
Medical University of Debrecen (*Debreceni Orvostudományi Egyetem*) Debrecen, 78 Nagyerdei Boulevard	------	1912	Dr. Pál Juhász
School of General Medicine	6		
Medical University of Pécs (*Pécsi Orvostudományi Egyetem*), Pécs, 82 Rákóczi Road	------	1912	Dr. Szilárd Donhoffer
School of General Medicine	6		
Medical University of Szeged (*Szegedi Orvostudományi Egyetem*), Szeged, 13 Dugonics Square	------	1872	Dr. Károly Tóth
School of General Medicine	6		
School of Pharmacy	4½		
School of Stomatology	4½		
University of Veterinary Medicine (*Állatorvostudományi Egyetem*), Budapest, 2 Landler Jenő Street	5	1782	Dr. András B. Kovács
III. POLYTECHNICAL UNIVERSITIES (*Műszaki Egyetemek*)			
Polytechnical University of Budapest (*Budapesti Műszaki Egyetem*), Budapest, 3 Műegyetem Rakpart	------	1782	Dr. Frigyes Csáki
School of Architectural Engineering (*Épitészmérnöki Kar*)	5		

See footnotes at end of table, p. 211.

Institution, schools, city, and street	Years of study	Year founded[2]	Rector or director
School of Chemical Engineering (*Vegyészmérnöki Kar*)	5		
School of Civil Engineering (*Epitőmérnöki Kar*)	5		
School of Electrical Engineering (*Villamosmérnöki Kar*)	5		
School of Mechanical Engineering (*Gépészmérnöki Kar*)	5		
School of Transportation Engineering (*Közlekedésmérnöki Kar*)	5		
Polytechnical University of Heavy Industry (*Nehézipari Műszaki Egyetem*), Miskolc	------	1949	Dr. János Zambó
School of Mechanical Engineering	5		
School of Metallurgical Engineering (*Kohómérnöki Kar*)	5		
School of Mining Engineering (*Banyamérnöki Kar*)	5		
University of Chemical Industry of Veszprém (*Veszprémi Vegyipari Egyetem*), Veszprém	------	1949	Dr. Pál Káldi
IV. AGRONOMIC UNIVERSITIES AND COLLEGES (*Agrár-Egyetemek és Főiskolák*)			
Agronomic University (*Agrártudományi Egyetem*), Gödöllő-Budapest	------	1945	Dr. Albert Kiss
School of Agricultural Mechanical Engineering (*Mezőgazdasági Gépészmérnöki Kar*)	5		
School of Argiculture (*Mezőgazdaságtudományi Kar*)	5		
College of Agronomy of Debrecen (*Debreceni Agrártudományi Főiskola*), Debrecen, 104 Böszörményi Road	5	1953	Dr. Ferenc Munkácsi
College of Agronomy of Keszthely (*Keszthelyi Agrártudományi Főiskola*), Keszthely, 16 Deák Ferenc Street	5	1797	Géza Láng
College of Agronomy of Mosonmagyaróvár (*Mosonmagyaróvári Agrártudományi Főiskola*), Mosonmagyaróvár, 2 Vár Street	5	1818	Dr. Géza Márton

See footnotes at end of table, p. 211.

Institution, schools, city, and street	Years of study	Year founded[2]	Rector or director
College of Horticulture and Viniculture (*Kertészeti és Szőlészeti Főiskola*), Budapest, 44 Ménesi Road	5	1853	Dr. Pál Kozma
University of Forestry and Lumber Industry (*Erdészeti és Faipari Egyetem*), Sopron, 4 Bajcsy-Zsilinszky Road	-----	1758	Dr. Gábor Pankotai
School of Forest Engineering (*Erdőmérnöki Kar*)	5		
School of Lumber Industrial Engineering (*Faipari Mérnöki Kar*)	5		
V. TEACHER-TRAINING COLLEGES (*Tanárképző Főiskolák*)			
Teachers College for Teachers of Handicapped Children (*Gyogypedagógiai Tanárképző Főiskola*), Budapest, 2 Bethlen Square	4	1924	Tibor Lovasz
Teacher-Training College of Eger (*Egri Tanárképző Főiskola*), Eger, 2 Szabadság Square	4	1949	László Szücs
Teacher-Training College of Nyiregyháza (*Nyiregyházi Tanárképző Főiskola*), Nyiregyháza, 16 Vasvári Pál Street	4	1962	József Kovács
Teacher-Training College of Pécs (*Pécsi Tanárképző Főiskola*), Pécs, 6 Ifjuság Road	4		Bertalan Márk
Teacher-Training College of Szeged (*Szegedi Tanárképző Főiskola*), Szeged, 6 Április 4 Road	4	1873	Dr. János Szendrey

See footnotes at end of table, p. 211.

Institution, schools, city, and street	Years of study	Year founded[2]	Rector or director
VI. COLLEGE OF PHYSICAL EDUCATION (*Testnevelési Főiskola*)			
College of Physical Education (*Testnevelési Főiskola*), Budapest, 44 Alkotás Street	4	1925	Endre Kerezsi
VII. COLLEGES OF ART AND MUSIC (*Művészeti és Zeneművészeti Főiskola*)			
College of Dramatic and Cinematographic Art (*Szinház- és Filmművészeti Főiskola*), Budapest, 2/c Vas Street	4	1865	Kálmán Nádasdy
College of Fine Arts (*Képzőművészeti Főiskola*), Budapest, 71 Népköztársaság Road	[3]4(3)	1871	Endre Domanovszky
College of Industrial Arts (*Iparművészeti Főiskola*), Budapest, 11-25 Zugligeti Road	[4]4	1880	Frigyes Pogány
Liszt Ferenc College of Music (*Liszt Ferenc Zeneművészeti Főiskola*), Budapest, 8 Liszt Ferenc Square	5(3)	1875	Ferenc Szabó

[1] Of the higher education institutions listed in the 1968 edition of the Guide to Hungarian Institutions of Higher Learning (see SOURCE OF DATA below), 48 are primarily postsecondary specialized schools engaged in training technicians or lower-elementary and kindergarten teachers (see appendix C).

[2] The year is the original date of founding, not the one in which the institution was reorganized to fit the requirements of the post-World War II regime.

[3] 4 years for artists; 3 years for teachers.

[4] 5 years for performers; 3 years for teachers.

SOURCE OF DATA: *Tájékoztató a Magyar felsőoktatási intézményekről 1968* (Guide to the Hungarian Institutions of Higher Learning 1968). Budapest: A Művelődésügyi Minisztérium Kiadványa, 1968, 207 p.; *International Handbook of Universities and Other Institutions of Higher Education 1965*. Paris: The International Association of Universities, 1965, p. 426-38; *Hungary. List of Persons Holding Important Positions in Party, State Administration, Public Life (Névsor azokrol, akik a pártban, államigazgatásban, közéletben fontos szerepet töltenek be)*. 10th ed. New York: Research Departments of Radio Free Europe, May 1967. 91 p.

Appendix C. Hungarian Education Institutions Primarily Specializing in Training Technicians or Lower-Elementary and Kindergarten Teachers: 1968

Institution	City and street	Years of study
I. HIGHER AGRICULTURAL *TECHNIKUMS* (*Felsőfokú Mezőgazdasági Technikumok*)[1]		
Higher Agricultural *Technikum (Felsőfokú Mezőgazdasági Technikum)*	Budapest 80 Maglódi Road	3
Do	Gyöngyös 1 Nemecz J. Square	3
Do	Hodmezővásárhely 17 Lenin Street	3
Do	Kaposvár Toponár	3
Do	Kecskemét 61 Bethlen Street	3
Do	Keszthely 1 Felszabadulás Street	3
Do	Kiskunhalas 43 Kossuth Lajos Street	3
Do	Körmend Rákóczi Road	3
Do	Mezőtúr 2 Tolbuchin Street	3
Do	Nagykanizsa 47 Ady Endre Street	3
Do	Nyiregyháza 69 Rákóczi Road	3
Do	Putnok Bajcsy-Zsilinszky Street	3
Do	Szarvas 1-3 Szabadság Street	3
Do	Zsámbék	3

See footnotes at end of table, p. 215.

Institution	City and street	Years of study
II. HIGHER INDUSTRIAL TECHNICAL *TECHNIKUMS* (*Ipari-Müszaki Felsőfokú Technikumok*)[1]		
Higher *Technikum* for—		
Automobile Transports (*Felsőfoku Gépjárműközlekedési Technikum*)	Budapest 14 Újhegyi Road	3
Chemical Industrial Mechanics (*Felsőfokú Vegyipari Gépészeti Technikum*)	Esztergom-Kenyérmező Wesselényi Street	3
Construction Industry (*Felsőfokú Építőipari Technikum*)	Budapest 74 Thököly Street	3
Construction Mechanics (*Felsőfokú Építőgépészeti Technikum*)	Debrecen Landler Jenő Street	3
Electrical Machines Industry (*Felsőfokú Villamosgépipari Technikum*)	Budapest 19 Nagyszombat Street	3
Food Industry (*Felsőfokú Élelmiszeripari Technikum*)	Budapest 46 Izabella Street	3
Light Industry (*Felsőfokú Könnyűipari Technikum*)	Budapest 18-20 Markó Street	3
Machine Industry (*Felsőfokú Gépipari Technikum*)	Budapest 8 Népszinház Street	3
Machine Industry (*Felsőfokú Gépipari Technikum*)	Kecskemét 10 Izsáki Street	3
Mechanics for the Construction and Construction Materials Industry (*Felsőfokú Épitő és Épitőanyagipari Gépészeti Technikum*)	Budapest 2-4 Szabó Ilonk Street	3
Metallurgical Industry (*Felsőfokú Kohóipari Technikum*)	Dunaújváros 1 Táncsics Street	3
Power Industry (*Felsőfokú Villamosenergia-ipari Technikum*)	Budapest 15 Üteg Street	3
Railways (*Felsőfokú Vasútforgalmi Technikum*)	Szeged 14 Marx Square	3
Surveying (*Felsőfokú Földmérési Technikum*)	Székesfehérvár 13 Pirosalma Street	2½

See footnotes at end of table, p. 215.

Institution	City and street	Years of study
Telecommunications *(Felsőfokú Távközlési Technikum)*	Budapest 22 Gyáli Road	3
Telecommunications and Instruments Industry *(Felsőfokú Híradás- és Műszeripari Technikum)*	Budapest 15-17 Tavaszmező Street	3
Water Management *(Felsőfokú Vízgazdálkodási Technikum)*	Baja 14 Bajcsy-Zsilinszky Street	3

III. HIGHER TECHNICAL SCHOOLS[1]
(Felsőfokú Szakiskolák)

Institution	City and street	Years of study
Higher Technical School of—		
Commerce and Restaurant Industry *(Felsőfokú Kereskedelmi és Vendéglátóipari Szakiskola)*	Budapest 9-11 Alkotmány Street	3
Finance and Accounting *(Felsőfokú Pénzügyi és Számviteli Szakiskola*	Budapest 10 Buzógány Street	3
Foreign Trade *(Felsőfokú Külkereskedelmi Szakiskola)*	Budapest 1 Néphadsereg Street	3

IV. INSTITUTES FOR TRAINING ELEMENTARY SCHOOL AND KINDERGARTEN TEACHERS
(Tanitóképző és Óvónőképző Intézetek)

Institution	City and street	Years of study
Teacher-Training Institute *(Tanitóképző Intézet)*	Baja 2 Szegedi Road	3
Do	Budapest 40 Kiss Jánosaltbgy Street	3
Do	Debrecen 3 Liszt Ferenc Street	3
Do	Esztergom 1-3 Makarenko Street	3
Do	Győr 42 Liszt Ferenc Street	3
Do	Jászberény 45 Rákóczi Street	3
Do	Kaposvár 10 Bajcsy-Zsilinszky Street	3
Do	Nyiregyháza 39 Bethlen Gábor Street	3

See footnote at end of table, p. 215.

Institution	City and street	Years of study
Do	Sárospatak 5 Eötvös Street	3
Do	Szombathely 4 Szabadság Square	3
Kindergarten Teacher-Training Institute *(Óvónőképző Intézet)*	Kecskemét 6-14 Kaszap Street	2
Do	Sopron 1-3 Ferenczi J. Street	2
Do	Szarvas 4 Szabadság Square	2

V. INSTITUTE FOR TRAINING INSTRUCTORS OF MOTOR-DISORDER VICTIMS
(*Mozgássérültek Nevelőképző és Nevelőintézete*)

Institution	City and street	Years of study
Institute for Training Instructors of Motor-Disorder Victims *(Mozgássérültek Nevelőképző és Nevelőintézete)*	Budapest 67 Villyani Road	4

VI. MILITARY COLLEGES OF THE HUNGARIAN PEOPLE'S ARMY
(*A Magyar Néphadsereg Katonai Főiskolai*)

Institution	City and street	Years of study
([2])	([2])	4

[1] In 1969, five higher *technikums* and one higher technical school were converted as shown below:

March 4: The higher *technikum* for the Electrical Machine Industry and the one for the Telecommunications and Instruments Industry were consolidated into a single institution—3-year Kandó Kálmán Technical College of Electrical Industry *(Kándó Kálmán Villamosipari Műszaki Főiskola)* (a).

July 19: The one for the Metallurgical Industry became the School of Foundry and Metallurgy *(Kohó- és Fémipari Főiskolai Kar)* operating within the framework of the Polytechnical University of Heavy Industry *(Nehézipari Műszaki Egyetem)* (b).

August 31: The one for the Machine Industry became the 3-year Banki Donat Technical College of Machine Industry *(Banki Donat Gépipari Műszaki Főiskola)* (c).

August 31: The one for the Machine Industry located at Kecskemét became the 3-year Technical College of Machine Industry and Automation *(Gépipari és Automatizálási Műszaki Főiskola)* (d).

August 31: The Higher Technical School of Commerce and Restaurant Industry became the 3-year College of Commerce and Restaurant Industry *(Kereskedelmi és Vendéglátóipari Főiskola)* (e).

Each conversion noted above resulted from a Decree of the Presidential Council of the People's Republic and/or a Resolution of the Hungarian Revolutionary Worker-Peasant Government and was published in *Magyar Közlöny* (Hungarian Gazette). The decree number and/or resolution number and the issue number, date, and page number of *Magyar Közlöny* for each conversion described above and labeled (a) through (e) are as follows:

(a) Decree No. 6 of 1969, Resolution No. 10007/1969. (III. 4.), and issue No. 17, March 4, 1969, p. 167-68.

(b) Resolution No. 1028/1969. (VII. 19.), and issue No. 55, July 19, 1969, p. 524.

(c) Decree No. 25 of 1969, Resolution No. 1033/1969. (VIII. 31.), and issue No. 67, August 31, 1969, p. 669, 676-77.

(d) Decree No. 24 of 1969, Resolution No. 1032/1969. (VIII. 3.), and issue No. 67, August 31, 1969, p. 669, 676.

(e) Decree No. 26 of 1969, Resolution No. 1034/1969. (VIII. 31.), and issue No. 67, August 31, 1967, p. 677.

[2] Hungarian official sources do not identify the military colleges. In 1968 the following three were in

operation: The Kossuth Lajos Military College *(Kossuth Lajos Katonai Főiskola)*, Budapest; The Zalka Máté Military Technical College (*Zalka Máté Katonai Műszaki Főiskola)*, Budapest; and the Kilián György Air Force Technical College *(Kilián György Repülő Műszaki Főiskola)*, Szolnok. See p. 173-74.

SOURCE OF DATA: *Tájékoztató a magyar felsőoktatási intézményekről, 1968* (Guide to the Hungarian Institutions of Higher Learning, 1968). Budapest: A Művelődésügyi Minisztérium Kiadványa, 1968, 207 p.; *International Handbook of Universities and Other Institutions of Higher Education 1965*. Paris: The International Association of Universities, 1965, p. 426-38; *Hungary. List of Persons Holding Important Positions in Party, State Administration, Public Life (Névsor azokrol, akik a pártban, államigazgatásban, közéletben fontos szerepet töltenek be)*. 10th ed. New York: Research Departments of Radio Free Europe, May 1967, 91 p.

Appendix D. Major Hungarian Research Institutes: 1963

Institute	Year founded	Located in—	Directed by—
Astronomical Observatory	1921	Budapest	Academy of Sciences
Central Institute of—			
Food Industry and Research	1959	do	Ministry of Food
Physics Research	1950	do	Academy of Sciences
Central Laboratory of Measuring Technics	1958	do	Ministry of Metallurgy and Machinery
Central Research Institute for Building Materials	1953	do	Ministry of Building
Central Research Institute of—			
Chemistry	1952	do	Academy of Sciences
Radiation Biology	1957	do	Ministry of Health
The Eötvös Loránd State Institute of Geophysics	1906	do	Academy of Sciences
Experimental Institute for Agricultural Machinery	1949	do	Ministry of Agriculture
Experimental Institute of the Hungarian Post Office	1891	do	Ministry of Transport and Communications
Hungarian Research Institute of Mineral and Natural Gas	1948	do	Ministry of Heavy Industry
Hungarian State Institute of Geology	1869	do	National Directorate of Geology
Institute for Farm Economics	1953	do	Academy of Sciences
Institute of—			
Agricultural Organization	1953	do	Ministry of Agriculture
Animal Husbandry	1949	do	Do.
Architecture and Construction	1948	do	Ministry of Building
Biochemistry	1950	do	Academy of Sciences

Institute	Year founded	Located in—	Directed by—
Biological Research	1950	do	Do.
Child Psychology	1902	do	Do.
Forestry Research	1949	do	National Directorate of Forestry
Genetics	1940	do	Academy of Sciences
Government and Legal Sciences	1949	do	Do.
Historical Sciences	1949	do	Do.
Linguistics	1950	do	Do.
Meteorology	1870	do	Council of Ministers
Pedagogy	1954	do	Ministry of Culture
Philosophy	1957	do	Academy of Sciences
Soil Mechanics and Agrochemistry	1950	do	Do.
Theatrical Art	1953	do	Ministry of Culture
National Institute for Alimentation and Nutrition	1949	do	Ministry of Health
National Institute of—			
Agrobotany	1954	Tápiószele	Ministry of Agriculture
Public Health	1927	Budapest	Ministry of Health
X-Ray and Radiation Physics	1956	do	Do.
National Research Institute of Health in Relation to Labor	1949	do	Do.
Observatory of Solar Physics	1958	Debrecen	Academy of Sciences
Research Institute for—			
the Instrument Industry	1950	Budapest	Ministry of Metallurgy and Machinery
the Iron Industry	1949	do	Do.
the Leather, Footwear, and Fur Industries	1949	do	Ministry of Light Industry
the Metal Industries	1948	do	Ministry of Heavy Industry
the Paper Industry	1949	do	Ministry of Light Industry
the Textile Industry	1949	do	Do.
Research Institute of—			
Agriculture	1950	Martonvásár	Academy of Sciences
Animal Health	1950	Budapest	Do.
Botany	1952	Vácrátót	Do.
Economics	1954	Budapest	Do.
Electrical Energetics	1949	do	Ministry of Heavy Industry
Experimental Medicine	1954	do	Academy of Sciences
Explosion Technique in Mining	1951	do	Ministry of Heavy Industry
Fur Animal Breeding	1952	Gödöllő	Ministry of Agriculture
High Pressure Equipment	1951	Budapest	Ministry of Heavy Industry
the History of Literature	1956	do	Academy of Sciences

Institute	Year founded	Located in—	Directed by—
Home Trade	1959	do	Board of Trade
Horticulture	1950	Budatétény	Ministry of Agriculture
Hydrological Economy	1952	Budapest	National Directorate of Hydrological Affairs
Inorganic Chemistry	1949	Veszprém	Ministry of Heavy Industry
Irrigation and Rice Cultivation	1956	Szarvas	Ministry of Agriculture
Labor Hygiene	1954	Budapest	National Council of Trade Unions
Mathematics	1950	do	Academy of Sciences
Medicinal Botany	1917	do	Ministry of Agriculture
Mining Industry	1949	do	Ministry of Heavy Industry
Motor Transport	1938	do	Ministry of Transport and Communications
Nuclear Physics	1954	Debrecen	Academy of Sciences
Organic Chemistry	1949	Budapest	Ministry of Heavy Industry
Plant Improvement and Cultivation	1955	Sopronhorpács-Fertőd	Ministry of Agriculture
Plant Protection	1949	Budapest	Do.
Railway Transport	1951	do	Ministry of Transport and Communications
Synthetic Materials	1950	do	Ministry of Heavy Industry
Technical Physics	1958	do	Academy of Sciences
Telecommunications	1953	do	Ministry of Metallurgy and Machinery
Thermotechnics	1949	do	Ministry of Heavy Industry
Timber and Wood	1949	do	National Directorate of Forestry
Transport and Roads	1956	do	Ministry of Transport and Communications
Scientific Institute of—			
Cinematography	1957	do	Ministry of Culture
Western Hungary	1943	Pécs	Academy of Sciences
Viticultural Research Institute	1950	Budapest	Ministry of Agriculture

SOURCE OF DATA: *Hungary.* Zoltán Halász, ed. Budapest: Corvina Press, 1963. p. 253-55.

For a more detailed listing and a description of the Hungarian research institutes operating within the framework of (1) the Hungarian Academy of Sciences, (2) the universities, and (3) government agencies, see *Directory of Selected Research Institutes in Eastern Europe*, prepared by Arthur D. Little, Inc. for the National Science Foundation. New York: Columbia University Press, 1967. p. 152-234.

Appendix E. Bibliography

Bibliographical Sources

APANASEWICZ, NELLIE *and* SEYMOUR M. ROSEN. *Eastern Europe Education: A Bibliography of English-Language Materials* (OE-14121). U. S. Department of Health, Education, and Welfare, Office of Education. Washington: U.S. Government Printing Office, 1966. 35 p.

"Iskolaügyünk 20 éves fejlődését irányitó főbb útmutatások, jogszabályok" (The Major Guides and Regulations Relating to the 20-year Development of Our Education). *Pedagógiai Szemle* (Review of Education). Budapest, XV:4:355-65. 1965.

ORSZÁGOS PEDAGÓGIAI KÖNYVTÁR. *Magyar pedagógiai irodalom* (Hungarian Pedagogical Literature). Budapest. 5 vols. 1959. 34, 43, 56, 88, and 92 p., respectively.

Legal Sources

BEDO, ALEXANDER KALNOKI *and* GEORGE TORZSAY-BIBER. *Legal Sources and Bibliography of Hungary.* New York: Praeger *for the* Free Europe Committee, 1956. 157 p.

FEKETE, WILLIAM SOLYOM. Laws on Public Education in Hungary After World War II. Washington: Library of Congress, 1959. 133 p. Mimeograph.

MACARTNEY, CARLILE AYLMER. *Hungary: A Short History.* Edinburgh: University Press, 1962. 262 p.

———. *October Fifteenth: A History of Modern Hungary, 1929—1945.* Edinburgh: The Edinburgh University Press, no date. 2 vols, 490 and 519 p., respectively.

SINOR, DENIS. *History of Hungary.* New York: Praeger, 1959. 310 p.

UNGER, MÁTYÁS *and* OTTÓ SZABOLCS. *Magyarország története* (History of Hungary). Budapest: Gondolat Kiadó, 1965. 418 p.

Statistical Sources

KÖZPONTI STATISZTIKAI HIVATAL. *Statisztikai évkönyv* (Statistical Yearbook). Budapest: Statisztikai Kiadó Vállalat: 1964, 1965, and 1966. p. 357-78, 432-33; 343-62, 416-17; and 339-61, 414-15, respectively.

Statisztikai időszaki közlemények—Magyarország kulturális helyzete, 1961 (Periodical Statistical Announcement—The Cultural Situation in Hungary, 1961). Budapest: Statisztikai Kiadó Vállalat, 1962-63. 145 p.

Statistical Pocket Book of Hungary 1967. Budapest: Publishing House for Economics and Law, 1967. p. 179-86.

Historical-Political Background

HALÁSZ, ZOLTÁN, *ed. Hungary*. Budapest: Corvina Press, 1963. 395 p.

HELMREICH, ERNST C., *ed. Hungary*. New York: Praeger *for the* Mid-European Studies Center of the Free Europe Committee, 1957. 466 p.

Hungary Today. New York: Praeger, 1962. 104 p.

KERTÉSZ, STEPHEN D. *Diplomacy in a Whirlpool. Hungary Between Nazi Germany and Soviet Russia*. Notre Dame, Ind.: University of Notre Dame Press, 1953. 273 p.

LENGYEL, EMIL. *1,000 Years of Hungary*. New York: J. Day Co., 1958. 312 p.

VÁLI, FERENC ALBERT. *Rift and Revolt in Hungary. Nationalism Versus Communism*. Cambridge, Mass.: Harvard University Press, 1961. 590 p.

ZINNER, PAUL E. *Revolution in Hungary*. New York: Columbia University Press, 1962. 380 p.

The Educational System: The Prewar Era

JÁNOSSY, DENNIS A. *Public Instruction in Hungary*. Budapest: Press of the Royal Hungarian University, 1929. 40 p.

JÓBORÚ, MAGDA. *Élet és iskola (A modern köznevelés történelmi és társadalmi háttere)* (Life and School: The Historical and Social Background of Modern Public Education). Budapest: Gondolat Kiadó, 1961. 152 p.

———. *A középiskola szerepe a Horthy-korszak művelődéspolitikájában* (The Role of the Secondary School in the Cultural Policy of the Horthy Era). Budapest: Tankönyvkiadó, 1963. 159 p.

KORNIS, GYULA [JULIUS]. *A magyar közoktatásügy története a világháború óta* (History of Hungarian Public Education Since the World War). Budapest: Magyar Pedagógiai Társaság, 1928. 555 p.

———. *Education in Hungary*. New York: Teachers College, Columbia University, 1932. 289 p.

KÖTE, SÁNDOR. *A magyar nevelésügy a polgári demokratikus forradalom és a tanácsköztársaság idején* (Hungarian Education at the Time of the Bourgeois Democratic Revolution and the Soviet Republic). Budapest: Tankönyvkiadó, 1963. 131 p.

MOSKOVITS, ARON. *Jewish Education in Hungary, 1848-1948*. Philadelphia: The Dropsie College for Hebrew and Cognate Learning, 1964. 357 p.

PEDAGÓGIAI TUDOMÁNYOS INTÉZET. *Tanulmányok a magyar nevelés történetéből, 1849-1944* (Studies on the History of Hungarian Education, 1849-1944).Budapest: Tankönyvkiadó, 1957. 323 p.

RAVASZ, JÁNOS, LÁSZLÓ FELKAI, BÉLA BELLÉR *and* GYÚLA SIMON. *A magyar nevelés története a feudalizmus és a kapitalizmus korában* (The History of Hungarian Education in the Era of Feudalism and Capitalism). Budapest: Tankönyvkiadó, 1961. 279 p.

SOMOGYI, JOSEPH. *L'Instruction publique en Hongrie* (Public Education in Hungary) (Publications du Bureau International d'Education, No. 87). Geneva: The Bureau, 1944. 122 p.

The Educational System: The Post-1945 Era

General References

HALÁSZ, ZOLTÁN. *Cultural Life in Hungary*. Budapest: Pannonia Press, 1966. 319 p.

HUNGARIAN PEOPLE'S REPUBLIC. *MINISTRY OF CULTURAL AFFAIRS Report on Educational Progress in 1965-66 Presented at the XXIXth Session of the International Conference on Public Education in Geneva, July, 1966.* [Budapest, 1966] 23 p.

———. *Report on Educational Progress in the 1966-67 Academic Year Presented at the XXXth Session of the International Conference on Public Education, Geneva, July 1967.* [Budapest, 1967] 36 p.

Nevelésügyünk húsz éve, 1945-1964 (Twenty Years of Our Educational System, 1945-1964). Budapest: Tankönyvkiadó, 1965. 601 p.

ORSZÁGOS PEDAGÓGIAI INTÉZET. *A közoktatásügy Europa szociálista országaiban* (Public Education in the Socialist Countries of Europe). Budapest: Tankönyvkiadó, 1965. 522 p.

PEDAGÓGIAI TÚDOMÁNYOS INTÉZET. *Tanulmányok a magyar népi demokracia neveléstörténetéből* (Studies on the History of Education of the Hungarian People's Republic). Edited by István Dancs and Gyula Simon. Budapest, no date. 2 vols., 329 and 669 p., respectively. Mimeograph.

SIMON, GYULA *and* JÓZSEF SZARKA. *A magyar népi demokrácia nevelésügyének története* (History of the Educational System of the Hungarian People's Republic). Budapest: Tankönyvkiadó, 1965, 195 p.

WIESSNER, R., H. BRAUER *and* W. MANN. *Hét szociálista ország oktatásügye* (The Educational System of Seven Socialist Countries). Budapest: Tankönyvkiadó, 1965, 84 p.

Adult Education

Első Országos Felnőttoktatási Konferencia (The First National Conference on Adult Education). Budapest: Táncsics, 1965.

Elementary Education

UNESCO. *INTERNATIONAL BUREAU OF EDUCATION. Primary School Textbooks.* (Publication No. 204). Geneva: The Bureau, 1959. p. 130-32.

———. *World Survey of Education: II. Primary Education.* Paris, 1958, p. 521-26.

Higher Education

The Development and Nowadays Situation of Hungarian Higher Education. Budapest: National Committee on Hungarian Student Organisations, 1958. 85 p.

International Handbook of Universities and Other Institutions of Higher Education 1965. Paris: The International Association of Universities, 1965. p. 426-38.

Tájékoztató a magyar felsőoktatási intézményekről, 1965 (Guide to the Hungarian Institutions of Higher Learning, 1965). Edited by László Szabó. Budapest: A Művelődésügyi Minisztérium Kiadványa, 1965. 147 p.

Tájékoztató a magyar felsőoktatási intézményekről, 1968 (Guide to the Hungarian Institutions of Higher Learning, 1968). Edited by László Szabó. Budapest: A Művelődésügyi Minisztérium Kiadványa, 1968. 207 p.

UNESCO. *World Survey of Education: IV. Higher Education.* New York, 1966. p. 583-93.

WORLD HEALTH ORGANIZATION. *World Directory of Medical Schools.* Geneva, 1963. p. 131-34.

Secondary Education

HABUDA, MIKLÓS, *ed. Középiskolai kollégiumi nevelés* (Collegium Education in the Secondary School). Budapest: Tankönyvkiadó, 1965. 262 p.

UNESCO. *World Survey of Education: III. Secondary Education.* Paris, 1961. p. 631-40.

Curriculums, Syllabuses, Rules, and Instructions

Elementary Education

MŰVELŐDÉSÜGYI MINISZTÉRIUM. *Tanterv és utasitás az általános iskolák számára* (Curriculum and Instruction for the General Schools). Budapest: Tankönyvkiadó. 670 p.

Secondary Education

MŰVELŐDÉSÜGYI MINISZTÉRIUM. *Tanterv és utasitás a gimnáziumok számára* (Curriculum and Instruction for the Gymnasiums). Budapest: Tankönyvkiadó, 1965.[1]

———. *Angol, francia, latin, német, olasz, és spanyol nyelv* (English, French, Latin, German, Italian, and Spanish). 118 p.

———. *Biológia* (Biology), 27 p. *Ének-zene* (Music-Singing), 22 p. *Fizika* (Physics), 24 p. *Földrajz* (Geography), 39 p. *Kémia* (Chemistry), 36 p. *Magyar irodalom és magyar nyelv* (Hungarian Literature and Hungarian Language), 87 p. *Matematika* (Mathematics), 38 p. *Orosz nyelv* (Russian), 23 p. *Osztályfőnöki óra* (Guidance), 27 p. *Pszichológia* (Psychology), 16 p. *Rajz- és műalkotások elemzése* (Drawing and the Evaluation of Masterpieces), 20 p. *Testnevelés* (Physical Education), 46 p. *Történelem* (History), 36 p. *Világnézetünk alapjai* (Foundations of Our World Outlook), 42 p.

ORSZÁGOS PEDAGÓGIAI INTÉZET. *A középiskolai tanulók tervszerű nevelésének programja. Nevelési terv* (Program of the Planned Education of Secondary School Students: Education Plan). Budapest: Tankönyvkiadó, 1965. 139 p.

UNESCO. *INTERNATIONAL BUREAU OF EDUCATION. Modern Languages* at General Secondary Schools (Publication No. 268). Geneva, The Bureau, 1964. p. 76-78.

Vocational Education

MŰVELŐDÉSÜGYI MINISZTÉRIUM. *Ipari és egészségügyi szakközépiskolák 1965-66. tanévi óratervei* (Programs of the Industrial and Health Vocational Secondary Schools for the 1965-66 Academic Year).

—————— *Művelődésügyi Közlöny* (Educational Gazette). Budapest. No. 13, 1965. Appendix p. 1-45 of the reprint.

Teachers Handbooks [2]

Elementary Education

Kézikönyv az általános iskolák 3. osztályának tanitói számára (Handbook for Third Grade Elementary School Teachers). Budapest, Tankönyvkiadó, 1966. 543 p.

Nevelőmunka az óvodában. Utmutatás óvónők számára (Education Work in the Kindergarten: Guide for Kindergarten Teachers). 5th ed. Budapest: Tankönyvkiadó, 1964.

Rendtartás az általános isokláк és a gimnáziumok számára (Regulations for Elementary Schools and Gymnasiums). Budapest: Tankönyvkiadó, 1964. 128 p.

Segédkönyv az osztályfőnöki munkához az általános iskolák nevelői számára (Guidebook for Home-Room Work for Elementary School Teachers). Budapest: Tankönyvkiadó, 1961. 414 p.

---

[1] The same address and publication date apply also to the remaining publications listed here of the *Művelődésügyi Minisztérium*.

[2] This bibliography lists only a few representative titles of the teachers handbooks available for every subject in every grade. As instructed by the Ministry of Culture, the *Országos Pedagógiai Intézet* (National Pedagogical Institute) has these handbooks prepared under its auspices.

Miscellaneous Subjects in Various Grades

Ének-Zene kézikönyv az általános iskolák 1. *osztályában tanitó nevelők részére* (Handbook of Music-Singing for First-Grade Teachers in the Elementary Schools). Budapest: Tankönyvkiadó, 1965. 87 p.

Környezetismeret kézikönyv az általános iskolák 4. *osztályának tanitói részére* (Handbook for Teaching "Knowledge of the Surroundings" for Fourth-Grade Teachers in the Elementary Schools). Budapest: Tankönyvkiadó, 1965. 127 p.

Tanári kézikönyv az orosz nyelv tanitásához az ötödik osztályban (Teachers' Handbook for Teaching Russian in the Fifth Grade). Budapest: Tankönyvkiadó, 1964. 119 p.

Tanári kézikönyv a 6. *osztályos fizika tanitásához* (Teachers Handbook for Teaching Physics in the Sixth Grade). Budapest: Tankönyvkiadó, 1965. 299 p.

Tanári kézikönyv az Élővilág cimű tantárgy tanitásához. 7. *osztály* (Teachers' Handbook for Teaching "The Living World." Seventh Grade). Budapest: Tankönyvkiadó, 1965. 127 p.

Testnevelés az óvodában (Physical Education in the Kindergarten). Budapest: Tankönyvkiadó, 1964. 204 p.

Party Documents

A Magyar Szociálista Munkáspárt Központi Bizottságának irányelvei időszerű ideológiai feladatokról (Guidelines of the Central Committee of the Hungarian Socialist Workers Party Concerning Present Ideological Tasks). Budapest: Kossuth, 1965, 63 p.

Mai kulturális életünk főbb kérdései (The Major Questions of Our Contemporary Cultural Life). Budapest: Kossuth, 1958.

Pártdokumentumok az ideológiai és a kulturális munkáról (Party Documents on Ideological and Cultural Work). Budapest: Kossuth, 1962. 275 p.

SIMON GYULA. *A Magyar Dolgozók Pártja fontosabb határozatai a közoktatásról* (The Important Decisions of the Hungarian Workers' Party Concerning Public Education). Budapest: Pedagógiai Tudományos Intézet, 1955. 112 p.

Specialized Studies

BÁRSONY, JENŐ, *ed. Az iskolai közösségi nevelés: Tapasztalatgyüjtemény* (Communal Education in the School: Collection of Experience). Budapest: Tankönyvkiadó, 1964. 334 p.

BORSOS, MARGIT, *et al. Falusi, tanyai iskolások* (Village and Farm Pupils). Budapest: Tankönyvkiadó, 1966. 64 p.

Demokrácia és köznevelés (Democracy and Public Education). Budapest: Országos Köznevelési Tanács, 1945.

GÁSPÁR, LÁSZLÓ. *Pedagógiai problemák egy tanyai iskolában* (Pedagogical Problems in a Farm School). Budapest: Tankönyvkiadó, 1963. 135 p.

HENCZ, AURÉL. *A Művelődési intézmények és a művelődésigazgatás fejlődése, 1945-1961* (The Evolution of Educational Institutions and Administration, 1945-1961). Budapest: Közgazdasági és Jogi Könyvkiadó, 1962. 515 p.

KELEMEN, LÁSZLÓ. *A 10-14 éves tanulók tudásszintje és gondolkodása* (The Level of Knowledge and Thinking of 10- to 14-Year-Old Pupils). Budapest: Akadémiai Kiadó, 1963. 351 p.

KÉTHLY, ANNA. *Demokratikus közoktatás* (Democratic Public Education) Budapest: Népszava, 1945. 15 p.

MAGYAR TUDOMÁNYOS AKADÉMIA. *A munkára nevelés hazai történetéből* (From the Domestic History of Education for Work). Edited by Béla Jausz, Szilárd Faludi, *and* Endre Zibolen. Budapest: Akadémiai Kiadó, 1965. 559 p.

———. Tanulmányok a neveléstudomány köréből—*1961, 1962, 1963, 1964, 1965.* (Studies From the Sphere of the Science of Education). (Separate studies for the indicated years.) Budapest: Akadémiai Kiadó: 1962, 1963, 1964, 1965—742, 583, 583, 646, and 451 p., respectively.

NAGY, SÁNDOR *and* LAJOS HORVÁTH, *eds. Neveléselmélet* (Theory of Education). Budapest: Tankönyvkiadó, 1965. 433 p.

PEDAGÓGIAI TUDOMÁNYOS INTÉZET. *Mit vár a társadalom az iskolai oktatástól* (What Society Expects of School Instruction). Edited by Mrs. Pál Komár. Budapest: Tankönyvkiadó, 1964. 368 p.

———————————. *Tanulmányok a neveléselmélet köréből* (Studies From the Sphere of Educational Theory). Budapest: Tankönyvkiadó, 1960. 199 p.

SALAMON, JENŐ. *Gyermekek gondolkodása a cselekvésben* (The Thinking of Children in the Course of Their Activities). Budapest: Akadémiai Kiadó, 1964. 316 p.

TIHANYI, FERENC, *ed. Oktatásügyünk továbbfejlesztéséért. Tanulmányok és dokumentumok* (For the Further Development of Our Educational System: Studies and Documents). Budapest: Tankönyvkiadó *for the* Pedagógiai Tudományos Intézet, 1961. 191 p.

Továbbképzés és demokrácia (Further Training and Democracy). Budapest: Egyetemi Nyomda, 1947.

Periodicals

Bibliographical

Magyar Pedagógiai Irodalom (Hungarian Pedagogical Literature). Budapest, irregular. Published by the *Országos Pedagógiai Könyvtár* (National Pedagogical Library).

English Language

East Europe. New York, monthly. Published by Free Europe Committee.

The New Hungarian Quarterly. Budapest.

Problems of Communism. Washington, D.C., bimonthly. Published by the U.S. Information Agency.

Slavic Review (formerly *The American Slavic and East European Review*). New York, quarterly.

Survey. London, quarterly.

General

Család és Iskola (Family and School). Budapest, monthly. Published by the Ministry of Culture *(Művelődésügyi Minisztérium)* and the National Council of Hungarian Women.

Köznevelés (Public Education). Budapest, semimonthly. Published by the Ministry of Culture.

Magyar Pedagógia (Hungarian Education). Budapest, quarterly. Published by the Pedagogical Committee of the Hungarian Academy of Sciences *(A Magyar Tudományos Akadémia Pedagógiai Bizottsága).*

Modszertani Közlemények (Methodological Announcements). Budapest, five times a year.

Népművelés (People's Education). Budapest, monthly. Published by the National Council of Popular Education (*Országos Népművelési Tanács*).

Pedagógiai Szemle (Review of Education). Budapest, monthly. Published by the National Pedagogical Institute (*Országos Pedagógiai Intézet*).

Pedagógusok Lapja (Teachers' Journal). Budapest, semimonthly. Published by the Teachers Union (*Pedagógus Szakszervezet*).

A Tanító Munkája (The Teacher's Work). Budapest, monthly.

Higher Education

Felsőoktatási Szemle (Review of Higher Education). Budapest, monthly. Published by the Ministry of Culture.

Kindergarten Education

Gyermeknevelés (Child Education). Budapest, published from January 1948 to January 1953.

Óvodai Nevelés (Kindergarten Education). Budapest, monthly.

Legal

Magyar Közlöny (Hungarian Gazette). Budapest, irregular. Official gazette published by the Secretariat of the Council of Ministers (*Minisztertanács Titkársága*).

Művelődésügyi Közlöny (Education Gazette). Budapest, irregular. Published by the Ministry of Culture.

Party Organs

Népszabadság (People's Freedom). Budapest, daily. Published by the Hungarian Socialist Workers' (Communist) Party (*Magyar Szociálista Munkáspárt*).

Társadalmi Szemle (Social Review). Budapest, monthly.

Statistics

Statisztikai Szemle (Review of Statistics). Budapest. Published by the Central Statistical Office (*Központi Statisztikai Hivatal*).

Subject-Matter Organs

Az Ének-Zene Tanitása (The Teaching of Music-Singing). Budapest, bimonthly.

A Fizika Tanitása (The Teaching of Physics). Budapest, bimonthly.

A Földrajz Tanitása (The Teaching of Geography). Budapest, bimonthly.

Az Idegen Nyelvek Tanitása (The Teaching of Foreign Languages). Budapest, bimonthly.

A Kémia Tanitása (The Teaching of Chemistry). Budapest, bimonthly.

Képes Nyelvmester (Pictorial Language-Master). Budapest, 10 times a year.

Középiskolai Matematikai Lapok (Journal of Secondary School Mathematics). Budapest, 10 times a year.

Magyartanitás (Teaching of Hungarian). Budapest, bimonthly.

A Matematika Tanitása (The Teaching of Mathematics). Budapest, bimonthly.

Rajztanitás (The Teaching of Drawing). Budapest, bimonthly.

A Testnevelés Tanitása (The Teaching of Physical Education). Budapest, bimonthly.

Történelemtanitás (The Teaching of History). Budapest, bimonthly.

Youth Organs

Ifjusági Magazin (Youth Magazine). Budapest. Monthly. Published by the Communist Youth League (*Kommunista Ifjúsági Szövetség*—KISZ).

Kisdobos (The Small Drummer), Budapest. Monthly. Published by the Association of Hungarian Pioneers (*Magyar Úttörők Szövetsége*).

Úttörővezető (Pioneer Leader), Budapest. Monthly.

Világ Ifjúsága (Youth of the World), Budapest. Monthly. Published by the World Federation of Democratic Youth.

☆ U. S. GOVERNMENT PRINTING OFFICE : 1970 O - 356-544